THE NEGRO
AND HIS MUSIC
*
NEGRO ART:
PAST AND PRESENT

Alain Locke

AYER COMPANY, PUBLISHERS, INC.
SALEM, NEW HAMPSHIRE 03079

Reprint Edition, 1991
Ayer Company, Publishers, Inc.
50 Northwestern Dr.
Salem, New Hampshire 03079

*

Library of Congress Catalog Card No. 69–18592

*

Negro Art: Past and Present reprinted from a copy
in the collection of Harvard College Library

*

Manufactured in the United States of America

AFRO-AMERICAN CULTURE SERIES

General Editor
ULYSSES LEE

Csb ISBN 088143-078-1
Pbk ISBN 0-88143-079-X

BIOGRAPHICAL NOTE

Born in 1886 in Philadelphia, Alain LeRoy Locke was educated at the Philadelphia School of Pedagogy, and Harvard University, where he was elected to Phi Beta Kappa and received a Ph.D. degree. In 1907, the first Negro to be awarded a Rhodes Scholarship, he traveled to England to study at Oxford University. After three years at Oxford, he studied for two years at the University of Berlin. In 1912 he returned to America and accepted a position as Professor of Education at Howard University. In 1917 he became a Full Professor of Philosophy, and later, Department Chairman, a post he held for forty years.

Locke was the author of a dozen or more books on Negro life and culture, his interests ranging from folk music to philosophy. He was a major force in the Negro cultural renaissance of the 1920's and his famous anthology, *The New Negro,* chronicled its early history as well as giving impetus to its later flowering. He founded the Associates in Negro Folk Education and edited its series of eight Bronze Booklets. In addition to *The New Negro* and two of the Bronze Booklets, Locke wrote *A Decade of Negro Self-Expression, The Negro in America,* and *Frederick Douglass.* He edited an anthology of Negro plays and one of Negro poetic works, and was coeditor of *When People Meet: A Study in Race and Culture Contacts.* He wrote many scholarly articles on native African Art and for two years before his death in 1954, was hard at work on a definitive statement on black contributions to American culture.

THE NEGRO and HIS MUSIC

by

ALAIN LOCKE, Ph.D.

*Professor of Philosophy,
Howard University.*

THE ASSOCIATES IN NEGRO FOLK EDUCATION
WASHINGTON, D. C.
1936.

PRINTED AND BOUND IN
THE UNITED STATES OF AMERICA
by THE J. B. LYON PRESS,
ALBANY, N. Y.

CONTENTS

THE NEGRO AND HIS MUSIC

EDITORIAL FOREWORD

The author of *"The Negro and His Music"* was born in Philadelphia, September 13, 1886, was educated there; and in college, graduate study and teaching has divided his interests between philosophy on the one hand and literature and art on the other. Following the former, after study at Harvard, Oxford and Berlin Universities, he has taught philosophy at Howard University since 1912, where he is professor of that subject. But avocationally, especially since editing *"The New Negro"* in 1925, he has been active as a literary and art critic and has become a spokesman and interpreter of the Negro's ever-increasing contribution to American culture and art.

I

THE NEGRO AND HIS MUSIC

INTRODUCTION

Is America Musical?—America is a great music consumer, but not as yet a great music producer. Music spreads over the whole surface of American life, but there are few deep well-springs of native music as in the folk music of many other countries. Negro music is the closest approach America has to a folk music, and so Negro music is almost as important for the musical culture of America as it is for the spiritual life of the Negro.

If we ask ourselves why America is not a musical nation, we find that it is because America is not a singing nation. Early colonial America was tuneful only in church, and then in a way neither spontaneous nor original. This was not due to the hardships of the colonial settlers and pioneers, for the people who had the most hardships in America,—the Negroes, turned out to be the songsters of the western world. If the rigors of the climate were responsible, we could never explain the Russians, with their great passion and ability for music. The best explanation is that early America was mostly Anglo-Saxon (more so even than present-day America)—and that meant a weak musical heritage, a very plain musical taste, and a puritan bias against music as a child of sin and the devil, dangerous to work, seriousness and moral restraint. So, early America could only open its throat in church in praise of God; in the daily routine of life, she hummed or whistled simple ditties or chewed and kept silent.

There was open and obvious joy in music only where the French or Spanish influence touched American life

1

as in Louisiana and Southern California, or later where German immigrants with their traditional background of music settled in considerable numbers. The beginnings of American opera were at New Orleans and the beginnings of our great orchestras and their cultivation of serious classical music are to be traced in most instances to German influences. It is doubtful if America would have produced much great or original music without these foreign minority influences.

America's Folk Music.—If American civilization had absorbed instead of exterminating the American Indian, his music would be the folk music of this country. It could have been, for it was a music very noble and simple, full of the spirit of the wind, woods and waters; as serious American musicians have discovered too late to preserve it in any great way. It fell to the lot of the Negro, whom slavery domesticated, to furnish our most original and influential folk music, and because of its contagious spread and popularity, to lay the foundation for native American music. Certainly for the last fifty years, the Negro has been the main source of America's popular music, and promises, as we shall see, to become one of the main sources of America's serious or classical music, at least that part which strives to be natively American and not derivative of European types of music.

Certain strains of folk music,—Irish and Old English, have lingered in our mountain country and the backwoods, and are still important as musical sources. But the Negro's music has gradually swept the field. In doing this, it has overcome a double handicap, for both music and the Negro were generally despised. America did not become song-conscious until the age of Stephen Foster, who was the Joel Chandler Harris of Negro music, breaking its dialect bonds and smoothing it out palatably for the general American ear.

2

Prior to this, Negro music had an idiom too strange and a rhythm too peculiar for popular imitation or appreciation. It was listened to and enjoyed, but as something funny and humorous. In its pure peasant form it was condescendingly known as "plantation music," the South heard it from the "big porch" as comic entertainment. In doctored form, it got its first chance at the general public through the minstel troupes of the 1840's and '50's. Stephen Foster came on the crest of this minstrel vogue to widen its appeal and to set the whole country humming, whistling, and eventually playing and singing Negroid,—that is, diluted versions of Negro melodies and dialect ditties. The real characteristic elements of Negro music, typical Negro rhythm and harmony were only later blended with the stock of American popular music in the age of "ragtime" and "jazz."

But before this, the deep underground stream of Negro folk music was flowing in the veins of the Negro peasant through the heart of the South. From close familiarity, it seeped under the skin of the Southern aristocrats, although as slave owners they had to formally despise it. The plantations were far from the theatres and music-halls; through the Negro they had entertainment and the proxy experience of the deep joys of making music. The South was thus made music-conscious by the Negro, and although its tastes have never been very sophisticated, the South loves music in an intimate and emotional way. So does the Negro; the only difference being that the Negro is by instinct and experience a music-maker. Starting as the South's dancing and singing entertainer, and broadening out to become the minstrel of the North and West, the Negro has gradually but surely become America's troubador.

3

How Musical is the Negro?—But the Negro is American as well as Negro. He has his musical shor' comings. If Negro music is to fulfill its best possibil. ties, Negroes must become musical by nurture and not rest content with being musical by nature. They must build up two things essential for the highest musical success;—a class of trained musicians who know and love the folk music and are able to develop it into great classical music, and a class of trained music lovers who will support by appreciation the best in the Negro's musical heritage and not allow it to be prostituted by the vaudeville stage or Tin Pan Alley, or to be cut off at its folk roots by lack of appreciation of its humble but gifted peasant creators. Our music should not be at the mercy of a popular fad, which may die down at any time, or be exploited, or even developed most seriously by other than Negro musicians. Of course, it is a common possession, a gift that we would not take back even if we could. The use to which the white musician has put Negro music, especially of late, when the most serious musicians of the land have been culti- vating it, is a tribute as welcome as it is deserved. But the final exponent of Negro music should be the Negro himself. Today it is admitted that he is, so far as the execution or performance of this music is con- cerned; but it is doubtful whether the Negro has yet become an undisputed master in the creative compo- sition of music based on his native racial idiom and tradition. So Negro music today needs some bitter tonic of criticism as well as its sweet mead of praise.

One of the handicaps of Negro music today is that it is too popular. It is tarnished with commercialism and the dust of the market-place. The very musicians who know the folk-ways of Negro music are the very ones who are in commercial slavery to the Shylocks of Tin Pan Alley, in artistic bondage to the ready cash

4

of our dance-halls and the vaudeville stage. They have no time for composition of a serious kind, and little chance to study great music for inspiration. On the other hand, our musicians with formal training are cut off from the people and the vital roots of folk music, and live uncreatively in the cloisters of the conservatories, many of them under the palling taboos of musical "respectability." Only lately have some of them learned to openly study and admire the folk music sources of what is most original and promising in Negro music.

It is time to realize that, though we are a musical people, we have as yet produced too few great musicians; perhaps no exceedingly great musician (although America herself scarcely has). Our creativeness on the folk level has not yet been matched by widespread instrumental mastery or great creativeness in musical composition of the more formal and serious kind. And because of this, many white musicians have had to be pioneers in developing certain phases of Negro music.

All this shows that the Negro must look to his musical laurels, and not go to sleep on his great heritage. A great folk music deserves and demands a great classical music. People with the folk gift of spontaneous harmony should breed great composers. A folk who can improvise great and moving choral orchestras, for that is what a Negro singing group really is, should eventually have great opera, expert symphony orchestras, and skilled virtuosi or technical master-musicians. We shall see signs of such developments in the later chapters of this booklet; but the development must be speeded up. Many schools of national music, now great, were once in this same retarded state. In the eighteenth Century, even France and Germany borrowed their music from Italy; in the nineteenth, Russia imported her formal music from the Italy and France. But in less than three-score years, great composers have developed these dormant bodies of folk music to world influence and recognition. Negro folk music and its derivatives in popular music,—jazz and ragtime, already have world vogue and acceptance. Our serious music is beginning to bud, but is for the most part at the stage of Russian music before Glinka, called the "father of Russian Music," or Hungarian music before Liszt and Brahms, or Bohemian music before Dvorak and Smetana.

So while we look at the past of Negro music, creditable and interesting as it is, we must have constantly in mind its future, if it is to realize its promise and successfully compete for the honor of being the basis of the great national music that America will some day produce.

QUESTIONS FOR DISCUSSION

Is America musical?—Is there a native American music? What strains of music could have been the basis for America's music? Why no great American Music? Is America becoming more musical, and why?

Is the Negro musical? By native endowment? By training?—How did Negro music come to favor in America?—Has its popularity been an unmixed blessing?—What effect has it had on Negro musicians?—Should Negro musicians study closely the folk-music?—Has classical musical training helped or hindered the creativeness of the Negro musician?—What are the prospects of Negro music?—Will "jazz" and "ragtime" end the vogue of Negro music or will a classical school of Negro music arise?

6

READING REFERENCES

Henderson, W. J.: *Why No Great American Music*—American Mercury, July, 1934.

Howard, John Tasker. *Our American Music*—Crowell,—1931.

Howard, John Tasker: *Native Elements in American Music*—American Scholar, May, 1934.

Johnson, James Weldon: *The Book of American Negro Poetry;*—Harcourt, Brace, 1922. Preface on *The Negro's Cultural Genius:* pp. 9–22.

Locke, Alain: *Toward a Critique of Negro Music*—Opportunity Magazine, November & December, 1934.

Vaughan—Williams, Ralph: *National Music*—Oxford University Press, N. Y., 1934.

II
NEGRO MUSIC: ITS TYPES AND PERIODS

Three Types: Folk; Popular; Classical.—There are three strands in the music of the Negro. One is his folk music, produced without formal musical training or intention by the greatest and most fundamental of all musical forces,—emotional creation. In the Negro's case, this creative force was deep suffering and its spiritual compensation in intense religious emotion and ecstasy. This rich and tragic vein of emotional expression not only has yielded us the "Spirituals," but has produced the most characteristic Negro musical idiom,—sad but not somber, intense but bouyant, tragic but ecstatic. Much of its irresistable appeal comes from such a unique and paradoxical combination of emotional elements.

The Negro's own natural reaction back to gaiety and humor and away from the intense reactions of his enforced sorrow and seriousness gave birth to the second strain of Negro folk music,—light, mock-sentimental, and full of pagan humor and pungent irony. Very little pure folk music of this lighter strain remains, because in highly diluted form, imitatively exploited by both white and Negro musicians, it has become the principal source and ingredient of American popular music. Indeed it has been the fate of both strains of Negro folk music to become crudely imitated and highly diluted with the tragic and heroic elements watered down to the sentimental and the comical and ironical flattened out into the burlesque and farcical. There is no truer test of what is genuine folk quality in Negro music than to remember this; to contrast, for example, the melodramatic sentimentality of a

8

manufactured spiritual like *"De Glory Road"* with the heroic simplicity of *"Go Down Moses"* or *"My Lord, What a Mornin',"* or again the contrast of the slapstick comedy of *"It Ain't Goin' Rain No More"* with the true folk humor of *"Oh, Didn't It Rain."*

The third strain is a strictly formal or classical type of music, properly styled Negro music only when obviously derived from folk music idioms or strongly influenced by them. Music in the universal mode without trace of folk idiom and influence earns cultural credit for the race when composed by Negro musicians and is properly mentioned in this or any other similar account, but is in no proper sense styled "Negro music." Contemporary "classical jazz," however, whether written by white or Negro musicians, is properly labelled "Negro music," because it is basically Negro in deriviation and inspiration. A rapidly growing amount of such "classical jazz" is an important part of our present-day typical or national American music, and it is to be reckoned as one of the Negro's major cultural contributions.

Thus we have three streams of musical expression to follow and explore,—all of folk origin, direct or remote, and a fourth separate strand of art music representing the Negro's participation in the general mainstream of cosmopolitan or classical music. We shall follow them in this order. First, the great dialect music of the Spirituals,—the true Negro folk-classics. Then the petty dialect of popular music, ragtime and jazz, and finally "classical jazz" and the transition to the universal speech of formal art music. Original folk spirituals, like *"Steal Away," "Go Down, Moses,"* or *"My Lord, What a Mornin',"* represent the folk classics or pure folk music. So in their way do the unadulterated secular ballads and genuine folk blues, like *"John Henry," "Steel Drivin Sam,"* the *"St.*

9

Louis Blues," "St. James Infirmary Blues" or "I'm an 'Easman." Then we have that broad but shallower stream of popular music, Negro and Negroid according to its degree of dilution, from "Swanee River" and "Alexander's Ragtime Band" to "Dinah" and "Minnie the Moocher." Occasionally, as with much of Stephen Foster's ballads or in close folk versions like Handy's "Careless Love," music of this popular strain achieves the level of the semi-classical and becomes the lasting classic of popular taste rather than the fugitive "hit of the season" or "money hit" of "Tin Pan Alley." On the next level, we have classical jazz such as Duke Ellington's "Black and Tan Fantasy" or his "Reminiscing in Tempo" or George Gershwin's "Rhapsody in Blue" and finally, the straight classics such as William Dawson's "Negro Folk Symphony," or Grant Still's "Afro-American Symphony" or Coleridge-Taylor's oratorio "Hiawatha."

The Ages of Negro Music.—Each type of Negro music we have mentioned has had a blossoming season. But that does not imply that under the spell of some genius or the sun of some revived interest, it cannot blossom again. In fact, we shall see a number of such cases. However, on the whole, each successive decade or so has had its characteristic and typical bloom. Though we have just about learned to appreciate it properly, the great heyday of our folk music is obviously over. Even the sultry and prolific jazz age begins to show some signs of change and decay. Nearly as obviously, we seem to be nearing another peak development, this time, of classical music based on Negro idioms and themes. But counting them in strict succession, there seems to have been about seven ages of Negro music from its infancy to the present; though we must hasten to add that, Shakespeare to the contrary, the seventh age is far from an age of decadence and decline. Although there is, of course, some over-lapping, these seven periods and their approximate dates are:

Before 1830—1. *The Age of Plantation Shout and "Breakdown."* Dominated by African Reminiscences and Survivals.

1830–1850—2. *The Age of the Sorrow-Songs: The Classic Folk Period:* The Great Spirituals and the Folk Ballads.

1850–1875—3. *The First Age of Minstrelsy:* Stephen Foster and the Sentimental Ballad.

1875–1895—4. *The Second Age of Minstrelsy:* Farce and Buffoonery;—the "Buck and Wing," the "Coon Song," the "Folk Blues."

1895–1918—5. *The Age of Ragtime:* Vaudeville and Musical Comedy.

1918–1926—*The Jazz Age:* The Stomp, the Artificial Blues and Dance Comedy.

1926 to date—*The Age of Classical Jazz;* with the dawn of Classical Negro Music.

Of course, exceptional cases are plentiful: a few Negro classical musicians quite anticipated the present day, when Negro music seems to be approaching real maturity on the plane of formal music. Spirituals are still being created, but no one doubts that the real age of the sorrow songs has passed. But in the main the growth of Negro music has travelled this course, and it will be used as a road-map in our historical review of the subject.

11

Once in a while we shall seem to go out of the way, because it will be necessary at times to follow separately the two strands of "folk" and "classical," and at other times to keep them clear from the merely popular. One of our main interests, even if we are interested in classical music, must be to follow closely the course of folk music. Because the musical experience of humanity has taught us that here are the roots of all great music, and that great geniuses when they arise almost invariably turn to it for source material and inspiration. Much classical music is folk music at second or third remove from the original source.

The Step-Ladder of Folk Music.—Folk elements do not necessarily make folk music. Only when pure and in the form originally used by the people for themselves, do they yield us true folk music. This is why real folk music is rare; but it is the most precious musical ore we have. When folk elements are stereotyped and artificially imitated, we have popular music with a folk flavor: from *"Yankee Doodle"* to *"Old Folks at Home."* When developed and blended with the technique of formal music, they are no longer content with the simple forms of the folk ballad or sentimental ballad, and yield classical music of folk origin; as Dett's *"Juba Dance"* or a concert arrangement of a "spiritual," or a *"Symphony on Folk Themes."* When so thoroughly blended as to be recognized only upon technical musical analysis, folk music has become completely universalized and has made its final contribution, as the German chorale in a Bach instrumental *Chorale* or a Polish folk dance in a *Polonaise.*

But though the great masters often use this highest kind of universal musical speech in which the layman does not recognize the folk elements, they themselves know it and often admit that the finest taproots of their art run down deep into the sub-soil of folk music.

12

Even after the themes, harmonies and color have been refined out, basic rhythms betray the original folk sources. Thus the forms of Italian opera come from provincial folk-songs; the great classical music of Germany from German folk songs and dances; Spain and Russia likewise. A song or a harmony which was originally at home in the mountain valleys of the Caucasus or the lonely Northern Steppes or the half-Asiatic towns of Russian Georgia would wind up finally on the pens of the great Russian composers of St. Petersburg and Moscow and on the grand opera stages of the Imperial Opera and Ballet. So when the folk songs of the Negro of the Georgia plantations or the Carolina rice-fields or the Mississippi bayous turn up as spirituals and blues in European concert-halls, as they do, or as ingredients in the symphonies of European composers like Dvorak, Delius, Milhaud or in the equally elaborate formal work of Negro composers like Dawson, Dett and Still, they are following a path common to all musical development.

Is Folk Idiom Racial or National?—The answer is both, because it is only a difference of degree. What for Negro music we call racial is only an intensified variety of the same elements that we called national. Likewise, if we call the Negro especially musical, he is so only in degree. As we approach the peasant stocks of the Irish, Italian, German and Russian nations, we see they all have their well-springs of folk music. It has simply been the lot of the Negro in America to be the peasant class, and thus to furnish the musical sub-soil of our national music. This has been true for a double reason. The Negro experience has led to a peculiar need for emotional expression. Also, the Anglo-Saxon stocks which have been the dominant forces in American civilization are not as highly endowed musically as other races, the Latin,

13

Scandinavian, Slav and Negro. All peoples produce as exceptions great music and great musicians, but we call a people musical, when in addition to this, they invent and sustain large volumes of spontaneous folk music. The Negro's musical claims have until recently rested mainly upon the latter. But now he has also begun to produce, in addition to folk music, worthy formal musicians and music of the classical type.

The Negro's Cultural Gifts.—Of the four gifts which James Weldon Johnson cites in his well-known preface to *"The Book of American Negro Poetry,"* three are musical. He says:

These creations by the American Negro may be summed up under four heads. The first two are the Uncle Remus stories, which were collected by Joel Chandler Harris, and the "spirituals" or slave songs, to which the Fisk Jubilee Singers made the public and the musicians of both the United States and Europe listen. The Uncle Remus stories constitute the greatest body of folk lore that America has produced, and the "spirituals" the greatest body of folk song.

The other two creations are the cakewalk and ragtime. We do not need to go very far back to remember when cakewalking was the rage in the United States, Europe and South America. Society in this country and royalty abroad spent time in practicing the intricate steps. Paris pronounced it the "poetry of motion." The popularity of the cakewalk passed away but its influence remained. The influence can be seen today on any American stage wherever there is dancing.

The influence which the Negro has exercised on the art of dancing in this country has been almost absolute. For generations the "buck and wing" and the "stop-time" dances, which are strictly Negro, have been familiar to American theatre audiences. A few years ago the public discovered the "turkey trot," the "eagle rock," "ballin' the jack," and several other varieties that started the modern dance craze. The dances were quickly followed by the "tango," a dance originated by the Negroes of Cuba and later transplanted to South America.

Rhythm as a Folk Gift.—Without doubt the Negro's chief native musical gift is his instinctive mastery of rhythm. Master also of pitch and harmony, as are all folk-singing peoples, he excels most all other races in the mastery of rhythm. One naturally wonders why! Many reasons have been given, but the most likely is the Negro's long and intimate contact with the original source of rhythm,—the dance. With him

14

dancing has always been a spontaneous and normal mode of expression rather than an artificial and formalized one. No matter how set the general pattern is, the Negro always improvizes as he dances, whether in solo or group dancing. And although much Negro dancing seems confined to foot dancing, really the rhythm always begins from within as a body vibration, and throughout the whole dance the body vibrates sympathetically. It is typical for any Negro audience to follow any rhythm it may be watching or hearing. Moreover, it is the typical Negro reaction to embroider whatever basic rhythm is set,—changing, doubling, skipping beats in a fashion bewildering to those less expert in rhythmic patterns and designs. Along with this, the Negro dance has the feature, characteristic of Russian, Polish and other Slavic folk-dances, of sudden changes of the pace and daring climaxes of tempo. These subtle ways of varying the simplest of rhythmic patterns is the secret of their unusual and basic musical ability. Modern jazz and dance artists have proved that this art can be learned after close study and familiarity with Negro performers and dancers; however, experts usually detect a more mechanical regularity to even the best Anglo-Saxon imitations. Many think the Negro expression of rhythm inimitable in its naturalness, lack of self-consciousness, its freedom and technical assurance.

The Dance Sources.—So as James Weldon Johnson has said: "The influence the Negro has exercised on the art of dancing in America has been almost absolute." Throughout the ages, the influence of the dance upon music has also been almost absolute. We know how much the gavotte, minuet, waltz, polka, mazurka and sarabande, as folk dances, have contributed to European music, popular and classical. This basis for American music has for the most part been laid down

15

by the figures, rhythm and tempo of Negro dances;
the "breakdown," the "buck and wing," and numerous
other "stop time" dances,—the "turkey trot," the
"eagle rock," "ballin' the jack," the "cakewalk," the
"Charleston," the "black bottom," the "shimmy," down
to the humble but contagious contemporary "truckin'."
As we come down the list to our own generation, this
influence is only too obvious. But what of it, from the
point of view of serious music? Well, musical history
tells us of a day when the waltz was too vulgar for
the court and the ballroom (and at that time, it was) ;
but what of the Viennese court at Schönbrun two
generations later, and the Strausses, the Schuberts and
Schumanns that made it respectable and musically
creative! It is the same story with the Negro folk
things that begin on plantations, levees and cabarets
and have triumphantly invaded in turn the stage, the
ballroom, the salon and finally the musical conservatories. When we add to these typical North American
Negro forms, the rather unknown fact that the "tango"
rhythm is of Afro-Cuban origin, one clearly sees that
American music and modernistic music have a Negro
basis.

So as we follow the ages of Negro music we shall
also be witnessing the gradual development of native
American music.

DISCUSSION QUESTIONS

What relation exists usually between folk music and
classical music? What is the relation of popular music
to folk music? What musical contributions is the
Negro said to have' made to America in general and
American music in particular? What historical reasons
and social conditions led to the Negro's becoming the
"peasant source of folk music in America?" In addition to these special experiences, was the Negro natively
endowed musically? In what directions? Is folk-

16

music racial or national in basis? Is the Negro influence on American dance forms musically important? Why? What reasons are there for thinking Negro folk music will follow the same course as other folk music? If so, will American music be Negro, Negroid or American? What are the main historical stages of Negro music?

READING REFERENCES

Johnson, Rosamond: *Rolling Along in Song*—Viking Press, N. Y., 1936. (Comprehensive Collection with music arrangements)

Odum, H. W. and Guy B. Johnson: *The Negro and His Songs*—University of North Carolina Press, 1925.

Odum and Johnson: *Negro Workaday Songs*—University of North Carolina Press, 1926.

Scarborough, Dorothy: *On the Trail of Negro Folk Songs*—Harvard University Press, 1925.

White, Newmon I: *American Negro Folk Songs*, 1928.

Work, J. W.: *Folk Songs of the American Negro*, 1915.

Folk-songs in the Making: Literary Digest 101, April, 1929.

Negro Spirituals in the Making: Musical Quarterly, 17—October, 1931.

17

III

THE SORROW-SONGS: THE SPIRITUALS

The Sorrow Songs.—The spirituals are the most characteristic product of Negro genius to date. They are its great folk-gift, and rank among the classic folk expressions in the whole world because of their moving simplicity, their characteristic originality, and their universal appeal. Although the products of the slave era and the religious fervor of the plantation religion, they have outlived the generation and the conditions which produced them. But they have not always been properly appreciated or understood. One of the proofs of their classic immortality lies in what abuses the spirituals have survived.

They have lived through the contempt of the slave-owners. It was only cultured observers with the Union armies like Wm. Allen and Colonel Thos. Wentworth Higginson who called them to the attention of music-lovers. Then, although they were never written down or formally composed in definite versions, they have survived imperishably. Evolved from hymns, they were again driven out of the church worship by the conventions of respectability and the repressions of Puritanism as the Negro church became more sophisticated. Finally, after enduring the neglect and disdain of second-generation respectability, spirituals have had to survive successive waves of false popularizations, first the corruptions of sentimental balladry, then a period of concert polishing, and finally the contemporary stage of being "ragged" or "jazzed."

How They Survived.—They were first given to the musical world not as slave songs, but as "jubilees." It

18

is a romantic story, told in Pike's *"Story of the Jubilee Singers,"* and retold in Professor Work's *"Folk Songs of the American Negro."* It is the tale of that group of singers who started out from Fisk University in 1871, under the resolute leadership of George L. White, to make this music the appeal of that struggling college for funds. With all the cash in the Fisk treasury, except a dollar held back by Principal Adam K. Spence, the troupe set out to Oberlin, where after an unsuccessful concert of current music, they instantly made an impression by a program of spirituals. Henry Ward Beecher's invitation to Brooklyn led to a national and international hearing, repeated tours all over America and Europe,—fame for the singers, fortune for the college, but most important of all, recognition for Negro folk music. Other schools, Hampton, Atlanta, Calhoun, Tuskegee and a host of others joined the movement, and spread the knowledge of these songs far and wide in their concert campaigns. Later they were recorded and saved permanently as collection after collection was published. Thus they were saved during that critical period in which any folk product is likely to be snuffed out by the false pride of the second generation. Professor Work rightly estimates this a service worth much more to the race and the nation than the considerable sums of money brought to these struggling schools. Indeed it saved a folk art, preserved the most perfect registration of the Negro folk temperament and the most unique embodiment of its folk experience. Still during this period the spirituals were too often treated sentimentally, and their deepest tragic feeling and their purest folk artistry overlooked.

Their Rediscovery.—Only since 1900 has the profundity and true folk character of the spirituals been gradually discovered and recognized. It was one of the great services of Dr. Du Bois, in his unforgettable

19

chapter on *"The Sorrow Songs"* to give them a serious and proper interpretation as the peasant's instinctive distillation of sorrow and his spiritual triumph over it in a religious ecstasy and hope. Men then began to realize that though naive and simple, they were really very profound. Underneath broken words, childish imagery, peasant simplicity, was an epic intensity and a tragic depth of religious emotion for which the only equal seems to have been the spiritual experience of the Jews, and for which the only analogue is the Psalms. The spirituals stand out, therefore, as one of the great classic expressions of all time of religious emotion and Christian moods and attitudes.

Shortly after this, Henry Krehbiel, one of the great music critics of his generation, gave the spirituals their first serious and adequate musical analysis and interpretaton in his *"Afro-American Folk Songs."* By this time, they had definitely come into their own and were recognized not only as unique folk music but as the main strand in American folk-song. Already they had been taken out of their original religious setting, and adapted to secular uses, some of them unworthy of their great dignity and spirituality. This was particularly true in their use as catch-penny sentimental appeals in the missionary campaigning of the Negro schools. Only with the original Fisk Singers was their real simplicity and dignity maintained. They were then carried still further from their proper sphere to the minstrel stage and the concert hall.

But just about this time they received the highest possible recognition,—that of being used as the thematic material for symphonic music through their incorporation in the epoch-making work of Anton Dvorak, the Bohemian composer, who chose them to represent American atmosphere in his symphony *"From the New World"* (1894).—Since then, the spirituals and even

20

the secular Negro folk melodies and their harmonic style have been regarded by most musicians as the purest and most valuable musical ore in America; the raw materials of a native American music. So gradually ever since, their folk quality and purity of style have been emphasized by real musicians. Eventually on another level, they will come back to their original power and purity. We should always remember that they are not sentimental nor theatrical, but epic and full of simple dignity. They are also essentially choral in character, and not at their best in solo voice or solo instrumental form. They will find their truest development, then, in symphonic music or in the larger choral forms of the symphonic choir, like the development which the great modern Russian composers have brought to Russian folk music. At this stage, on a higher level, they will reachieve their folk atmosphere and epic spirituality.

But let us go back to the originals,—the true spirituals. Many songs called spirituals are far from being so. The term is often very inaccurately used, especially to denote later artificial compositions which imitate the folk spirituals or dress them up in sentimental and concert versions. Yet age alone is not the hallmark of a true spiritual; for although the last generation of slavery from 1845-65 was their hey-day, genuine spirituals are composed in primitive Negro communities even today. However, a genuine spiritual is always a folk composition or a group product, spontaneously composed as a choral expression of religious feeling, or as Miss Zora Hurston aptly puts it,—"by a group bent on the expression of feelings and not on sound effects." She coins the useful term "neo-spirituals" to describe the artificial derivatives which we are all familiar with in the entertainment spirituals of the concert-hall and glee-club rendition. These "reno-

21

vated spirituals," she says correctly, "are a valuable contribution to the musical literature, but they are not the genuine thing. Let no one imagine they are the true songs of the people as sung by them."

Negro spirituals thus are not originally solo or quartette material. They are congregational outbursts under the pressure of great religious emotion,—choral improvisations on themes familiar to all the participants. Each singing of the piece is a new creation, and the changes, interpolations, variations defy the most expert musician's recording. Before they completely vanish in their original form, this congregational folk-singing, with its unique breaks and tricks, should be recorded by phonograph, the only way their full values can be gotten.

Needless to say, the early four-part hymn harmony versions were mere approximations and travesties of the real folk singing. Both the rhythm, phrasing and harmony are much more complex and irregular. Only recently have we recaptured in any art oganization the true flavor and manner of these songs. But a record of the Eva Jessye Choir or the Hall Johnson Singers will give us our closest reproduction of the genuine Negro way of singing these songs. Both of them, it will be noticed, have the actual mechanics of improvised Negro choral singing, with its syllabic quavers, off-tones and tone glides, improvised interpolations, subtle rhythmic variation. In most conventional versions of the spirituals there is too much melody and formal harmony. Over-emphasize the melodic elements of a spiritual, and you get a sentimental ballad à la Stephen Foster. Stress the harmony and you get a cloying glee or "barber-shop" chorus. Over-emphasize, on the other hand, the rhythmic idiom and instantly you secularize the product and it becomes a syncopated shout, with the religious tone and mood completely evaporated. It is

22

only in a subtle fusion of these elements that the genuine folk spiritual exists or that it can be recaptured.

At present, spirituals are at a very difficult point in their career; they are caught in the transitional stage between a folk-form and an art-form. Their increasing popularity has brought a dangerous tendency to sophistication and over-elaboration. Even Negro composers have been too much influenced by formal European idioms and mannerisms in setting them. This is slightly true of the work of Mr. Henry T. Burleigh, who must be credited, however, as the musician who won for the spirituals the acclaim and acceptance of the concert stage. He is the father of the art spiritual, even though some of his settings have overlaid the folk spirit with concert furbelows and alien florid adornments.

This does not mean that there is only one style of rendering spirituals. The folk itself has many styles. It only means that the folk quality and atmosphere should be preserved as much as possible. To realize this, one has only to compare the robust and dramatic rendering of the Negro baritone Paul Robeson with the subdued, ecstatic and mystic renderings of Roland Hayes. Both are great interpretations; and each typical of a vein of Negro singing. As long as the peculiar quality of Negro song is maintained and the musical idiom kept pure, there can be no valid criticism. Complaint cannot legitimately be made against the concert use and the art development of the spirituals, but only against the glossed-over versions characteristic of those arrangers and singers who have not closely studied the primitive Negro folk-ways of singing.

Solo vs. Choral Versions.—In spite of the effectiveness of the solo versions, especially when competently and reverently sung in the true Negro manner, it is being realized more and more that the proper idiom of these songs calls for choral arrangement. The vital sustained background of accompanying voices is important. The younger Negro musicians Nathaniel Dett, Carl Diton, Ballanta Taylor, Edward Boatner, Lawrence Brown, Hall Johnson and Eva Jessye, while they have written effective solo versions, are turning with increasing interest to the choral form. Herein lies the significance of the newer types of Negro choral choir that are beginning to appear or re-appear, among them the excellent choral organizations led by Eva Jessye and Hall Johnson. They have about restored the spirituals to their primitive choral basis and their original singing style. Developed along the lines of its own originality, we may expect a development of Negro folk song that may equal or even outstrip the phenomenal choral music of Russia.

Negro music should be expected to flower most naturally in the field of vocal music, since its deepest folk roots are there. Commenting critically on a recent Carnegie Hall concert of a well-known and well-trained Negro University Chorus, Mr. Olin Downes, prominent music critic, soundly advised more singing in the true Negro idiom and less effort at imitation of other types of choral singing. Some interpreted this advice as a biased curtain-lecture to Negro singing groups to stick to their own limited province. But this was not the real issue. No one could ban from Negro groups the whole range of universal music. It was rather the advice to develop a great and unique musical style out of the powerful musical dialect which we have in our most characteristic folk-songs; as such organizations as the Ukrainian Singers, the Russian Symphonic Choir, the Don Cossack's Chorus have done from the Russian folk music and its unique styles of singing. Two Victor recordings of the Hall Johnson Chorus illustrate how this double uniqueness of singing style and folk melo-

24

dies can be effectively used. Eventually choral works of an entirely new sort can and must come from Negro sources. While seculars like *"St. James Infirmary Blues," "Water Boy"* and *"I'm an Eastman"* are used in this particular recording similar choral arrangement of the Spirituals has been tried and found successful. Someday too a great creative composer might develop a great liturgical music out of the musical materials of the Spirituals.

So these "sorrow songs" are more than a priceless heritage from the racial past, they are promising material for the Nego music of the future. And they are the common possession of all, part of the cultural currency of the land, as their popularity and universal appeal only too clearly proves. A "Society for the Preservation of the Spirituals" organized in Charleston, S. C. by a white singing organization is a striking symbol of this common duty to restore them to dignity and respect.

DISCUSSION QUESTIONS

Why are the spirituals a "classic expression of the Negro folk-spirit"? What generation's experience do they represent? Can they be understood by a generation lacking that experience? To what extent are they racial? To what extent universal? Have Negroes always appreciated them? What reasons have there been and to what uses have they been put that would tend to obscure their meaning? What changes of singing style have occurred in their rendition? What is the original style? Is this original style best and how has it been recaptured by modern musicians? What organizations and leaders have been prominent in this movement? Are the spirituals best as choral or as solo music? What similarity is there between them and Russian folksongs? Will a great school of choral music

25

arise from their further cultivation? What sentiments
and moods do they reflect?

READING REFERENCES

Burlin, Natalie Curtis: *Negro Music at Birth*—Musical Quarterly,
January, 1919.

Dett, Nathaniel: *"Religious Folk Songs of the Negro"*—Hampton Press,
1927.

DuBois, W. E. B.: *The Sorrow Songs* in *"Souls of Black Folk;"* 1903.

Higginson, T. W.: Chapter IX in *"Army Life in a Black Regiment"*—
Boston, 1870.

Jessye, Eva: *My Spirituals*—Robbins-Engel, 1927.

Johnson, Hall: *"The Green Pastures Spirituals:"*—1932.

Johnson, James Weldon & Rosamund J. Johnson:
The Book of American Spirituals—Viking Press, 1925.
The Second Book of Negro Spirituals—Viking Press, 1926.

Krehbiel, H. E.: *Afro-American Folk Songs.* Scribner, N. Y., 1914.

Locke, Alain: *The Spirituals* in *The New Negro,* 1925.

McIlhenny, E. A.: *Befo' the War Spirituals.* Christopher Pub. Co.

Taylor, Ballanta, Nicholas: *St. Helena Spirituals.*

RECORD ILLUSTRATIONS

"City Called Heaven" (arranged Hall Johnson); *"Lord I Can't Stay
Away* (arr. Roland Hayes); *"Heaven, Heaven"* (arr. Burleigh)
sung by Marion Anderson—Victor 8958.

"Were You There" and *"Steal Away"* sung by Paul Robeson—Victor
19742.

"Sometimes I feel Like a Motherless Child" (arr. Lawrence Brown)
and *"On Ma Journey"* (arr. Edward Boatner)—Robeson—Victor
20013.

"My Lord What a Mornin'" (Burleigh) and *"Weepin' Mary"* and
"I Want to be Ready" sung by Paul Robeson—His Master's Voice
—B 2897.

Choral Versions:

Hall Johnson Chorus: *Three Spirituals:* Victor 36020.

Fisk Jubilee Singers: *"Ezekiel Saw the Wheel"* and *"Little David"*—
Columbia 818 D.
"Every Time I feel de Spirit" and *"Steal Away to Jesus"*—
Columbia 562 D.

Birmingham Jubilee Singers: *"I Heard the Preachin' of the Elders"*—
Columbia 14345.
"Where are You Runnin', Sinner?"
"Do You Call that Religion" and *"Home in that Rock"*—Columbia
14163 D.

Dixie Jubilee Singers: *"'I Couldn't Hear Nobody Pray"* and *"Roll,
Jordan, Roll"*—Brunswick 2773.

"Neo-Spirituals" or *Religious Songs Modelled on "Spirituals":*

Pace Jubilee Singers: *"Every Time I feel the Spirit"*—Victor 38019. *"Seek and You Shall Find"* and *"God's Goin' a Move this Wicked Race"*—Victor 21705.

Hattie Parker: *"I Do, Don't You"*—Victor 26226 B.

Blind Willie Johnson: *"I Know His Blood Can Make Me Whole"* and *"Jesus Make Up My Dying Bed"*—Columbia 14276 D. *"Mother's Children Have a Hard Time"* and *"If I Had My Way, I'd Tear this Building Down"*—Columbia 14343 D.

Lawrence Tibbett: *De Glory Road*—(Wolfe)—Victor 7486.

John Charles Thomas: *'Gwine to Hebb'n.* Victor 1544.

IV

SECULAR FOLK SONGS

THE BLUES AND WORK-SONGS

The Other Folk Strain.—Second only to the spirituals is the secular or non-religious folk music of Negro peasant origin. For generations it was neglected and despised. Indirectly it has come into its own through its influence on popular music of the ragtime and jazz era. But "rag" and "jazz" are only diluted versions of it; far from representing its true strength and quality. People who rave over its equivalent in foreign lands have until recently looked down on it and so we have let most of it die out unrecorded. Now the musical folk-lorist is trying hard to preserve its last remnants and to reconstruct the older primitive versions from the "fancy" popularizations that are still current. It has now become fashionable to collect Negro folk ditties and work-songs; and even the "blues" have taken on musical respectability. We now see in them unique expressions of Negro emotion, folk-wit and musical inventiveness.

The Secular Themes.—This material·is far more fragmentary than the spirituals, but being a combination of folk poetry and folk music, the words are welded closer to the music than in the case of the spirituals. For they were more of a direct improvization than the spirituals, which in thought were too influenced by the evangelical hymns after which they were originally modelled. Some Negro seculars also were dialect versions of old ballads current in colonial days. Many of the "mountain ballads," now equally prized after generations of neglect, can be found in parallel Negro

28

and white versions; "Frankie and Johnnie" is an instance. However, most Negro ballads are very racy and quite original. They deal even more often with unrequited love, though there are a number glorifying risky and dare-devil adventure. The Negro love themes are almost invariably treated more ironically and less sentimentally, however, than their Caucasian analogues. Whatever the theme, whether it be the sob or the laugh, the plea or the threat, despair or revenge, defeat or triumph, the mood is registered in pithy phrases and vivid imagery having the elemental force of life itself. "Joe Turner" says "Ef yo' don't believe Ah'm leavin', jes count de days Ah'm gone;" the deserted girl ironically wails "Ticket agent, ease your window down, De man I love done lef' dis town;" or " 'Twa'n't for powder an' fo' store-bought hair, De man ah love wouldn't a-gone nowhere," or even more poetically:

> "We wreck our love boats on the shoals,
> And in the wreckage of desire,
> We sigh for wings like Noah's dove
> To fly away from loveless love."

The Music.—But for every dozen labor and work-songs and folk ballads still preserved, we have unfortunately only one genuine folk tune. Most of the folk-lorists interested in this material were not skilled musicians and could only transcribe the words. Yet here was folk music of the first water. Growing up as part of the workaday rhythms of daily toil, with genuine, unsophisticated moods, these work songs have a swing which is irresistible and a philosophy which is elemental. The classic of this type is *"John Henry,"* which exists in scores of versions. The levee songs are another important variety; likewise a few of the older ballads, which are rare. As we shall see later, "blues"

29

are not a part of this original folk-saga; but are a later product of the same folk spirit, being often a "one-man affair originating typically as the expression of a single singer's feelings." Whereas the oldest seculars were group songs and often group compositions, in which one person took the chant lead, but the body of the song was moulded in improvised chorus. The railroad and chain-gang singing is the last survival of this practice which once was universal on the levees, in the cotton-fields, as well as in the plantation meetings and the first generation camp-meetings and revivals. *"Water-Boy"* is a late synthetic version of this original and typical folk thing.

Zones of Negro Seculars.—We must never forget that Negro folk music is regional. That is, it belongs to a particular locality and has many local differences. Close comparative study has not yet been made. But we can safely divide Negro secular folk-songs into six zones or provinces, each with its characteristic flavor and musical idiom. They are:

I. Virginia and the Upper South—

Melodic—earliest to gain favor—heavily influenced by Irish and English folk ballads and dances—the school that finally gave us Jim Bland and *"Carry Me Back to Ole Virginny."*

II. The Creole South—

Also a mixed tradition—melodic—influenced by Spanish French and Cuban idioms—"lullaby" and Negro version of French folk ballad typical. Examples: *"Petite Ma'mselle"*—*"M'sieu Banjo."*

30

III. The Seaboard Lower South—

A more racy strain of folk-balladry—product of the Carolinas and Georgia—realistic, less sentimental—road songs—pickin'-songs — shouts — game-songs — blues—ballads. Examples: *"John Henry"—"Casey Jones."*

IV. The Mississippi Strain—

Levee and Delta music—racy—sentimental—the tap-root of jazz—*"Joe Turner,"* *"Memphis Blues"—"St. Louis"* and *"Gulf Coast Blues."*

V. The Southwest—

The Kansas, Oklahoma, Missouri strain—heavy influence of the cow-boy and Western ballad style—*"St. James Infirmary Blues."* Negroid, not pure Negro—parallel versions.

VI. The Mountain Music—

Parallel Negro versions of Hill Ballads—Kentucky and Virginia Highlands—Negroid—*"Frankie and Johnnie"—"Careless Love."*

Obviously the first four are the more typically racial and important. The Upper South influenced the music of the first and second age of minstrelsy and also gave us the spirituals, for the most part. Jazz, by common knowledge sprang from the Mississippi strain. A complete geography of Negro folk music has yet to be worked out, however.

"Joe Turner" and *"John Henry." "John Henry"* is supposed to be the grandaddy of the Negro ballads as *"Joe Turner"* is of the 'Blues." The work-song

31

type is composed of several short lines repeated with pauses intervening for the stroke of a pick or hammer, and is usually sung by a group; while the classical blues form is "a three line verse with exact or slightly variant repetition of the first line, and a climactic third line finishing off the mood with a proverbial twist or epigram."

"John Henry said to his captain,
Well—a man ain't nuthin but a man,
And before I'll let your steam-drill beat me down,
I'll die wid' my hammer in my hand,
I'll die wid' my hammer in my hand."

and

"You'll never miss the water till de well runs dry,
Never miss the water till the well runs dry,
An' never miss Joe Turner 'till he says good-bye.

"Sweet babe, I'm going' to leave you, and the time ain't long,
No, the time ain't long,
If you don't believe I'm leavin', count the days I'm gone.

Dr. Guy Johnson says: "John Henry is the Negro's greatest folk character. . . . The songs, of a narrative ballad type, sung most frequently as a solo with banjo or guitar accompaniment, are the heart of the legend which has sprung up around him. . . . No description of the harmonic and rhythmic beauties of the Negro work song can do the subject justice. The concerted movements, the grunts emerging at each stroke of pick or hammer, the off-pitch, slurring, sliding attacks made on the tones, the unsteady harmonic patterns, these have to be seen and heard in order to be understood."

Miss Scarborough has found many examples of folk material both in the copied Anglo-Saxon four-line ballad form and in the more characteristic Negro three-line "blues" form. The latter, with its epigrammatic flavor, has a folkiness all its own. The dominant blues mood is a lament, beginning in a sentimental expression of grief or hard luck, sometimes ending on an intensification of the same mood and sometimes turned to ironical self-ridicule or fatalistic resignation. Self-pity

32

tends to dominate. But irony and bitter disillusionment also occur.

> 'Gwine lay my head right on de railroad track,
> 'Gwine lay my head right on de railroad track,
> 'Cause my baby, she won't take me back.

> 'Gwine lay my head right on de railroad track,
> 'Gwine lay my head right on de railroad track,
> If de train come 'long, gwine snatch it back.

or
> Boll-weevil, where you been so long?
> Boll-weevil, where you been so long?
> You stole my cotton, now you wants my cohn!

Making mirth of one's sorrow, "laughing the blues away,"—has become the fixed stereotype of the artificial blues, of which there are legion to the few older folk ones.

The musical rhythm and harmony of the blues is as characteristic and simple as their verse form and idiom of thought. The tunes are built around a succession of three common chords on the key-note, the sub-dominant and the chord of the dominant seventh. The form is admirably adapted to impromptu songs and impromptu versifying. The repetition of the second line gives emphasis, a chance for improvised variation, leaving a wait in which originally to think up the last line, and later in which to improvise and vary the rhythm before returning to the regular pattern of the original theme. This interval is the original "break,"—the narrow cradle for improvised rhythm and eccentric tone intervals from which jazz was born. From such simple swaddling clothes that terrific giant of modern popular music has grown. Later in the chapter on jazz, we shall hear the story of how W. C. Handy, "Father of the Blues," made them famous and started the avalanche of artificial blues composition.

But we must never forget the folk originals without which no such music would have been. Later, "blues" because a generic name for all sorts of elaborate hybrid Negroid music. But that is only since 1910. Before

33

that, it was the work-songs, the love-ballads, the "over-and overs," the slow drags, pats and stomps that were the substance of genuine Negro secular folk music. And the lower Mississippi is the home of the most deeply characteristic forms, though as we have seen, each section has added a rich crop of its own.

DISCUSSION QUESTIONS

Why were the secular songs neglected? How have they been recovered? Do we have them in their earliest forms? Are "Blues" or folk ballads older? What are the distinctive verse and musical forms of each? What are the "zones of Negro folk music and their characteristics? Is the musical structure of the blues original? And racial? How racially distinctive are the moods? Even where the themes are common to Anglo-Saxon folk ballads, are there differences? What is the John Henry saga? What is the "home of the Blues"? Who is called the "Father of the Blues"? Are the later "artificial blues" different? Whose work are they?

READING REFERENCES

Brown, Sterling. *The Blues as Folk Poetry*—in "Folk-Say"—Norman Oklahoma, 1930.

Hare, Maud Cuney: *Negro Musicians and Their Music*—Assoc. Publishers, Washington, D. C.,—pp. 64–112.

Lomax, John: *Self-Pity in Negro Folk Song*—"The Nation," Vol. 105, pp. 141–145.

Lomax, John and Allan: *Negro Folk Songs*—Macmillan, N. Y., 1936.

Lomax, John and Allan: *American Ballads and Folk Songs*—Macmillan, 1934.

Niles, Abbe & W. C. Handy: *Blues: An Anthology*—A & C Boni, N. Y., 1926.

Sandburg, Carl: *America's Song Bag*.

Van Vechten, Carl: *The Blues*—in "Vanity Fair," August, 1925 & March, 1926.

RECORD ILLUSTRATIONS: BLUES AND SECULAR FOLK-SONGS

Vocal:

"*Gulf Coast Blues*" sung by Eva Taylor—Okeh 3055 B.
"*Gulf Coast Blues*" sung by Bessie Smith—Columbia 3844 A.
and "*Down Hearted Blues*" (arr. by Clarence Williams).

34

"*St. Louis Blues*" sung by Bessie Smith—Columbia 14064 D. and "*Cold in Hand.*"

"*John Henry*" sung by Henry Thomas—Vocalion 1094 A. and "*Cottonfield Blues.*"

"*Steel Drivin' Sam*" sung by Clara Smith—Columbia 14053 D. and "*He's Mine, All Mine.*"

"*Tough Luck Blues*" sung by "Ma" Rainey—Vocalion 12735 B (also 20885) and "*Screech Owl.*"

"*Boll-Weevil Blues*" sung by Bessie Smith—Victor 81671.

"*Black Snake Blues*" sung by Victoria Spivey—Okeh 8338 A.

"*Jorgie Blues*" sung by Edna Winston—Victor 20654 B. and "*Ever After On.*"

"*Grievin' Me Blues*" sung by Tampa Red and Georgia Tom—Vocalion 1216 and "*It's Light Like That.*"

"*I'm Gonna Start Me a Graveyard*" sung by Jim Jackson—Vocalion 1164A and "*I'm a Bad, Bad Man.*"

"*If You Only Knowed*" (arr. by Porter Grainger)—sung by Bessie Smith—Columbia 14058 D.

"*Ticket Agent, Ease Your Window Down*" (arr. by Spencer Wiliams) —Columbia 14025 D.

"*Careless Love*"—W. C. Handy—Decca 132; also sung by Bessie Smith —Columbia 14083.

Instrumental:
"*St. Louis Blues*"—by Duke Ellington's Orchestra—Brunswick 4936.

"*Chicago Blues*" — by Jimmie Johnson and Orchestra — Columbia 14334 D.

"*Blues in G*"—guitar solo by Lonnie Johnson—Okeh 8575.

"*Low Down Rounder Blues*" and "*Rock and Gravel Blues*"—(guitar) Peg Leg Howell—Columbia 14320.

"*Johnny Dunn's Cornet Blues*"—by Johnny Dunn—Decca 124 D.

"*Shadow of the Blues*"—clarinet solo by Wilton Crawley—Okeh 8619.

Choral Versions:
"*St. James' Infirmary Blues*"—Hall Johnson Choir—Victor 30647 A.

"*Water Boy*" and "*I'm an Eastman*"—Hall Johnson Choir—Victor 36047 B.

Seculars:
"*Oh, Rock Me, Julie*" and "*Oh, Didn't it Rain?*" (Burleigh) sung by Paul Robeson—His Master's Voice—3033 B.

"*Water Boy*" (arr. by Avery Robinson) and "*Lil' Gal*" (Rosamond Johnson)—Victor 19824.

"*The Lonesome Road*" and "*Wake Nicodemus*" (arr. by Shilkret)— sung by Frank Crummit—Victor 21098.

"*Way Down That Lonesome Road*" and "*Crowin' Rooster Blues*"— Lonnie Johnson—Okeh 8574.

"*I'm Comin' Virginia*" (Heywood-Marion Cook)—sung by Ethel Waters —Columbia 14170.

"*He's Gone Home*" and "*I Wonder What This New Year's Gonna Bring*" (arr. by Porter Grainger)—Columbia 14269 D.

In this selected list, the author has had constructive suggestions from his colleague, Professor Sterling Brown.

V

EARLY NEGRO MUSICIANS

We turn away for a chapter from the folk music of the race to the few but significant formal musicians who early pointed the way to higher attainment in music. They were as sophisticated as the folk music we have been discussing was primitive, and there was a complete gulf between. They were cut off, like the earlier Negro poets and writers, from the folk tradition. Their story is one, therefore, of isolated promise and achievement.

Chevalier St. Georges.—Taking them chronologically,—for they have no group significance, there was first a West Indian mulatto, Chevalier Saint-Georges, born in the town of Basse-Terre, Guadeloupe. Educated in Paris, and skilled in other fashionable arts, he became the music student of Gossec and wrote two concertos for violin and orchestra and numerous quartettes. Much of his music is preserved in manuscript in the library of the Paris Conservatory, including a manuscript opera, "*L'Amant Anonyme.*" Lawrence declares that "Gossec and Saint-Georges were the first French musicians to write string quartettes." St.-Georges died in Paris June, 1799.

Bridgetower.—Another mulatto, George Augustus Bridgetower was born at Biola, Poland in 1779. He became one of the eminent violinists of his generation, after taking his degree of Bachelor of Music at Cambridge, England, in 1811. Seven years before that he had played the first performance of the famous Kreutzer Sonata, with the composer Beethoven at the piano in Vienna. Afterward there was an estrangement between the two men, who at that time were close friends and musical associates. A full account of Bridgetower may be found in Thayer's Life of Beethoven. He died in England in 1845.

Edmund Dede.—Dede, a New Orleans Negro, born there in 1829, was able to enter the Paris Conservatory and graduated in 1857 with high rank as a violinist. He composed numerous orchestral works, of which the most ambitious was *"Le Palmier Overture."* Later he died at Bordeaux where he was conductor at the Municipal Opera and of the orchestra of L'Alcazar. This was also the era of the vogue in New Orleans of the famous musical family of the Lamberts, all pupils of a talented father, Richard Lambert. Lucien Lambert, one of the sons, was one of the outstanding composers of his time, when as a matter of fact America was producing almost no composers.

Joseph White.—Born at Metanzas, Cuba, this Negro violinist was sent to Paris in 1855 on the advice of Gottschalk and became a prize virtuoso under Alard. He composed a violin concerto and numerous other concert pieces and in 1864 became professor of violin at the Paris Conservatory. He visited America in 1876, playing in Boston and New York with great success. He died in Paris in 1920.

Gottschalk.—The story of Louis Moreau Gottschalk is graphically put in the words of Louis Antheil, the modernist composer. He says: "I should like at this moment to go into a lengthy song of praise of Louis Gottschalk, the first American composer to become known in Europe, whose work Chopin himself praised, and who had a considerable furore in his day, but who, because of our American habit of discounting our great men, has fallen into the limbo of forgotten genius. . . . Gottschalk was a mulatto. In looking over his work recently I was astonished to find a *"Cubana"* which was, without a shadow of a doubt, the celebrated *"Peanut-Vendor"* rumba, note for note! But it was written

37

over three-quarters of a century ago and with what astonishing ingenuity and pianistic brilliance! Truly Europe must have been astonished and the salons through which Chopin walked electrified by this dark and slender American, who left his white gloves intentionally upon the piano (for the ladies afterwards to tear apart)." In spite of the florid salon style of musical taste in his day and of being the composer of the romantic *"The Last Hope"* and *"The Dying Poet,"* Gottschalk must be credited with an appreciation of the native folk music of Louisiana, witness his other compositions,—*"Bamboula," "Negro Danse," "Le Bananier," "The Banjo," "La Savane,"* and the aforementioned *"Peanut-Vendor Rumba."*

It was in Louisiana, that the pianist Gottschalk commenced to compose in a tone-painting vein, at the age of thirteen, when his senses were freshly impregnated with the luxuriant surrounding of a semitropical climate, when still a stranger to Parisian life, and before he became acquainted with Schumann and the apostles of musical progress in Leipzig. To the end of a prematurely closed and wandering existence, he never quite got rid of the banjo in his music, of the mournful cries of the banana seller, or of the melancholy impressions of the Savannah.

Elizabeth Taylor Greenfield.—Miss Greenfield, or as she was called the "Black Swan," was born in Natchez, Miss., in 1809 and died in Philadelphia in 1876. The interval between was one of the sensational musical careers of the century. Taught by amateur teachers in Philadelphia, she made such a sensational impression in her concert debut in Buffalo in 1851 that she was immediately compared with the greatest soprano voices of the time,—Sonntag, Patti, Parodi and Jenny Lind. Moreover it was a voice with a sensational compass of three and a quarter octaves, yet with pure soprano tones in the upper register. She toured the free states triumphantly for two years, and then left in 1853 for Europe and instruction under the famous teacher, Garcia, with a farewell audience in New

38

York of four thousand persons. After a year, she made a series of appearances in England under distinguished patronage, including a command performance at Buckingham Palace, and returned to America for a concert career that only the turmoil of the Civil War broke into. Her later appearances were successful, but more and more she devoted herself to teaching. She had complete command of the standard concert repertory of her day.

The Hyers Sisters.—Anna and Emma Louise Hyers, natives of California, after training under Professor Sank and Madame D'Ormy, made a sensational concert debut in Sacramento in April, 1867. Anna sang the high soprano parts; while Emma possessed a phenomenal voice compassing mezzo-soprano and so low and deep a contralto that it was billed as "tenore." These were analyzed as true voice effects by competent musical authorities and not falsetto or trick effects. Beginning at Salt Lake City in 1871, they made a continental tour of the American music centers, culminating in tumultuous receptions in New York, New England and Canada. Their repertory was operatic for the most part, and they were counted among the great vocal artists of their generation.

"Blind Tom."—Thomas Green Bethune, born blind in Columbus, Ga., was a musical genius of another order. Entirely untaught, with a sense of absolute pitch and a prodigious sound memory, he became a musical phenomenon. But in spite of the rather circus atmosphere that his curious combination of blindness, illiteracy and musical genius provoked, he was, by the testimony of experts, a master musician. He could play flawlessly any composition he heard played, usually on once hearing it, could improvise correctly and expressively, and is said to have had a repertory of several thousand pieces including the difficult virtuoso piano

39

literature of the day, compositions by Thalberg, Gott-schalk, Moscheles, Mendelssohn, Rossini. But Bach and Beethoven were frequent items on his programs, revealing a more than superficial and mechanical com-prehension of music. Of course, he toured everywhere as a prodigy,—England, Scotland, France, Canada and the entire United States.

These are typical of the individual achievements of the first and second generation of Negro musicians on the art-level, at a time when even the folk music had not yet broken through to recognition. There were others, for whom we have only space for brief mention before passing on to typical instances of group achieve-ment in formal music during this early period 1800–1880. Such careers as the Luca Brothers, Justin Hol-land, Thos. Bowers, Madame Selika, Sisseretta Jones, called the "Black Patti" can be traced from the refer-ences by those particularly interested in the Negro musical pioneers.

There were also many troupes and musical organiza-tions, of which two should be mentioned especially. They were path-breakers in early Negro music. The standard musical organization of the mid-century was not the orchestra but the band. Some of the crack military bands were really first-rate musical organiza-tions. But before there was any such thing as a Negro military regiment to give this type of music support, several Negro bands had won their way to premier rank. By far the most famous and long-lived of these was a Philadelphia organization, led by an accom-plished conductor, arranger and composer, Frank John-son, protégé of P. S. Gilmore, the "bandmaster of America." Johnson's band was organized in 1839, and by 1843 had won such acclaim as to have made a con-cert tour of England, Scotland and Ireland. After a command performance, Johnson was presented with a silver trumpet by Queen Victoria, for he was a phenomenal soloist on this instrument. He died early at the height of his fame in 1846; but the band continued under Joe Anderson till his death in 1874, and then split into two quite famous organizations, the Excelsior Band and Frank Jones' Orchestra. Practically all of the membership were trained musicians, and they had a skilled string section in the later days for selections of the concert music type.

The other organization has already been briefly mentioned, but its role in winning an international hearing for Negro music must be stressed. The Fisk Jubilee Singers, starting out on a risky venture, became the most travelled and internationally acclaimed American musical organization of its time. After a first European tour in 1874, and a second more extensive one in 1877, this group of eighteen singers, ten women's voices and eight men, travelled as far as Australia, New Zealand and South Africa, brought in $90,000 for the erection of Jubilee Hall on Fisk University campus, and put Negro music and musicianship on the path of world recognition.

When we realize what this really meant, its significance increases. These early Negro musicians had to compete in a double contest,—first to gain the respect of musicians and at the same time win the public ear. For only in terms of overwhelming public interest was it possible to compel the attention of managers and critics. Only a combination of native talent and technical proficiency could do this. But the general result was that those who came out of curiosity for a new sensation remained to wonder and admire on a strictly musical basis. It is to be noticed also how many of the voices were phenomenal, especially in range. This is almost a peculiarity of the Negro voice; today as yesterday we have singers whose voice range is so unusual

41

that they hardly fit the fixed classification of voices. The extraordinary range of Paul Robeson and Marion Anderson today had its historical parallel in the phenomenal range of Elizabeth Greenfield, Emma Hyers, Madame Selika, and others in the past. With technical skill added to such natural equipment, and the discipline of classical music added to the powerful originality of the folk music, an almost unmatched combination is made that appeals both to the musical layman and the musical expert. This wide appeal accounts for the triumph of Negro music, which as we have seen, was well established in the North and in Europe almost before the Negro masses were out of the "house of bondage."

DISCUSSION QUESTIONS

What gulf was there between the early Negro musicians and their racial heritage of folk music? Were they outstanding according to the musical standards of their day? What unique contributions did they make to early European classical music? To early American music? What sections of America received and recognized them? Did their fame spread to Europe and what was the reaction in America to their European reputations? Were there more vocalists than instrumentalists? What peculiar features of voice range is noteworthy, and does it still persist among Negro singers? Who were some of these pioneer musicians?

READING REFERENCES

Hare, Maud Cuney: *Negro Musicians and their Music*—pp. 197–238.
Johnson, James Weldon: *Black Manhattan*—pp. 94–101—1930.
Lovingood, Penman: *Famous Negro Musicians*—Press Forum Co., Brooklyn, N. Y., 1921.
Trotter, James M.: *Music and Some Highly Musical People, Boston,* 1878.

42

VI

THE FIRST AGE OF MINSTRELSY: 1850-1875

Minstrelsy,—What Is It?—One may well ask, especially if we give it an important place in the history of American and Negro music. For it was not primarily music: the early minstrel, black or white, was no lyric troubadour, but an improvising clown. Music was in the bottom of his bag of tricks; his main show was antics, capers and eccentric dancing. And stage minstrelsy preceded the musical age of minstrelsy by fifteen or twenty years just as plantation minstrelsy had preceded it for generations. However, the tradition which gave American music "Dixie" (Dan Emmett, its author, was a minstrel)—"The Old Folks at Home" (Stephen Foster was a minstrel's bard)—"Listen to the Mockin' Bird," and "Carry Me Back to Old Virginny" (James Bland, its Negro composer, was a minstrel) —commands the attention of the musical historian and the music-lover.

Minstrelsy's Origin.—Minstrelsy originated on the slave plantations of the South. Weldon Johnson tells us: "Every plantation had its talented band that could crack Negro jokes, and sing and dance to the accompaniment of the banjo and the 'bones'—the bones being the actual ribs of a sheep or other small animal, cut the proper length, scraped clean and bleached in the sun. When the planter wished to entertain his guests, he needed only to call his troupe of black minstrels." At times these bands became semi-professional and travelled around a circuit, but the limitations of chattel slavery set definite bounds to that.

Negro minstrelsy came to the American stage, however, in a counterfeit imitation of this by white actors,

43

who began comic Negro impersonations as "black-face" acts before 1830. But in that year in Louisville, Dan Rice, the father of stage minstrelsy, put on an act copied from a Negro stable hand, named Crow reputedly, which was such a success that it was introduced at the old Bowery Theatre in New York, November 12, 1832, to begin formally what was to be the entertainment vogue of two generations of the comic American stage and what has been correctly called "one of the most completely original contributions America has made to the theatre." But as a stage tradition, minstrelsy was and remained a caricature of Negro life and ways, and when Negroes themselves came into stage minstrelsy, the mould was too set to be radically changed. They had to accept "almost wholly the performance pattern as it had been worked out and laid down by the white minstrels during the preceding twenty-five years, even to blacking their faces, an expedient which, of course, never entered the minds of the original plantation artists" (Johnson).—However they brought to the fore not only a more genuine and cleaner humor and a new vivacity, but brought music and instrumental expertness on many instruments besides the banjo to add to the main attractions and appeals of orthodox minstrelsy. But before that in 1843 a quartet of white men had appeared in New York City as "The Virginia Minstrels": their tenor was Dan Emmett, the composer of *"Dixie,"* which ironically enough was Negro before it was "Confederate." Its first official title was: *"Dixie-Land: Ethiopian Walk 'round."*

Minstrelsy was instantly popular and profitable. Rice was not only the box-office success of his day, but spread the minstrel vogue by several trips abroad. In 1833, he introduced Thomas Jefferson at the age of four to the stage as a co-minstrel singing the same "Jim

44

Crow." Even the elder Booth at the time was not above Negro character parts. He appeared in several with his life-long friend and associate Rice, who died in 1860. Despite the fact that "this first native form of stage entertainment" was launched by white comedians and that where the "white man began by imitating the Negro, the Negro began by imitating him in turn," the first Negro troupes brought a real contribution to the "Minstrel Show." The two really great Negro minstrel troupes of these days were *"Lew Johnson's Plantation Minstrel Company"* and the *"Georgia Minstrels."* The latter was the first successful all-Negro group and was founded in 1865 by Geo. B. Hicks, a native Georgian. This company, with many changes of management, name and personnel made extraordinary contributions to the American stage and American music. Reorganized first under a white manager, it was known until 1878 as *"Callender's Original Georgia Minstrels,"* then bought by Jack Haverly, it was managed by Gustav Frohman as *"Haverly's European Minstrels,"* and finally in 1882 reorganized by Charles Frohman as *"Callender's Consolidated Minstrels."* Three series of European tours in 1876, in 1880 and 1882, made them world-famous.

But celebrated managers were matched by celebrated comedians, singers, dancers and instrumentalists. The greatest of the early Negro comedians, Billy Kersands and Sam Lucas were members of this troupe. James Bland, the composer of *"Carry Me Back to Ole Virginia"* and other less known but really important melodies, was a star performer in the Haverly period. The celebrated Bohee Brothers, perhaps the most sensational banjoists of generations, were crack instrumentalists in this troupe. At the height of its success, about 1876, the *"Georgia Minstrels"* were an aggregation of twenty-one performers, most of them trained musicians, who really so dignified the tradition that they played in concert halls and attracted the attention of the cultivated musical public. They introduced serious music on their programs, to the best of their ability to work it in with the stereotype of minstrelsy, and were recognized for their contrast with the slap-stick school of minstrels. In fact it may be said that minstrelsy was born in the slap-stick of burlesque and died in the straw of the circus. There was a period in between when it rose to a sturdy, healthy prime of clean comedy and pleasantly diluted folk music. This was its romantic period, and it was minstrelsy's musical hey-day as distinguished from its vaudeville phase. There were two stellar geniuses of this romantic period, one white, one Negro,—Stephen Collins Foster and James Bland.

Foster, the Troubadour.—A native of Pittsburgh, Stephen Foster was by main intention a maker of drawing-room ballads, suited to the sentimental taste of the 1850's. But his sensitive musical genius was caught by an idealized fascination for the plantation. Son of a former mayor of Pittsburgh, he saw more of the stage Negro than the genuine article. It has been said: "Strangely, the man who wrote the greatest songs of the Southland was not a Southerner. He stood afar off and caught the spirit of the cane-field and cabin, the porticoed mansion and the white seas of cotton." It is just as ironical that Foster was not a Negro, for his real success and lasting fame came not through the balladry by which he set such store, but through the Negroid folk ballads which came out of his curious fascination with a romantic and half-mythical South. In fact "*Old Folks at Home*" was the title of America's most famous song which he wrote in 1851, but everyone knows it as "*Swanee River*" or "*Way Down Upon the Swanee River.*" Foster had to ask his brother to look up in the atlas a "good two-syllable name" for a

Southern river. But Foster had gone at an impressionable period to Cincinnati, just across the river from the Kentucky he made famous later in *"Ole Black Joe,"* *"My Old Kentucky Home,"* and *"Way Down South."* And the Negro influence registered deeply.

Foster evidently came into first hand contact with Negro plantation singing. It was known that he visited out from Cincinnati, especially at the old Kentucky manor-house of his kinsfolk, the Rowan family at Bardstown. At any rate he caught enough of the unique flavor of Negro folk song to give vitality and deep sentimental appeal to his music, yet had enough tincture of the fashionable style of his day to give his songs immediate vogue and popularity. In this respect his relation to Negro folk-song is very like Joel Chandler Harris's relation to Negro folk-lore. Both watered the original down just enough to give it the touch of universality, and yet not enough to destroy entirely its unique folk flavor. But neither service, as we shall soon see, was an unmixed blessing.

In the straight vein of the sentimental ballad without Negro elements, there is scarcely a song of Foster's long list of 160 that has survived in more than the title. No one hears them except *"Come Where My Love Lies Dreaming," "Jennie With the Light Brown Hair." "Ah, May the Red Rose Live Alway,"* and the like are scarcely known. But *"Uncle Ned"* (1848), *"De Camptown Races"* (1850), *"Swanee River"* (1851)—written, by the way for Christy's Minstrels, *"Massa's in the Cold, Cold Ground"* (1852), *"My Old Kentucky Home"* (1853), and *"Old Black Joe"* (1860) are known and will be known as long·as American popular music has admirers. His biographer says: "Without the minstrels, Foster would probably have died keeping books for his father's business." With the vogue of these songs the sentimental side of the plantation legend wormed its way into the heart of America for better or worse, mostly worse. For with its shallow sentiment and crocodile tears went an unfortunate and undeserved glorification of the slave regime. Only recently has anyone dared question, musically or otherwise *"Is it true what they say about Dixie?"* Foster and his music did more to clinch this tradition than all the Southern colonels and novelists put together, ironically enough: a tribute to the power of music in general and the power of Negro folk song idioms in particular.

One additional proof of the probability that the Foster melodies are folk melodies polished down to the sentimental taste of the day lies in a song, equally popular, perhaps more so in its time, actually written by a Philadelphia Negro, Richard Milburn. This song—*"Listen to the Mockin' Bird,"* definitely proved as Milburn's in Weldon Johnson's *"Black Manhattan"* (p. 112), by the copyright edition of 1855, has much of the same flavor and quality of the Foster classics.

James Bland.—A little later, in the 70's in fact, when the minstrel style was turning from melody to jig rhythm, a last brilliant strain of romantic music poured from the prodigal and careless genius of James Bland. His life was as tragic as Foster's; both were reckless and irresponsible troubadors. Neither were Southerners; Bland was born on Long Island of mixed Negro, Indian and white parentage, and after several years at Howard University, ran away, as Will Marion Cook puts it: "banjo under arms, to join Callender's Minstrels, and to become, at the height of his fame in the United States, London and Paris, the brightest and most versatile star of the heyday of minstrelsy." Research about Bland's career and revival of his music ought to be one of the major projects in the history of Negro music. He was far more than a great song-

48

writer. However, it is as the composer of "*In the Morning by the Brightlight*," "*In the Evening by the Moonlight*," "*Oh, dem Golden Slippers*" and "*Carry Me Back to Ole Virginny*" that he will be best remembered. His contemporaries testify to his great composing talent as well as his extraordinary musicianship, especially to his way of playing these songs so differently from their now popular versions that to these men they are "scarcely the same songs." This is so often the case with the work of Negro musicians. It results from the double handicap that so many of them were careless, extemporizing talents who let their publishers rob and edit them, and from the fact that many of the virtuoso tricks of Negro musicians cannot be put down in black and white notation. For years, Foster's "*Swanee River*" was passed off as a composition of Edwin Christy's, the minstrel magnate; how much of Jim Bland's music has been filched or lost will never be known.

It is interesting to note, even as early as the minstrel period, the double strand in Negro music which today divides it as "sweet jazz" and "hot jazz." Then it was the twanging, swift "banjo music" and the more stately, sugary "guitar music." As the minstrel tradition drew toward its close, the burlesque motive dominated and the banjo-picker was in the ascendant; but Foster and Bland were the sweet minstrels responsible for the romantic Southern legend and the sentimental ballad that for two generations dominated American song. Tracing its derivation, Goldberg (p. 87) says: "Traveling southwards, along the banks of the great river and its tributaries,—(the Mississippi) we encounter a decidedly new and more melancholy and refined musical element. Its sadness blended with the strains of the English ballads of fifty or sixty years ago, and reproduced, with a certain indescribable charm, in one or two

49

of the more ancient Christy Minstrel's ditties. The element we speak of proceeds doubtless from the Creole stock in Louisiana, and is, perhaps, mixed with the tango of the Cuban Negro."

To say that one of these strands is more Negro than the other is entirely out of place, even though the melodic vein may have fused with old English forms and the 17th and 18th Century tunes transplanted by the colonists. Because when the Negro fusion came, it brought a glow and emotional warmth that is easily recognized as different and more compelling. Even after its heyday, it has reechoed powerfully through later American music in the lullaby and the "pickaninny croon," suffering usually from atrociously sentimental and silly ditties for words, whereas most of the original renditions were wordless croons and humming phrases.

Although this more melodic and melancholy element in Negro song is nowadays associated with the deeper South, particularly Louisiana, Foster and Bland prove that it was just as native to Kentucky and Virginia. Without it we would never have had such art songs as the later "*Go to Sleep, My Little Pickaninny*," "*Lil Gal*," or even "*Mighty Lak a Rose*." Isaac Goldberg rightly comments that there are two strands in Negro music,—"music of the heels" and "music of the heart" as he calls them. He is also right in tracing the sentimental strain in American popular song to a Negro main source, long before the vogue of the Irish sentimental ballad. He quotes Gus Kahn as thus explaining the vogue of the romantic South in our popular music: "The South is the romantic home of our Negro; he made it a symbol of longing that we, half in profiteering cold blood, but half in surrender to the poetry of the black, carried over into our American song." Much, therefore, that is typically American in mood

and sentiment was precipitated in the minstrel period
and by the minstrel tradition.

DISCUSSION QUESTIONS

How did the minstrel tradition start on the American Stage? Did it have a plantation beginning? Was
the picture of the Negro a true one or a caricature?
Was the picture of the South and the plantation regimé
true or distorted? Were the Negro minstrels able to
break the mould of the minstrel tradition when they
appeared? What stereotypes did they have to accept?
What did they add? What troupes were important
musically? And which period was the musical heyday
of minstrelsy? What was the musical background of
Stephen Foster and James Bland? Of Dan Emmett?
What contributions did minstrelsy make to American
music? To the American popular mind? How Negro
was this music? Is the musical tradition of the Negro
single or composite?

READING REFERENCES

Burnett, J. G.: *National Elements in Stephen Foster's Art*—1922.
Goldberg, Isaac: *Tin Pan Alley*—John Day, N. Y., 1930—Chapter 3;
pp. 31–59.
Johnson, James Weldon: *Black Manhattan*—Alfred Knopf, N. Y., 1930,
pp. 74–103.
Howard, John Tasker: *Stephen Foster, America's Troubadour*—Crowell,
N. Y., 1935.
Parkman, Darley & Sigmund Spaeth: *Gentlemen, Be Seated: A Parade
of Old-Time Minstrels*, 1936.

RECORD ILLUSTRATIONS

Foster, Stephen:
"Stephen Foster Melodies"—Orchestral Medley arr. Shilkret—Victor
Masterwoks Album 9246-47-48 and 49.
"Massa's in the Cold, Cold Ground"—choral version—Gramophone
B 4394.
"My Old Kentucky Home"—Paul Robeson—Gramophone B 3653.
"Old Black Joe" and *"Uncle Ned"*—L. Tibbett and chorus—Victor 1265.
"Old Folks at Home" ('Swanee River')—Columbia 5015 M.
"Carry Me Back to Ole Virginny" (Jim Bland) same record and
Columbia 50120 D—sung by Paul Robeson—Gramophone B 3664.
"Mighty Lak a Rose"—Ethelbert Nevin—Victor 1320 B.

51

VII

THE SECOND AGE OF MINSTRELSY:
1875-1895

Copper and Brass.—The period following the golden age of minstrelsy can barely be described as silver, it was an age of copper and brass. Musical taste generally was not high in America before 1875, but the cheapening effect of commercialism had not yet touched what music there was. But 1875–1895 was the circus age in American life, and music was hitched to the circus chariot; it became gaudy and cheap. There is no wonder that in these days there was such a bitter feud between popular and classical music. But for the triumphant vindication of the genuine folk music by the re-discovery of the spirituals through the work of the Jubilee Singers, true Negro music would have been extinguished. Thus, the best Negro musicians of this period had to make common cause with "classical music" in self defense. The music thought representative of the Negro by the general public was the "jig," the "clog"—a terrible hybrid of Negro and Irish dance figures, the "Double Shuffle," the "Pigeon Wing" and their musical companions,—the "minstrel ballad," usually a slap-stick topical ditty and the "coon-song." The minstrel tradition died down to a long twilight of burlesque and buffoonery, in spite of carrying along with it considerable talent which it seriously dimmed.

An Age of Caricature.—From 1875–1895 then was a period of artistic decline even in the midst of an increasing popularity of the minstrel tradition. Note that it was an age of slap-stick caricature, and that the burlesque spirit, once the vogue began, spread from the Negro folk types to the Irish and the Jewish in quick succession. Music declined in quality with this cheapening of the content of the stage. Oddly enough as the emphasis on Negro mannerisms and traits grew stronger, the actual racial characteristics in song, dance and speech idiom were lost sight of and caricature versions substituted. Much of the minstrel stock in trade had its Negro, Irish and Jewish versions that underneath separate false dialects were pretty much the same. Dr. Goldberg is right in saying: "The old minstrel show, truth to tell, for all the sentimental memories that are linked to it, must have been a pretty dull affair. Its wheezes were old when Cleopatra was a child. Read them, if you have the courage, in the sere chapbooks. Its tunes were undistinguished, for the greater part, though they had the country by the ears. The words of its ditties chiefly served to fill space." . . . "And yet," he continues, "it is from the minstrel show that we get our patterns of modern popular song. And if, even today, an Al Jolson or an Eddie Cantor seems somehow not himself without the blackface make-up (and Goldberg could have added 'Amos and Andy'), it is because he got his start in these troupes of pseudo-minstrels. Almost every song-and dance man of note, from the times of Harrigan and Hart down to our own sophisticated day, began behind the burnt cork."

Pseudo-Negroes.—"Pseudo-Negroes" is an inspired term. Not only were these latter-day minstrels predominantly white performers in make-up, but they were pseudo-Negroes spiritually. Even the real Negro minstrels were, too, in the psychological sense. Superficially they reflected some of the characteristic traits of the Negro, but instead of his real peasant humor, his real folk farce, his amazing ribaldry, the minstrels made a decoction of their own of slap-stick, caricature and asininity. It was this period that fixed the unfortunate stereotype of the Negro as "an irresponsible,

53

happy-go-lucky, wide-grinning, loud-laughing, shuffling, banjo-picking, dancing sort of being." It should be noted how different the Negro types of the Foster era were in mood, traits and sentiments. If anything, the Negroes of the first age of minstrelsy were too pathetic and romantic and too serious, just as those of the second period were too comic and over-ridiculous. Eventually the full blast of the circus tradition struck the minstrels and there was little difference; everything was freakishly exaggerated, squeeky music and falsetto singing were almost standard, fat men impersonated "colored cook-ladies, horse-play was more and more emphasized and if there had been good music, it would have been drowned out in continuous convulsions and explosions of laughter. Certain musical interludes were provided, usually barber-shop quartets, equally unrepresentative of the Negro folk singing they were supposed to derive from.

So pseudo-Negro characterization led to misrepresentative music. In this interval between the old-time ballads which, in their way, had folk flavor and rag-time, which was even more folky and genuine, the popular types of Negro music and song were bad and superficial. Even serious singing took on the trite form of the "barber-shop quartet"; Negro harmony was supposed to be the "barber-shop chord," and you could make any song Negro by sprinkling it with Negro dialect. Negro musical taste itself became seriously corrupted as the common notions prevailed. We took to the melodeon organ and the piano, instruments not suited to folk music even as well as the banjo and the guitar. Not until the jazz age did genuine Negro harmony and rhythm conquer the piano or Negro techniques of singing and playing re-appear. For a long time, then, Negroes played and sang not as they originally did but as they were supposed to sing and play.

This was inevitably a time of decadence for both Negro music and American music too. For when popular music becomes cut off from sound roots in folk music, and good music has to wall itself about to keep from being contaminated by popular music, music is in a precarious condition all round. This was the situation in American music, with few exceptions, between 1875 and 1895.

But underground there were streams or rather reservoirs of pure folk music waiting to be tapped. In the very midst of this musical drought the gusher of the spirituals was unexpectedly "brought in." A considerable time would elapse before it would creatively kindle native American musical composition, but in the meantime it received, as we have seen, immediate acceptance from the serious musical public. Then from another source came the quickening tradition of the waltz and the waltz ballad in the early nineties to found the fame and fortune of early Tin Pan Alley with the hits of Charles K. Harris, composer of *"After the Ball is Over,"* Von Tilzer and Victor Herbert. It is interesting to note that Tin Pan Alley's second ride to fortune was to be in the wake of the Negro cake-walk and the rising tide of ragtime, and that exactly what the genius of Victor Herbert did with the dying and sterile tradition of the Irish comedy song of the Chauncy Olcott ballad, the next generation of Negro musicians did with the stiff minstrel "cake-walks" and the sentimental ditties first called "coon-songs."

In the second period of minstrelsy, Negro music was doing little beside marking time and tuning up its audience. Meanwhile from Christy to.Weber and Fields, "Bones," "Tambo," "Interlocutor" and the minstrel formula were dominating popular entertainment and laying the basis for the great American vogue of burlesque, vaudeville and musical comedy.

55

What changes set in toward the end of the minstrel age? What damage did it do to American popular music? How has the false tradition of the Negro as set by this period hamper the artistic and particularly the musical development of the Negro? How did Negro music eventually escape the double pitfalls of sentimental romance and slap-stick burlesque? What trends and which Negro musicians broke the minstrel straight-jacket? What relation did Tin Pan Alley sustain to the Negro music of this period? Has the influence of Tin Pan Alley on Negro music been favorable? Unfavorable? In what respects?

Eaton, Walter P.: *Negro Minstrels*—The American Scholar—March, 1935.

Goldberg, Isaac: *Tin Pan Alley*—Chapter 4—pp. 60–83.

Hare, Maud Cuney: *Negro Musicians and Their Music*—Chapter 3, pp. 38–53.

VIII

RAGTIME AND NEGRO MUSICAL COMEDY
1895–1925

The Returning Tide.—After this ebb of real Negro music, there set in about 1895 a sudden flood-tide of new life and vitality. It became the rising tide of ragtime and after two decades, the flood-tide of jazz. It was a movement on the level of popular music, and its chief sponsor and beneficiaries were *"Tin Pan Alley,"* the commercial music market of New York with its subsidiaries all over the country and "Broadway," the commercial amusement stage and its syndicates throughout America. However, serious music ultimately was influenced and took in the new substance and energy as the age of ragtime and jazz passed over into the present-day phase of "classical jazz" and native American music.

How It Began.—The break with minstrelsy came first in 1891. The *"Creole Show"* opened that year with a nucleus of veteran minstrels,—Sam Lucas, Fred Piper, Billy Jackson and Irving Jones, doing a refurbished minstrel entertainment, but with a chorus of attractive Negro girls in smart dances and fancy costume and a singing chorus of the best musical talent. That not only broke the tradition of "blackface" somewhat, but brought the straight appeal of music and dance to the foreground. This show played a whole season in Chicago during the World's Fair in 1893, where also, oddly enough, a strain of genuine Negro music that was to revolutionize American music had come up from Memphis and the Mississippi. For W. C. Handy had come to the World's Fair with *Mahaly's Minstrels* seeking a fortune they did not get but with a future they could not have dreamed of.

57

For a time these two forces, destined ultimately to fuse, went their separate ways. Eventually, however the tap-stream of undiluted folk music and dance was going to be channeled into American life and entertainment through the stage talent of vaudeville and Negro musical comedy. The Mississippi was preparing a musical flood which is not over yet.

One was to lead to Cole and Johnson, Williams and Walker, Ernest Hogan, Miller and Lyles, Eubie Blake, Florence Mills, Ethel Waters, and the other, to Handy's *St. Louis* and *Memphis Blues* through the blues-singing Bessie, Clara and Mamie Smiths to the Fletcher Hendersons, Duke Ellingtons and "Cotton Club" of contemporary jazz. Moreover, it was to produce Jim Europe, Will Marion Cook, and many other creative pioneers of Negro music. In fact, it was to usher in the age of Negro music, in contrast to which the periods we have reviewed to date must be put down as merely an age of Negroid music. At first it would seem that the revival of the spirituals would be the exception to point this rule; but only a few organizations like the original Fisk Jubilee Singers had any conception of the spirituals as "folk music" to be presented pure and undefiled. The popular rage of the spirituals in the 80's and 90's called for highly diluted and doctored versions. Not until ragtime and jazz had opened the way, did the spirituals come into their full heritage and complete appreciation.

"*The Creole Show*" was followed in 1895 by "*The Octoroons*," also presented by John W. Isham, a Negro manager who knew and believed in the musical possibilities of Negro talent. In 1896, evidently leaning backward to avoid the tradition of black-face, he presented the first all-colored show to play Broadway under the title "*Oriental America*" at Wallack's Theatre. Into it he put Sidney Woodward, a native

58

of Memphis, who had already won a reputation as a concert tenor, J. Rosamond Johnson, the composer, Wm. C. Elkins, who had an honorable part in developing serious Negro folk choirs, and others of an order of talent and training not recognized before by the burlesque and variety stage. We might say that Negro musical comedy made its way by luring its audience with comedy farce and then ambushing and conquering them with music. This was eminently true of the next success, *"Black Patti's Troubadours,"* that was written and scored by the talented Bob Cole and had as its star attraction Madame Sisseretta Jones, who was really one of the great soprano voices of her generation and who already had an international reputation. "Black Patti," as she was called interrupted her concert career for this show, which ran several years and toured the entire country, but she made no other concessions to vaudeville; she sang her operatic and concert repertory, with ensemble numbers with what was one of the first really good Negro stage choruses.

Ragtime's Cradle.—While ragtime's audience was being captured, it itself was in the making. "Rag" made a Cinderella appearance in the mid-nineties in the humble rags and ashes of the "coon-song." But behind her at the magic hour was a golden slipper for Tin Pan Alley and a coach and prancing horses for Negro music. The "coon-song" was a relic of the worst minstrel days; slap-stick farce about "razors, chickens, watermelons, ham-bones, flannel shirts, and camp-meetings." But the appeal was not in what they said, but in the rhythm and swing in which they said it. The public was either tiring of the sentimental waltz ballads in which early Tin Pan Alley had gotten its hold on the public ear and purse, or else the Negro thing was in itself more compelling. Anyhow, as early

59

as 1893, astute entertainers like Geo. M. Cohan, May Irwin, Marie Cahill Harris and von Tilzer knew that the new black music had a future. They skimmed off the new rhythm to ditties like May Irwin's *"Hot Tamale Alley"* and the notorious *"Ta-ra-ra Boom de Ay."* Meanwhile the Negro comedians were countering with *"Smokey Mokes"* and *"I Don't Care if You Never Comes Back."* This was Gussie L. Davis, a former Haverly's Minstrel, who knew his plantation rhythm. Then finally in the cake-walk performances of the increasingly successful Negro shows this rhythm took up its conquering sway. For the Negro performers on Broadway had as much and more to do with starting this vogue than Tin Pan Alley.

The Negro Tempo.—Just at this juncture the Negro composer and song-writer picked up the baton and gave America its first experience of genuine Negro tempo. Goldberg says (page 151):—"The earlier ragtime, for all its debt to the white writers and the white performers, was definitely and refreshingly black. The rule of the white upon the pseudo-Negro minstrel stage was virtually over. The Negro upon the vaudeville and musical stage was achieving a certain revindication." In 1898, Bob Cole presented his *"A Trip to Coon-Town,"* much more pretentious than the name,— since an authority thinks it "the first Negro show to make a complete break from the minstrel pattern; the first that was not a mere potpourri, the first to be written with continuity and to have a cast of characters working out a plot, therefore, the first Negro musical comedy." Out of this success grew the partnership of Bob Cole and Billy Johnson and later the still more famous trio combination of musical comedy talent, Bob Cole, James Weldon and J. Rosamund Johnson. Negro song-writers and composers began to spring up as if by magic. Will Marion Cook with his *"Dark-*

60

town Is Out Tonight," Al Johns with *"Go Way Back and Sit Down,"* Will Accoe, Hillman and Perrin, Tom and Charles Turpin, and many another. Will Marion Cook, who will be mentioned again later, along with Bob Cole was the guiding genius of the movement. A thorough musician, trained in the violin and harmony under Joachim at the Berlin Conservatory (Hochschüle der Musik), Cook saw the serious potentialities of Negro ragtime music. As early as 1898 he wrote the score for the next great musical success *"Clorindy, the Origin of the Cake-Walk,"* with the collaboration in the lyrics of Paul Laurence Dunbar. *"Clorindy"* was years ahead of its time, its hints of the symphonic development of Negro syncopation and harmony were not to be realized for another ten or fifteen years. In many ways the American ear was just being broken in to the Negro tempo; and its subtleties were missed in the consternation over the new fast pace and swing of "raggin' " tunes.

The White Pioneers.—While the Negro performers and songsters were pioneering on the stage, the white pioneers were staking the fortunes of ragtime in Tin Pan Alley. Many Negro performers were too close to the subject to sense its originality and its financial prospects. They often gave the canny Tin Pan Alley scribes real nuggets of gold by letting them "set their stuff." Ernest Hogan's immortal *"All Coons Look Alike to Me"* was set to a "rag accompaniment" by a certain Max Hoffman, and one of the first musical notations of "rag" appeared in D. A. Lewis's setting in 1896 of Bert Williams' *"Oh, I Don't Know, You're Not So Warm."* Rag was reduced to a technique of piano writing and made a popular song vogue in this way, and soon America would be trying to imitate this syncopation swing. Ben. Harney, credited with being the first white to transcribe ragtime for the piano,

61

published his *"Ragtime Instructor"* in 1897. Goldberg says: (p. 147) "Harney had served as accompanist to a Negro and had toured the West and the Middle West long before he came East to start the rage of ragtime in Gotham." What passed for ragtime was not the full rhythmic and harmonic idiom of the geniune article as used, for example, by Will Marion Cook and the Negro musical comedy arrangers who had chorus and orchestra at their disposal, but the thin and rather superficial eccentric rhythm as it could be imitated on the piano or in the necessarily simplified "accompaniments" of popular sheet music of the day. Still a few artists, like the famous Scott Joplin wrote real rag in compositions like his *"Maple Leaf Rag"* (1898) and *"Palm Leaf Rag"* (1903). Also, Kerry Mills, with his *"Georgia Camp Meeting,"* (1897); *"Rastus on Parade,"* *"Whistlin' Rufus"* set the pace that was to catch the whole country and culminate in that instrumental classic of matured ragtime—Irving Berlin's *"Alexander's Ragtime Band."* Two outside forces of great significance combined to re-enforce the contagious singing and dancing of the Negro performers and the salesmanship of the Tin Pan Alley magnates, now growing rich on popularizing ragtime. The first was the sudden vogue of the cake-walk as a fashionable dance, and the second was that the hectic enthusiasms of the Spanish-American war music were to be seasoned with the new condiment of ragtime. Its most popular marching song was *"There'll Be a Hot Time in the Old Town Tonight,"* hybrid ragtime, and all America stepped to it until it began stepping still faster and higher to

"Come on and hear; come on and hear
Alexander's ragtime band. . . .
If you care to hear the Swanee River
    played in ragtime,
Come on and hear; come on and hear,
Alexander's Ragtime Band."

The Real Roots.—But although there is much conflicting legend about *"There'll Be a Hot Time in the Old Town Tonight,"* all the stories agree in at least one particular,—that it is a polished-up version of a less polite Negro cabaret song and dance from St. Louis. George Cohan ascribes it, perhaps most reliably, to a dressed-up version of a tune popular in Babe Connor's all-colored resort in St. Louis of the early 90's, heard by old theatrical troupers there and brought East. Theodore Metz, the copyright composer, got the main theme somewhere. The importance of this is not merely to document the Negro source of a tune that after all is no musical gem, but to show that ragtime, like its successor, jazz, is a child of the Mississippi bends and levees, and Memphis and St. Louis in particular. From these catch-pools, this music followed a circuitous route, spreading to places like Cincinnati and Chicago, and thence to New York. Williams and Walker, it will be remembered, came out of the West to bring the most genuine brand of Negro humor that had reached us to that date. From 1896 to 1909 they had only Cole and Johnson as rivals in presenting authentic Negro music, tempered, of course, to Broadway's taste. Considering purely commercial control, it is rather remarkable that there was as little dilution as there was. In the jazz age a decade later, the box-office had a tighter grip on Negro talent. But irrespective of that Ernest Hogan, Bob Cole, George Walker, Alex. Rogers, Will Marion Cook, Ada Overton (later Mrs. Walker), Jim Europe, were artists to the core, most unmercenary,—to a fault in fact, in view of the financial exploitation of their wares by others. They also wrote their own shows for the most part, often managed them, and several of them "walked out" rather than compromise or submit to managerial dictation. They were their own best critics, knew the effects they wanted, and Bert Williams was the only one to survive into the era of organized profits and regimentation.

So to the commercial successes of the ragtime era, there can fortunately be added such serious musical contributions as Will Marion Cook's *"Mandy Lou," "Exhortation," "Rain Song," "Swing Along, Children,"* Rosamond Johnson's *"Since You Went Away," "Lit'l Gal,"* Cole and Johnson's musical operettas *"Trip to Coon Town"* (1901), *"The Shoofly Regiment"* (1906); *"The Red Moon"* (1908); Cook's shows for Williams and Walker *"In Dahomey"* (1902); *"In Abyssinia"* (1906) and *"In Bandanna Land"* (1907). Much of the truly artistic possibilities of this period were snuffed out prematurely with the death of George Walker in 1909 and that of Bob Cole in 1911.

From Ragtime Band to Syncopated Orchestra.—We have so far only discussed the music makers. Let us turn briefly to the music itself. The musical vehicle in the minstrelsy days was a band, and a not too skillful one at that. The ragtime era continued the tradition of a band. But with a difference, the leader became a conductor, not an antic-playing drum-major. In the Negro musical shows real musicians were the arrangers and conductors of the orchestras and their conception of instrumentation and playing began to affect even dance and amusement music.

The peculiar combinations of instruments known to the jazz age had not yet made their appearance, but the best leaders insisted on characteristic Negro harmony and swing; that is, when they were not held in the leash as many times they were. Handy, "Father of the Blues," in the mid-nineties had to do fancy cornet variations in florid concert style and operatic selections (and as a thorough musician could do them).

64

Not until 1903 did he get a chance to organize a Negro band after his own heart's desire. Will Marion Cook had many a scene before he could get what he wanted in his revolt against the minstrel tradition on the one hand and apeish imitation of florid classics on the other; for the classics of the nineties did not mean the great masters. Not until 1905 did Cook get his chance, when he trained the *"Memphis Students"* for their Proctor's Theatre debut that year. This organization was the first truly genuine Negro playing unit; like the original *Jubilee Singers* they blazed a trail to Europe their first season and with their demonstration of the difference, real jazz was in the making and Negro music had burst the Nordic strait-jacket unwise imitation had imposed. The name Memphis was well-chosen; it was the early tribute of those who knew the true folk source of this musical style. The band was actually composed of twenty of the best musicians who had gravitated to New York from everywhere. It was doubtful if any were from Memphis. It was a folk orchestra like the Gipsy or Bailaika groups, using their own characteristic combinations of instruments, chiefly banjos, mandolins, guitars, saxophones, trumpets, trombones, a violin, double-bass and drums. Will Dixon was the conductor, but the genius of Will Marion Cook was back of the whole thing. In less than ten years he was to organize his own *"American Syncopated Orchestra"* that really began symphonic jazz, no matter what claims may be made for Paul Whiteman and Gershwin's *"Rhapsody in Blue"*—and no discredit to them, either, for as we shall see later, they also have done tremendous pioneer services to Negro and American music.

However, the point is that in New York between 1905 and 1912 or 1915, four Negro conductors and arrangers of genius organized Negro music out of a

65

broken, musically-illiterate dialect and made it a national and international music with its own peculiar idioms of harmony, instrumentation and technical style of playing. They did it so gaily that few knew the effort, the endless rehearsing, the feverish experimentation that lay behind it. Negroes played and sang that way, but without any realization of the revolutionary musical significance. But these men saw the future of Negro music; they had the courage to be original. They had swift vindication; in less than ten years Europe knew that musically something new had come out of America. Their names? Ford Dabney, James Reese Europe, Will Marion Cook and W. C. Handy. Dabney revolutionized the Negro dance orchestra and started the musical fortunes of Florenz Ziegfeld when he was experimenting with roof-garden shows. Jim Europe, a member of the *Memphis Students,* alternated with Cook as musical director of the Cole and Johnson shows, organized the famous *"Clef Club Orchestra"* and music center in 1910. Later Europe was to vindicate Negro music in two other ways—to make it preferred for rhythm and accord in the new dance vogue of the American stage started by the celebrated Vernon and Irene Castle (who insisted on Negro orchestras for their accompanists) in 1913–15, and by the still more important vogue for Negro music which Europe started abroad by the uniqueness of the 15th Regiment (367 U. S. Infantry) Band which he organized and led during the War, 1917–18. Mrs. Irene Castle McLaughlin says: "It was Jim Europe who suggested the fox-trot to us, and for all I know he invented it and deserves all of the credit for the most popular dance of today. I cannot trace the origin of the name, but I do know that the tempo was the invention of his ingenious musical mind." Marion

66

Cook not only gave Negro music its first serious orchestral ambitions, but with his "syncopated orchestra" surprised and converted the European music centers by his concerts in London, Paris, Berlin, in 1919–20. This venture, in spite of great artistic success, was financially unsuccessful, primarily because of the size of the group upon which Mr. Cook insisted. In the long run, he was wise, since he was challenging comparison with classical music and the traditional symphony orchestra. As to Handy, it is well-known how between 1909 and 1912 he championed simon-pure and despised Mississippi folk music and finally in the latter year loosed the overwhelming flood of the "Blues."

Others are reaping today what these men sowed; for the most part their careers had an element of tragedy. Europe, always a strict disciplinarian, was killed by a resentful, unruly dismissed musician; Cook was almost broken in the struggle to realize a vision more than a generation ahead of its time. Handy, making millions for the song-brokers, himself went bankrupt, but in Goldberg's words: "rather than go into bankruptcy and evade moral obligations that might easily have found legal relief, sold his beautiful New York residence, and ruined both his health and his sight in the unremitting labor of meeting his debts. Today happily he has regained both. He is still the undaunted 'Daddy of the Blues,' carrying on in his humbler Broadway quarters." The leaders of this generation of Negro musicians had ideal goals and moral loyalties; theirs was not merely inborn musical talent and musical luck.

Carnegie Hall: May, 1912: In 1905, "ragtime" rated only a vaudeville introduction at *Proctor's Twenty-third Street Theatre;* a sceptically offered chance, a novelty risk and experimental dare. It was, as we have

67

seen, an immediate success that reached Europe within the year, but as a novelty and curiosity after all. But by 1912, three Negro conductors led a syncopated orchestra (today we would say a jazz orchestra), of a hundred and twenty-five Negro musicians in a "Concert of Negro Music." The formal coming-out party was at Carnegie Hall, the audience, the musical elite of New York, the atmosphere and the comparison challenged that of any concert of "classical music," and the compositions conducted by their own composers or arrangers. Perhaps the transformation was too sudden; many did not recognize this folk music in full dress. Some thought it was incongruous (and some of it was), but all those who with shorter memory remind us of of the epoch-making significance of Paul Whiteman's famous concert of "Classical Jazz" in 1924 or of a similar concert of the Vincent Lopez orchestra the same year, ought to remember the historically more significant concert of *The Clef Club* at Carnegie Hall, May, 1912. For that night the Cinderella of Negro folk music found royal favor and recognition and under the wand of Negro musicians put off her kitchen rags. At that time ragtime grew up to full musical rank and the golden age of jazz really began. To that we now turn.

DISCUSSION QUESTIONS

What broke the minstrel tradition? What shows and what producers did this? What rôle did Negro musicians play in the early history of Tin Pan Alley? In the Broadway vogue for musical comedy? What were the individual contributions of John Isham? Ernest Hogan? Bob Cole? Rosamond and Weldon Johnson? Ford Dabney? Will Marion Cook? James Reese Europe? Williams and Walker? Ada Overton Walker? The *Memphis Students?* The *Clef Club?*

68

The American Syncopated Orchestra? What were the principal Negro musical comedies of the period? When and how did ragtime come to the attention of the serious musical public? What are the main differences of "Ragtime" and "Jazz"? Did ragtime music evolve into jazz?

READING REFERENCES

Goldberg, Isaac: *Tin Pan Alley*—Chapter 6, pp. 139–177.

Hare, Maud Cuney: *Negro Musicians and Their Music*—Chapter 8, pp. 157–177.

Johnson, James Weldon: *Black Manhattan*—pp. 96–125.

Johnson, James Weldon: *Along This Way*—Viking Press, 1935—pp. 156–162; 170–201.

Little, Arthur W.; *From Harlem to the Rhine*—Covici Friede, N. Y., 1936, pp. 108–125. (Jim Europe).

McLaughlin, Irene Castle: *Jim Europe: A Reminiscence.*—Opportunity Magazine, March, 1930.

Marks, E. B.: *They All Sang*—Viking Press, N. Y., 1934.

RECORD ILLUSTRATIONS

"Alexander's Ragtime Band" (Irving Berlin). Victor 25455.

"Maple Leaf Rag" (Scott Joplin). Victor 22608.

"Kitten on the Keys" (Confrey).

"Tiger Rag"—La Rocca and Original Dixieland Orchestra—Victor 25403.

"Clarinet Marmalade" and *"St. Louis Blues"* recreated by Benny Goodman Orchestra—Victor 25411.

"Exhortation" (Marion Cook)—His Master's Voice 3409 B.

"Swing Along" (Marion Cook).

Bert Williams: *"Not Lately"* and *"You Can't Trust Nobody"*—Columbia 3589 A.

Bert Williams: *"Elder Eatmore's Sermon"*—*"Oh, Death Where is Thy Sting"* and *"When I Return"*—Columbia 2652 A.

IX

JAZZ AND THE JAZZ AGE: 1918-1926

The Birth of Jazz.—Although 1918 is the official birthday of jazz, jazz had an embryonic start much before that. In fact, jazz was carried in the bosom of ragtime and, as has been said, is only ragtime more fully evolved. The Negro folk idiom in melody and syncopated rhythm gives us "ragtime," carried over to harmony and orchestration, it gives us "jazz." It is one and the same musical spirit and tradition in two different musical dimensions. In fact, if Isaac Goldberg's analysis of ragtime and its connection with the spirituals is correct, we may actually have on our hands, in seemingly quite different things, one essential Negro style of music with three different dimensions,—the spirituals, ragtime, jazz. Strange, it may seem! But before coming to that, any close observance of the intermediate period between ragtime and jazz will convince us that at least ragtime is the mother of jazz, not just merely its predecessor. When we realize this, we can then quite clearly see that the Carnegie concert of 1912 was truly the birthday party of jazz, while the Whiteman concert of 1924 from which we have seemed to take credit, actually deserves credit in another connection, for it was the "coming of age" party for jazz.

The Continuity of Negro Music.—Goldberg suggests, following no less an authority than W. C. Handy, that the spirituals, ragtime and jazz form one continuous sequence of Negro music, being just different facets of the same jewel. Says he: (p. 141)—"Handy, the recognized pioneer of the 'blues' insists that ragtime, essentially, is nothing more than a pepped-up secular version of the Negro spirituals. He recalls how in the old minstrel days they rendered such haunting exhorta-

70

tions as *'Git on Board, Little Chillun.'* To sing it in the traditional fashion of the earnest if ecstatic spiritual was too tame. So sung faster, to the accompaniment of eccentric hand-clapping and gestures, it becomes the 'spiritual' disintegrating, breaking up into its ragtime successor" . . . (in fact, in the camp-meeting style of jubilation, the dividing line between the spiritual and ragtime almost completely breaks down) — "Today," he continues, "hearing Handy jazz up the invitation to a ride on the heavenly railroad, one would exclaim, 'Why, he's simply jazzing it.' In Handy's minstrel days, they called it 'jubing,' from the word 'jubilee.'" Ragtime, then, is already found lurking beneath the ecstasy and the rhythms of the more jubilant songs to the Lord, just as in the slower-paced spirituals, one hears the mood, though not the peculiar pattern of the "blues.' And when we recall how jazz budded out of the improvised break interval of the blues, this theory grows even more plausible. For then we have approximately the same contrast between the stately spiritual chorale and the jubilant spiritual camp-meeting shout in the religious music that in the secular music we have between the slow swaying melancholy blues and the skipping rag and fast-rocking jazz. The extreme contrast but common root of the slow and the fast elements of the Hungarian Czardas is another case in point and, clearly, a close analogy. As Goldberg later says: "Ragtime is then, in part, the pagan release of the Negro from his own addiction to holiness, and his rhythms brought to us something of that profane deliverance. It is in brief a balancing of the psychological accounts . . . The spirituals translate the Bible; ragtime translates the other six days of the week."

The Raciness of Jazz.—Time and again, in spite of the obvious development of ragtime and jazz from Negro sources and the pioneer artistry and tricks of Negro

71

dancers and musicians, the question comes up in sceptical quarters: how Negro is it after all? No one will deny that the elements of ragtime and jazz can be found elsewhere in the world, not only in other folk music, but as a device of syncopation, in some of the most classical music,—Beethoven, for instance. But in spite of this, jazz and ragtime are distinctively Negro, in fact, the further back one goes the more racial it is found to be. Today's jazz is a cosmopolitan affair, an amalgam of modern tempo and mood. But original jazz is more than syncopation and close eccentric harmony. With it goes, like Gipsy music, a distinctive racial intensity of mood and a peculiar style of technical performance, that can be imitated, it is true, but of which the original pattern was Negro. Moreover it is inborn in the typical or folky type of Negro. It can be detected even in a stevedore's swing, a preacher's sway, or a bootblack's flick; and heard equally in an amen-corner quaver, a blue cadence or a chromatic cascade of Negro laughter. An authority insists rightly that it is what he calls "a rubato of pitch as well as of accent," that is a subtle irregularity of interval of tone quality and pace of rhythm that once was a Negro secret and still is a Negro characteristic. "It began," this critic says, "in the restless feet of the black; it rippled through his limbs and communicated itself to every instrument upon which he could lay his hands. . . . It still remains a racial accent which the white, for all the uncanny skill with which he has translated it from its original black, has not fully mastered. And yet, by paradox, it is the white, the Northern white (and we should add, the Jew) in association with the Negro, who has developed ragtime and jazz to their fuller (not yet their fullest) possibilities." So jazz is basically Negro, then, although fortunately, also human enough to be universal in appeal and expressiveness.

Jazz at Home.—But as jazz has spread out from its Mississippi headwaters and become the international ocean it now is, it has become more and more diluted, more cosmopolitan and less racial. It was the early jazz that was the most typically racial—and musically the most powerful. To sense the difference instantly, one has only to contrast, for example, one of the early blues, like Bessie Smith's old version of the *"Gulf Coast Blues"* with any up-to-the-minute cabaret blues or to compare a real folky rendition of the *"Memphis Blues"* with some modern fancy-dress version. Jazz is more at home in Harlem than in Paris, unless Paris imports Harlem to play, sing and dance it as she used to do; but beyond that, jazz is more at home in its humble folk haunts even than in Harlem. "The earliest jazz-makers were the itinerant piano players who wandered up and down the Mississippi towns from saloon to saloon, from dive to dive. Often wholly illiterate, these humble troubadours knew nothing about written music or composition, but with minds like cameras they would listen to the rude improvisations of the dock laborers and the railroad gangs and reproduce them, reflecting perfectly the sentiments and moods of these humble folk. Seated at the piano with a carefree air that a king might envy, their box-back coats flowing over the stool, their Stetsons pulled well over their eyes and cigars at a forty-five degree angle, they would 'whip the ivories' to marvelous chords and hidden racy meanings, evoking the intense delight of their hearers who would smother them at the close with huzzas and whiskey."

The same commentator, J. A. Rogers, writes about the exact origin of jazz: "More cities claim its birthplace than claimed Homer dead. New Orleans, St. Louis, Memphis, Chicago, all assert the honor is theirs. But jazz, as it is today, seems to have come into being

73

this way. W. C. Handy, after having digested the airs of the itinerant musicians referred to, experimented with the blues form from 1909 until 1912, and by 1912 had evolved the first jazz classic, '*The Memphis Blues.*' Then came, as a fairly authentic legend has it, Jasbo Brown, a reckless musician of a Negro cabaret in Chicago, who played this and other blues, blowing his own extravagant moods and risqué interpretations into them, while hilarious with gin. To give further emphasis to his veiled allusions he would make his trombone 'talk,' by putting a derby hat and later a tin can at its mouth. The delighted patrons would shout, 'More, Jasbo! More, Jas, more!' And so the name originated."

"*Father of the Blues.*"—William C. Handy was born November 16, 1873, in Florence, Ala., the son and grandson of Methodist ministers. None of the family was musical (except no doubt in church), and his father disapproved of his ambition for a musical career. As a boy, he would steal down to the locks to hear the laborers sing or to the barber shop to hear the new tunes at quartet and band rehearsals. By ear, he became a good cornetist at nineteen in the interim of teaching public school. Later he worked in the pipe foundry at Bessemer, Ala., and heard the folk tune which is the basis of his later published "*Harlem Blues.*" In 1893, he organized a quartet which hoboed its way to the World's Fair at Chicago. After a successful but spendthrift experience with this group, Handy found employment with "*Mahara's Colored Minstrels*" as band leader and solo cornetist. They had to conform to the minstrel formula, Irish ditties of the type popularized by Chauncey Olcott, Virginia reels and "coon songs." At the time he was interested in classical music and performed it well. It was in 1897 that Handy discovered experimentally the popular ap-

74

peal of the real "down-home" music (at least with the gallery), by the success of his playing of *"Georgia Camp Meeting"* while on tour in California.

In 1903, he organized his own band in Clarksdale, Miss. In Cleveland, according to his own story, he was confronted at a dance engagement with a rival "sidewalk orchestra" of "three seedy-looking Negroes equipped respectively with guitar, mandolin and bass viol," who played a backyard "over-and-over" wail that brought more in tips from the audience than his uniformed band received in pay. Some weeks later, Handy started on his search for folk music seriously and took down first a version of the *"Joe Turner"* blues heard at a country railroad station. This lesson in the folk idiom led to his adopting it as the novelty feature of the Pythian Band which he organized in Memphis, 1905, the same year, it will be remembered, that the Memphis Students band was making its debut at Proctor's, New York.

In Memphis in 1909, a hotly contested municipal election campaign involved the competition of three Negro bands, Eckford's, Bynum's, and Handy's. Jim Mulcahy, saloon-keeper and ward leader, backer of candidate Crump, had hired Handy. As a street-corner opener, Handy introduced a lively or "hot" tune made up from his memories of the lively tunes he had heard, set to the tavern ditty:

> "Mister Crump won't 'low no easy-riders here,
> Mister Crump won't 'low no easy-riders here.
> I don't care what Mister Crump don't 'low
> I'm gwine to de barrel-house anyhow,—
> Mister Crump can go an' catch hisself some air!"

It became the craze of the town and helped elect the candidate. Handy was convinced about the popular appeal of the genuine folk music. His first two blues had been unsuccessful. "Mr. Crump," his third, was also turned down by one New York firm after the other,

75

"because there were four bars missing to the strain." In 1912, Handy himself brought out a first edition of a thousand copies of the most famous of all blues, "*The Memphis Blues*," that has done millions since. It did not take immediately and was bought outright from Handy in 1912 by T. C. Bennett, a white Memphis promoter, for $100. (Let us remember Stephen Foster's $100 for his "Oh, Susanah.") In a garbled version, in which the rhythm was simplified and words added, it was republished in New York and has reaped a fortune for its copyright owners. Handy was even refused permission by the present copyright owner to use "*The Memphis Blues*" in his "*Blues Anthology*," published in 1926, thirteen years after. Thus Handy became the "father of the blues" although the greed and plagiarism of Tin Pan Alley disinherited him of much of his just rewards.

"The success of the '*Memphis Blues*,'" Abbe Niles says in his excellent preface to the "*Blues Anthology*," "resulted very shortly first in the borrowing of the magic word, and then, of the jazz idea and the 'blue note.' The 'blue note' is in official music the invention of W. C. Handy to devise a musical notation for representing the typical Negro voice slur or 'break' and its characteristic treatment of the tonic third. Stereotyped as the introduction of the minor third into melodies based on the prevailing major, this interpolated minor third has become the famous 'blue note.' Later the harmony of such a suspended third or seventh was introduced as the concluding harmony instead of the major tonic in compositions of the later period of sophisticated jazz, 1922-29. A similar treatment of the seventh note is the secondary 'blue note' (Niles, p. 16), and has been extensively used. It was responsible for the device of ending up a tune on a diminished seventh chord as in Gershwin's opera, '135th Street,' and more lately the added sophistication of the 'chord of the ninth.' "

"*Blue-Notes and Jazz Breaks.*"—Another cradle element of jazz was in Handy's "*Blues.*" It was the *habanera* or tango rhythm, an eighth and two-quarter note's sequence, first used by him in the original "*Memphis Blues.*" The justification for the use of the tango rhythm as characteristically Negro, and its popularity among Negroes becomes very plausible when it is realized that this is originally an Afrcan rhythm—(the native word for it is "Tangana"—Niles, p. 16), and that it probably became Spanish through the Moors. This is corroborated by the fact that this same tango rhythm is basic in the purest and oldest strains of the Afro-Cuban music, in the folk music of Mexico and Brazil where the Negro influence has been dominant, and in Negro dances of even the Bahamas and the Barbadoes. Further, an authority, Friedenthal, traces the Charleston to a compounding of this rhythm to the regular two-four beat. Says he: "Clap your hands on the dotted quarter and the eighth note which follows it, pat your feet regularly, four times to the bar, and you have the Charleston rhythm."

But in addition to jazz rhythm and harmony, jazz improvisation came rocketing out of the blues. It grew out of the improvised musical "filling-in" of the gap between the short measure of the blues and the longer eight bar line, the break interval in the original folk-form of the three-line blues. Such filling in and compounding of the basic rhythm are characteristic of Negro music everywhere, from deepest Africa to the streets of Charleston, from the unaccompanied hand-clapping of the street corner "hoe-down" to the interpolations of shouts, amens and exclamations in Negro church revivals. Handy's own theory of jazz is that it is, in essence, "spontaneous deviation from the musical

77

score," in other words an impromptu musical embroidery woven around and into the musical tune and the regular harmony. In short, daring and inspired musical play. When this style was incorporated into orchestral music, instrumental jazz was born out of the folk jazz which was its origin. Thus jazz is but a towering and elaborate superstructure built upon the basic foundation of the blues.

This fact disposes of the controversy as to whether jazz is a new type of music or simply another method of playing music, because it shows the difference between mere surface jazz and the real solid variety. The one is a mere set of musical tricks by which any tune whatsoever can be "ragged" or "jazzed"; the other is an organic trinity of jazz rhythm, harmony and creative improvisation. Surface jazz is the cheap alloy of Tin Pan Alley; many are the classical compositions that have suffered this trick adulteration. Beethoven, Verdi, Mozart, Tchaikovsky have all paid their unprofitable toll as the "high-brow" music of the elect has been stepped down for popular consumption as "the music of the millions." Nevertheless it is only half true to say as Gilbert Seldes does: "There is no such thing as jazz music; jazz is a method of playing music." Eccentric tone distortion and rhythmic antics are only one side of jazz, and the more superficial side at that. What is deeper is the mood out of which it is generated and the instinctive gift of doing it spontaneously. No really Negro musical group worries about what the other musicians are going to do; they are just as apt to vary and embroider at will and whimsy, with nobody put out on musical base, so to speak, as to follow score. No one approaching it from the side of experience rather than academic debate could be in doubt about the racial color and feeling of jazz; it is just as unique and characteristic as Gipsy is Gipsy. As a matter of fact, in the world of musical idiom, it has no other serious rival.

Niles puts it neatly. He says: "Up to this time, every other type of orchestra had played as best it could what was set before it in black and white. Successive and competitive improvisation was unknown and a heresy. After this, it was different." Louis Armstrong, in his clever recent book, "*Swing That Music*," (p. 121) says "to become a front rank 'swing player,' a musician must 'learn to read expertly and be just as able to play to score as any 'regular' musician. Then he must never forget for one minute of his life that the true spirit of swing music lies in free playing and that he must always keep his own musical feeling free. He must try to originate and not just imitate. And if he is a well-trained musician in the first place, he will be able to express his own musical ideas as they come to him with more versatility, more richness and more body. . . . To be a real swing artist, he must be a composer as well as a player." Most of the members of today's Negro jazz orchestras are highly trained musicians, but more of their pieces are worked out by ear in improvised experiment than are played from set arrangements. The arranger, more often, just copies down the good "break" or the happy inspiration so that it won't get forgotten.

For the process of composing by group improvisation, the jazz musician must have a whole chain of musical expertness, a sure musical ear, an instinctive feeling for harmony, the courage and gift to improvise and interpolate, and a canny sense for the total effect. This free style that Negro musicians introduced into playing really has generations of experience back of it; it is derived from the voice tricks and vocal habits characteristic of Negro choral singing. Out of the voice slur and quaver between the flat and the natural came

79

the whole jazz cadenza and all of the myriad jazz tone tricks, and out of the use of a single sustained voice tone as a suspension note for chorus changes of harmony came the now elaborate system of jazz harmonic style. It is most interesting to note that the African has this same fluid shifting musical scale, even more subtle than the scale shifts of American Negro folk music. In fact, it seems that the American Negro musical traits are the original African ones toned down and held in leash somewhat by the more regular patterns of European music. These basic racial idioms are more apparent in the simpler earlier forms of jazz, and still more in the vocal rather than the instrumental pieces. Some day, when Negro folk music is being scientifically studied, the old cheap discarded Okeh and Columbian records of *"The Memphis Students,"* the *McKinney Cotton Pickers," "The Chicago Rhythm Kings," "The Dixieland Orchestra"* and of the early "Blues-singers"—Bessie, Clara and Mamie Smith and Ma Rainey, will be priceless material in showing how jazz was created.

The Saxophone Intrudes.—Meanwhile a musical revolution was brewing: the saxophone was about to usurp the jazz throne. With the full vogue of the jazz age, the traditional and previously characteristic Negro instruments, the guitar, the fiddle, the banjo were pushed into the background of the jazz orchestra by the saxophones, the trumpets, trombones and clarinets. Only the bass fiddle and the drums have vigorously survived, and they with completely changed technique. Why was it? One reason is: not that here was a relatively unused instrument waiting a chance, but that it was suitable for creating the closest imitation of voice harmony possible. Fletcher Henderson in New York and Will Stewart in Chicago had a great deal to do with demonstrating the mellow song-like possibilities of

80

the sax. But these possibilities could not have been realized except for the astonishing revelations of new techniques of playing all the wind and brass instruments that came from the pioneer jazz players. "Sweet jazz" broke through on the saxophone; what subsequently became known as "hot" jazz on the trombone and trumpet. Jim Europe and Will Vodery were great influences in consolidating these new instrumental set-ups and timbres to the balanced orchestra; the jazz era was then officially on its way. Europe's 15th Regiment Band that he took to France during the World War was the musical wonder of the decade. The European musicians could not believe until Jim Europe's musicians played on borrowed instruments that they did not use special instruments quite different from theirs. Such agility, variability of tone, odd intervals, widened tone range were, indeed, a revelation. Of course, some of these jazz effects will never rise above the level of mere musical tricks, amusing, fascinating or arresting, but others are musical in a masterful way. The jazz revolution was a technical one and ushered in the first wave of the new modernistic harmony. After this, no limit could be set to the amazing variety of modern instrumental combinations and their new effects, the possibilities of which jazz-players demonstrated. This was perhaps their most important musical contribution.

The Jazz Epidemic.—Perhaps it would be truer to characterize jazz as an epidemic than as a revolution. The vogue spread so rapidly that the original source was hardly traceable. Within a very few years, American popular music was so innoculated with the new spirit and tempo that few people could recall when it had ever been different. The sugary sentimentality of the Harris-Olcott-Dresser period was quickly forsaken for the slangy, vernacular realism of the new song style. Technically, too, melody slipped back to second place

81

and snappy accompaniment and novel harmony became the standard by which music and songs found favor. Incidentally this new tempo was really more representative of the life and pace of our hectic times. Within a few years of the startling musical innovations of the Negro bands and players, white performers and arrangers and conductors had learned the new tricks and were feverishly and successfully competing in carrying the jazz style to a rapid perfection. Among these were several important pioneers of jazz and they deserve bracketed credit with the Negro pioneers; men like Lewis Muir, Ben Harney, Scott Joplin and later a relay of phenomenal jazz performers, Leon Beiderbecke, Jack Teagarden, Frank Teschmaker, Rademan, the originator of the "trombone laugh," Eddie Lang, Gene Krupa, Jack Stacey, Jess Stacey, Joe Venuti, Bennie Goodman and many others. It is remarkable to note how quickly the new style developed its own virtuosos, whom the expert critics of jazz know by their individual tone and style and rate with the enthusiasm and partisanship of classicists rating their favorite composers. There is no more interesting feature of this movement than the way in which the white musicians studied jazz, and from a handicap of first feeble imitation and patient hours in Negro cabarets listening to the originators finally became masters of jazz, not only rivaling their Negro competitors musically but rising more and more to commercial dominance of the new industry.

So jazz, in spite of its racial origin, became one great interracial collaboration in which the important matter is the artistic quality of the product and neither the quantity of the distribution nor the color of the artist. The common enemy is the ever-present danger of commercialization which, until quite recently, has borne with ever-increasing blight upon the healthy

82

growth of this music. The public taste is a notoriously poor judge of quality in this field; jazz experts will insist on reversing many of its preferences. They can never consent to a rating of jazz by the dollar intake, or the bestowals of titles and false claims by high paid publicity agents. The golden age of jazz artistically occurred long before the flood of popularity and profit. The pioneer jazz artists, black and white, between 1922 and 1928 were true artists, more often than not, with the artist's usual fate of a few discerning admirers, an early death and belated fame. Half of the pioneers mentioned died prematurely; the rest enjoyed more fame than fortune. Lately, improved taste and understanding has forced the re-publication of the recordings of such men, notably the Biederbecke Memorial Album, with its illuminating manual by Warren Scholl; the new pressings of La Rocca's Dixieland Orchestra and other signs of posthumous appreciation reversing the hasty and unjust verdict of the crowd.

The Genealogy of Jazz.—Only when we trace jazz to its humble roots can we comprehend the succession of styles that have given us the various schools of jazz, or understand why the critics prefer early "pure" jazz to the concocted, artificial and more sophisticated variety. Part of this early history is well traced in Geo. W. Lee's *"Beale Street: Where the Blues Began,"* tracing the Memphis beginnings; another, the equally important New Orleans school, is vividly told by Armstrong in *"Swing That Music."* The Memphis strain goes back to just after the Civil War. West Dukes began it with an orchestra that was famous both before and after the war. He was followed by Jim Turner; Handy was Turner's pupil and began as alto horn player and tenor in Turner's vocal quartet. Turner and Handy together organized the *"Mahara*

83

Minstrels." At the same time Charles Bynum, reputed to be the first to have played the blues orchestrally, was the leading bandmaster on Beale Street. Then in succession came Alex. Green, Charles Holmes, J. Leubrie Hill, Robert Henry and Will Stewart. This succession will not impress the reader until he learns later how by a system of apprenticeship this tradition has come steadily down from one musical generation to the next as a young member of one band has branched out to found his own orchestra and develop his individual style. Just to anticipate with two striking instances, Wm. Grant Still, perhaps today the most outstanding Negro composer in symphonic forms and Jimmie Lunceford, the latest word in jazz orchestra music, both trace back to a Beale Street apprenticeship. Considerably later, the powerful New Orleans strain got under way, and spread up the river on the famous old backwheeler excursion boats; La Rocca's Dixieland Orchestra, Keppard's Creole Band, Perez's Band, Ory's Jazz Orchestra, King Oliver's Band, the master of the phenomenal Louis Armstrong. It is like a great musical Mississippi, only running north.

Will Stewart, just mentioned, was largely responsible, according to Mr. Lee, for transplanting the blues to Chicago just as Handy transplanted them to Tin Pan Alley and New York. Thus after leaving its humble sources in the delta, the levee, the Memphis dive and "barrel-house" saloon, jazz divided into two streams. Chicago became the reservoir of the rowdy, hectic, swaggering style of jazz that has since become known as "hot jazz;" while New York (and Paris and London) has furnished the mixing bowls for the cosmopolitan style of jazz notable for stressing melody and flowing harmony as "sweet jazz." Then later still came the development of the sophisticated hybrid style that we know as "classical jazz." Curiously

84

enough, most of the notable white jazz musicians were disciples of the Chicago school; Biederbecke, Teschmaker, the Staceys and scores of others learned their jazz in the Chicago cabarets. But the New York school was polished and sophisticated from the early days of Ford Dabney, Will Marion Cook, Jim Europe and Fletcher Henderson. It was fortunate after all, for these men were the ambassadors who carried jazz to Europe and the haughty citadels of serious music. So their smoother, more mellow jazz was the first to become world famous and to have international influence.

European musicians, on the look-out for a new modernistic style in music, seized eagerly upon it and a mixed style dominated by jazz was born, giving us first the Continental classical jazz of European composers like Honegger, Weiner, Darius Milhaud, Kurt Weill, Krenek, and then considerably later, the American jazz classicists,—Copland, Chiafarelli, Gruenberg, John Alden Carpenter and George Gershwin. Later, of course, "hot jazz" reached New York and Europe in a second wave of fashion and popularity with the vogue of Duke Ellington and Louis Armstrong. When it did, it took so furiously it almost swamped its less torrid and peppery rivals: today, the leading devotees of jazz, especially in Europe, are violent partisans of "hot jazz" or as the latest phrase has it, "swing music." However, we must never forget that jazz has three styles "hot," "sweet" and "classical" and, historically at least three capitals, Chicago for the first, New York, the second, and Paris, the third.

Schools or Styles?—But the matter of "jazz schools" is more a problem for critics and a feud among imitators than a serious division or confusion for Negro musicians and the original geniuses of Negro music. They pass back and forth almost at

85

will from one to the other, changing moods and styles where others would be crossing frontiers or raising barricades. For in spite of commercially imposed specialization, Negro bands and composers are very versatile. Louis Armstrong, now the arch-apostle of "hot jazz" and Coleman Hawkins, its arch exponent in Europe, both played for several years in the orchestra of Fletcher Henderson. Fletcher Henderson, so important a popularizer of "sweet jazz" could on occasion be a path-breaker of the other style as in his *"Carolina Stomp"* and the sensational *"Everybody Loves My Baby."* Duke Ellington turns from the delicate sophistication of *"Sophisticated Lady"* and *"Mood Indigo"* to the frenzy of *"The Mooche," "Hot and Bothered"* and *"The Birmingham Breakdown,"* and then moves over at will to classical jazz in selections like *"Creole Rhapsody"* and *"Reminiscing in Tempo."* In short, what to the white musicians are different schools and contrasted techniques of jazz are to the Negro musicians, and a few whites thoroughly saturated in the tradition, interchangeable varieties of style. This versatility has had its drawbacks, however. The white musicians, proceeding oftener with a guiding thread of theory, have often been able to go farther by logic in the development of the more serious aspects of jazz than the Negro musicians have, moving too much under the mere guidance of instinct. Besides too great familiarity has bred, if not contempt, at least a certain short-sighted perspective on the best possibilities of jazz. Thus, it has been white musicians and critics who for the most part have capitalized jazz, both commercially and artistically.

Jazz and Morals.—Calling jazz an epidemic, brings out another important aspect of the matter; the connection between jazz and that hectic neurotic period of our cultural life, not yet a completely closed chapter,

86

—the "jazz age." The Negro, strictly speaking, never had a jazz age; he was born that way, as far as the original jazz response went. But as a modern and particularly as an American also, he became subject to the infections, spiritual and moral, of the jazz age. The erotic side of jazz, in terms of which it is often condemned, is admittedly there. But there is a vast difference between its first healthy and earthy expression in the original peasant paganism out of which it arose and its hectic, artificial and sometimes morally vicious counterpart which was the outcome of the vogue of artificial and commercialized jazz entertainment. The one is primitively erotic; the other, decadently neurotic. Gradually the Negro singers and musicians succumbed to the vogue of the artificial and decadent variety of song, music, dance which their folk-stuff started, and spawned a plague, profitable but profligate, that has done more moral harm than artistic good. The early blues-singers, for instance, were far from elegant, but their deadly effective folk speech was clean and racy by contrast with the mawkish sentimentality and concocted lascivity of the contemporary cabaret songs and dances. When they were "blue," they were really "down-hearted;" when they were revengeful and defiant they

> "Had the world in a jug
> The stopper in my hand
> I'm a goin' to hold it, till
> You come under my command."

Ironical, or plain sarcastic, they wailed:

> "Some o' you men, don't you make me tired,
> Yes, some o' you men, yo' jes' make me tired,
> You got a mouthful of 'gimme'—and
> A handful o' much-obliged'."

The only contemporary blues singer who retains much of this earlier effectiveness and folk flavor is Ethel Waters, and she has been forced by managerial

87

control or suggestion too far out of the line of the original tradition. The older generation sang not for the night clubs and "hot spots" of Harlem and its Broadway imitations that have spread all over the world of commercialized entertainment, but to the folky people for whom this racy idiom was more a safety valve of ribald laughter than a neurotic stimulant and breaker of Puritan inhibitions. Thus jazz is an emotional narcotic in one background and a stimulant in another; healthy paganism in one case, morbid eroticism in the other. As the latter, it is an expression of modern hysteria, common to both black and white sophisticates in our hectic, neurotic civilization of today.

So, even those who violently condemn jazz and its influence are partly right. Its cult does have a direct relationship to the freer sexuality of this age. However, instead of blaming it on jazz, the vogue of jazz should be regarded as the symptom of a profound cultural unrest and change, first a reaction from Puritan repressions and then an escape from the tensions and monotonies of a machine-ridden, extroverted form of civilization. In such dilemmas and their crises, Negro emotional elements have been seized upon, and jazz has become one of the main channels of emotional exhaust and compensation. Its devotees, especially at the height of the craze, rationalized this in a complete creed and cult of primitivism. But it was not original and genuine primitivism; only a sophisticated substitute. We must remember that in the cultural history of England and France such "break-down" periods as the Jacobean Restoration and the Bourbon debacle took place without any Negro inoculation. It is, therefore, unsound to speak of the Negro jazz vogue as the cause of modern eroticism, when in fact, it is mainly a

88

symptom, although it must be admitted, sometimes a compounding factor.

Jazz and the Modern Spirit.—For better or worse, jazz is, however, the spiritual child of this age. Phases of it will disappear with the particular phase of civilization which gave birth to it; but some permanent contributions to music and art will have been made. More than that, jazz will always be an important factor in interpreting the subtle spirit of our time, more so after it has passed into history. One naturally wonders, why it is that jazz has become so characteristic an expression of the modern spirit.

There are many interpretations; each perhaps with its share of the truth. George Antheil, himself an important modernistic composer, stresses jazz as a gift of "primitive joy and vigor." "Negro music," he says, "appeared suddenly (in Europe) after the greatest war of all time . . . it came upon a bankrupt spirituality. To have continued with Slavic mysticism (Russian music was the great vogue when the World War broke out), would in 1918 have induced us all to commit suicide. We needed the roar of the lion to remind us that life had been going on for a long while and would probably go on a while longer. Weak, miserable and anaemic, we needed the stalwart shoulders of a younger race to hold the cart awhile till we had gotten the wheel back on. . . . The Negro taught us to put our noses to the ground, to follow the scent, to come back to the elementary principles of self-preservation."

Then, there is the theory of emotional escape, seemingly contradicting this first theory of emotional rejuvenation. Jazz, according to these theorists, was a marvelous antidote to Twentieth Century boredom and nervous exhaustion, a subtle combination of nar-

89

cotic and stimulant; opium for the mind, a tonic for the feelings and instincts echoing the quick nervous tempo and pace of the hectic civilization of ours, which had originally caused that neurasthenia and disillusionment. It would be a curious fact if jazz really was such a cultural anti-toxin, working against the most morbid symptoms of the very disease of which it itself was a by-product. Many competent observers think it is.

In some important way, jazz has become diluted and tinctured with modernism. Otherwise, as purely a Negro dialect of emotion, it could not have become the dominant recreational vogue of our time, even to date, the most prolonged fad on record. More importantly, jazz in its more serious form, has also become the characteristic musical speech of the modern age. Beginning as the primitive rhythms of the Congo, taking on the American Negro's emotional revolt against the hardships and shackles of his life, jazz became more than the Negro's desperate antidote and cure for sorrow. It incorporated the typical American restlessness and unconventionality, embodied its revolt against the drabness of commonplace life, put pagan force behind the revolt against Puritan restraint, and finally became the Western World's life-saving flight from boredom and over-sophistication to the refuge of elemental emotion and primitive vigor. This is the credit side of the jazz ledger, against which the debit side we have already mentioned must be balanced, according to one's judgment and temperament and taste. Both detractors and enthusiasts must admit the power and widespread influence of jazz. It is now part Negro, part American, part modern; a whole period of modern civilization may ultimately be best known and understood as "The Jazz Age."

In what respects does jazz reflect the Negro and his temperament? In what respects does it represent the modern age, its moods and tempo? What were the origins of jazz and how were the "blues" related to it? What technical elements in the "blues" contributed to jazz harmony and jazz technique? What was Handy's relation to jazz as "father of the blues"? Why is jazz essentially connected with a free style and improvisation? What changes in modern musical harmony can be traced to jazz? What changes in the make-up of the modern orchestra? Why was the saxophone a factor in the evolution of jazz? What main differences are there between the folk-blues and the artificial blues of the cabarets? What are the main jazz capitols? Are the three styles of jazz,—"sweet," "hot" and "cosmopolitan" related to different styles of jazz playing and how? Who were the pioneers of the Chicago group and school of jazz? Of the New York group? Of the Continental European school? Of "classical jazz?" Who were some of the white pioneer jazz musicians? Who were more important among the early Negro jazz musicians and composers? On what basis do we speak of a "jazz classic?" What is the difference between real "folk jazz" and "cabaret jazz?" To what different groups are they directed? Are the emotional reactions of these respective audiences different? How? Is jazz a "mad and dangerous cult of eroticism?" In what ways does jazz express Negro eroticism? Modern eroticism? What can be said on the debit and credit sides of the jazz account? Has jazz done more moral harm than artistic good? What direct connections are there between jazz and the crises of modern civilization? Why does jazz reflect the American tempo and the modern mood as

91

well as Negro feeling? Is the Jazz Age over? Or waning?

READING REFERENCES

Armstrong, Louis: *Swing That Music*—Longmans, N. Y., 1936— pp. 1-87.

Goldberg, Isaac: *Tin Pan Alley*—pp. 234-296.

Milhaud, Darius: *Jazz Band and Negro Music*—Living Age, No. 323, 1924—p. 169.

Niles, Abbe: *Blues: An Anthology*—Boni, N. Y., 1926 Introduction, pp. 10-39.

Niles, Abbe: *Article on Jazz* in *Encyclopedia Britannica;* 14th Edition.

Osgood, Henry O.: *So This is Jazz*—Brown Little & Co., Boston—1926.

Panassie, Hughes: *Hot Jazz*—Witmark, N. Y., 1936.

Whiteman, Paul: *Jazz*—J. H. Sears & Co., N. Y., 1926.

RECORD ILLUSTRATIONS: EARLY JAZZ

The Bix Biederbecke Memorial Album—Victor.

La Rocca's Dixieland Orchestra: *"Tiger Rag"*—Victor 25403; *"Clarinet Marmalade"*—Victor 25411; *"Did You Mean It"*—Victor 25420.

McKinney's Cotton Pickers Orchestra: *"Miss Hannah"*—Victor 38133; *"Hullabaloo"*—Victor 22511.

Jimmie Noone: *"I Know That You Know"*—Vocation 1184.

King Oliver and Orchestra: *"Nagasaki"*—Brunswick 6429; *"I Got Rhythm"*—Brunswick 6233.

Chicago Rhythm Kings—Brunswick 500205.

"Darktown Strutter's Ball"—Paul Whiteman—Victor 25192.

Compare also: Porter Grainger, Clarence Williams and Spencer Williams accompaniments to early "Blues" records listed Chapter IV.

X

FROM JAZZ TO JAZZ CLASSICS: 1926–1936

From Jazz to "Jazz Classics."—For many persons, "classic" is a high-brow stick with which to spank so-called "low brow" music, because traditional music is more grown-up and authoritative. But let us listen to what may be said from the side of jazz in self-defense; and then realize, perhaps, that the important distinction is not between jazz and classical music but between the good, mediocre and bad of both varieties. Jazz has its classics; and the classical tradition has its second, third and fourth raters. By such standards a fine bit of writing or playing in the popular idiom and forms should outrate a mediocre attempt in the "classical" forms.

Louis Armstrong puts the case for good jazz plainly and sensibly. "Swing musicians worked hard for a quarter of a century, and against odds, to bring swing to the top; and swing musicians today have their work cut out for them to carry their art forward, to develop swing music into a broad and rich American music. . . . The way I look at swing music as it stands today is that it is America's second big bid to bring forth a worthwhile music of its own. The first big attempt was in the early days of jazz. We can now look back and see the mistakes and see about where jazz got side-tracked. We won't have many excuses to make if we let today's swing music go the same way. Jazz lost its originality and freshness and stopped growing. It stopped early. Jazz went down the easiest road where the big money was. . . . The writers of jazz have not developed jazz music much during all these years, although a few men must be given credit. But for the most part, the new songs that have been coming out of 'Tin Pan Alley,' which is Broadway's music publishing district, are really not new at all. They are the same old melodies and rhythms just twisted around in a different way and with different words. Coarse beats or sticky-sweet phrases, and all that, year after year. It makes a good musician tired, for they are the very ones who are doing most to break up these worn-out patterns. The reason swing musicians insist upon calling their music 'swing music' is because they know how different it is from the stale brand of jazz they've got so sick of hearing. But in the early days, when jazz was born, jazz wasn't that way at all."

So what we have said and quoted in defense and praise of jazz is by no means meant for the cheap low-browed jazz that is manufactured for passing popular consumption. But imbedded in this mass of mediocrity and trash are many compositions and versions of compositions that may justly be styled "jazz classics." One version of a song or dance tune may be cheap, trite and stereotyped and another version distinguished, original and highly musical. It depends on who "arranges" or recomposes it, and also upon who plays it. Some clownish rendition of *It Don't Mean a Thing* or crooner's wail of *Stormy Weather* will be musical trash, while an Ethel Waters or a Duke Ellington version must really be rated a "jazz classic," both for technical musicianship and for typically racial or "pure" style. It may take the connoisseur or expert to point it out to us, but after that, the difference is easily recognized.

Jazz has now developed its serious devotees and critics. They collect records, classify periods of style, trace developments of new technique, have their critical quarrels over favorites, have their special journals and their occasional "Jazz Recitals." Thus

94

the nameless musical foundling of the slums and dance halls has, within less than a decade, acquired musical respectability, a pedigree, and such standing in serious musical circles as in previous musical history no popular music has ever received. Later we shall quote several of the most authoritative jazz critics,—Henri Prunieres and Robert Goffin of Paris, Constant Lambert, the English composer. In passing, it will be enough to refer to Hugues Panassie's book,—*"Le Jazz Hot,"*—recently translated, which traces and analyzes jazz like a combined encyclopedia and hall-marking guild register.

The Title.—However, the most convincing praise of jazz will not come from the "jazz fans," but must come from the ranks of the orthodox musicians. And it is from such sources that jazz of the better sort has received great consideration. Kreisler, Rachmaninoff, Koussevitzky and Stokowski are certainly names authoritative enough. "Jazz," says Serge Koussevitzky, famous conductor of the Boston Symphony, "is an important contribution to modern musical literature. It has an epochal significance—it is not superficial, it is fundamental. Jazz comes from the soil, where all music has its beginning." And Leopold Stokowski, of the Philadelphia Orchestra, says more pointedly: "Jazz has come to stay because it is an expression of the times, of the breathless, energetic, super-active times in which we are living,—it is useless to fight against it. . . . Already its new vigor, its new vitality is beginning to manifest itself. . . . America's contribution to the music of the past will have the same revivifying effect as the injection of new, and in the larger sense, vulgar blood into dying aristocracy. Music will then be vulgarized in the best sense of the word, and will enter more and more into the daily lives of people. . . . The Negro musicians of America

95

are playing a great part in this change. They have an open mind and unbiased outlook. They are not hampered by conventions or traditions, and with their new ideas, their constant experiment, they are causing new blood to flow in the veins of music. The jazz players make their instruments do entirely new things, things finished musicians are taught to avoid. They are pathfinders into new realms."

We have to reckon with two types of worthwhile jazz, as distinguished from the trashy variety. First that which, rising from the level of ordinary popular music, usually in the limited dance and song-ballad forms, achieves creative musical excellence. This we may call the 'jazz classic;" and will consider it in this chapter. The other is that type of music which successfully transposes the elements of folk music, in this case jazz idioms, to the more sophisticated and traditional musical forms. This latter type has become known as "classical jazz," and will be considered in due course. Both the jazz classic and classical jazz are examples of the serious possibilities of the Negro's music, and both have been vital contributions to the new modernistic music of our time.

Jazz Contributions.—Jazz has thus seriously influenced modern music in general. It has educated the general musical ear to subtler rhythms, unfinished and closer harmonies, and unusual cadences and tone qualities. It has also introduced new systems of harmony, new instrumental techniques, novel instrumental combinations, and when fully developed, may lead to a radically new type of orchestra and orchestration. Thus jazz has been a sort of shock troop advance, which the regular line advance of modernistic music has intrenched and consolidated. In accounting for its originality and force, Mr. Stokowski has already referred to the Negro jazz musician's freedom from the

96

shackles of musical conventionality. But he could also have mentioned another factor. Much of the musical superiority and force of jazz comes from the fact that the men who play it create it. In the typical Negro jazz band, the musicians compose as a group under the leadership of a conductor who is also a composer or at least an arranger. The music comes alive from the activity of the group, like folk-music originally does, instead of being a mere piece of musical execution. There is the story that Rossini, the great Italian composer, often composed in bed, and that when a manuscript slipped down to the floor on the wall-side, he would think up another melody because it was easier than picking up the strayed manuscript. Improvising is an essential trait of the genuine jazz musician: with the assurance that "there is plenty more where it came from," he pours his music out with a fervor and freshness that is unique and irresistible. This titanic originality of the jazz orchestras has only to be harnessed and seriously guided to carry jazz to new conquests.

The Jazz Orchestra.—With all the changes of style and all the feverish experimenting, the jazz orchestra has remained relatively stable in its make-up. Usually a combination of from eleven to fourteen musicians, it is composed usually of three trumpets, two or three trombones, three or four saxophones, one or two clarinets, interchangeable with bassoon, a bass-fiddle, guitar, violin or banjo, and the two basic instruments, a piano and the "traps" or drums and percussion. The conductor traditionally is the pianist, though not always, and usually plays or alternates between conducting "in front" or at the piano, although more and more, the vogue is calling for the dangerous theatricality of the virtuoso or stunt conductor. Usually the Negro combinations are smaller and less formally

97

organized than the white jazz orchestras, and get similar or greater effects with fewer musicians.

Of course, their number is legion. Even to mention the outstanding organizations is difficult; but no jazz fan would omit Fletcher Henderson, Earl Hines, Luis Russell, Claude Hopkins, "Fats" Waller, Cab Calloway, Louis Armstrong, Don Redman, Jimmy Lunceford or Duke Ellington from the list of great Negro jazz combinations. Similarly, experts single out among the great white jazz groups, the 1926 orchestra of Jean Goldkette, Paul Whiteman's early aggregation, Ben Pollack's, Red Nichols', Ted Lewis, the Casa Loma orchestra, Jimmy Dorsey and finally Bennie Goodman. Many a popular and lucrative jazz combination is omitted, but they are the vendors of diluted and hybrid jazz, which the experts frown on as mere popular amusement music lacking real jazz character and distinction.

And when it finally comes to the blue ribbon of the fraternity, Ellington's band has usually received the expert's choice, although for a racier taste, Louis Armstrong has always had his special praise and rating. The Continental critics, with the advantage perhaps of distance, always argue Ellington versus Armstrong warmly, generally to conclude that Armstrong is the most phenomenal jazz player of today but that Duke Ellington is the greatest jazz composer.

Duke Ellington.—Constant Lambert, himself a modern composer of note and one who has used jazz idioms in his own compositions like the symphonic suite *"The Rio Grande,"* has this to say about jazz in general and Ellington and Armstrong in particular:

An artist like Louis Armstrong, who is one of the most remarkable virtuosi of the present day, enthralls us at first hearing, but after a few records one realizes that all his improvisations are based on the same restricted circle of ideas. . . . The best records of Duke Ellington, on the other hand, can be listened to again and again because they are

98

not just decorations of a familiar shape but a new arrangement of shapes. Ellington, in fact, is a real composer, the first jazz composer of distinction, and the first Negro composer of distinction. His works, apart from a few minor details, are not left to the caprice or ear of the instrumentalist; they are scored and written out . . . and the best American records of his music may be taken definitively like a full score, and they are only jazz records worth studying for their form as well as their texture. Ellington, himself being an executant of second rank, has probably not been tempted to interrupt the continuity of his texture with bravura passages for the piano, and although his instrumentalists are of the finest quality, their solos are rarely demonstrations of virtuosity for its own sake.

The real interest of Ellington's records lies not so much in their color, brilliant though it may be, as in the amazingly skillful proportions in which the color is used. I do not only mean skillful as compared with other jazz composers, but as compared with so-called high-brow composers. I know of nothing in Ravel so dextrous in treatment as the varied solos in the middle of the ebullient *"Hot and Bothered,"* and nothing in Stravinsky more dynamic than the final section. The combination of themes at this moment is one of the most ingenious pieces of writing in modern music. It is not a question, either, of setting two rhythmic patterns working against each other in the mathematical Aaron Copland manner—it is genuine melodic and rhythmic counterpoint which, to use an old-fashioned phrase, "fits perfectly". . . .

He has crystallized the popular music of our time and set up a standard by which we may judge not only other jazz composers, but also those high-brow composers, whether American or European, who indulge in what is roughly known as "symphonic jazz."

Extravagant and eccentric as such praise might seem coming from only a single voice, however distinguished, it becomes something quite different when echoed here and there independently by the most competent European and American critics and composers. On such a basis, I think we must agree that in addition to being one of the great exponents of pure jazz, Duke Ellington is the pioneer of super-jazz and one of the persons most likely to create the classical jazz toward which so many are striving. He plans a symphonic suite and an African opera, both of which will prove a test of his ability to carry native jazz through to this higher level. Many of his more spectacular competitors have changed their style repeatedly, proof of musical versatility, but Ellington's has developed more solid maturity, especially as shown by

99

the lately published four-part *"Reminiscing in Tempo."*
Critics had said previously: "His one attempt at a
larger form, the two-part *'Creole Rhapsody'* is not
wholly successful, although it does develop and inter-
weave a larger number of themes than usual in his
work. It is here that Ellington has most to learn."
The later record proves that he has learned or is
learning. So one can agree with Robert Goffin that
"the technique of jazz production has been rationalized by Ellington" and that "he has gradually placed
intuitive music under control."

Jazz has been as fickle a medium as acting, and but
for recording would have vanished in thin air. Its
most extraordinary achievement, as has been said, is
"the dissociation of interpretation from a stenographic
execution of a work," to "improvise upon a given
rhythmic theme with changes of tone, combinations of
voices and unexpected counterpoints (spontaneous
interpolations)." Someone had to devise a technique
for harnessing this shooting geyser, taming this wild
well. R. D. Darrell's tribute to Ellington is probably
an anticipation of what the future critics will judge.
He says:

"The larger works of Gershwin, the experiments of Copland and
other serious composers are attempts with new symphonic forms stem-
ming from jazz but not of it. Not forgetting a few virtuoso or im-
provisatory solos (by Zez Confrey, V. Venuti and Lang, Jimmie Johnson
and others), one can truthfully say that a purely instrumental school
of jazz has never grown beyond the embryonic stage . . . Ellington's
compositions gravitate naturally toward two types, the strongly
rhythmed pure dance pieces (*'Birmingham Breakdown,'* *'Jubilee
Stomp,'* *'New Orleans Low Down,'* *'Stevedore Stomp'*) or the slower
paced lyrical pieces with less forcefully rhythmed dance bass (*'Mood
Indigo,'* *'Take it Easy,'* *'Awful Sad,'* *'Mystery Son,'* etc.) Occasionally the two are combined with tremendous effectiveness, as in the
'East St. Louis Toodle-O,' *'Old Man Blues,'* or *'Rocking in Rhythm.'*
The most striking characteristic of all his works, and the one that
stamps them as ineradicably his own, is the individuality and unity
of style that weld composition, orchestration and performance into one
inseparable whole. . . . Within an Ellington composition there is a
similar unity of style of the essential musical elements of melody,
rhythm, harmony, color, and form. Unlike most jazz writers, Ellington

never concentrates undue attention on rhythm alone. . . . Delightful and tricky rhythmic effects are never introduced for sensational purposes, rather they are developed and combined with others as logical part and parcel of the whole work. . . . Harmonically Ellington is apt and subtle, rather than obvious and striking, and in the exploitation of new tone and coloring, he has proceeded further than any other composer—popular or serious, of today."

Such praise would be too much if it were entirely true of Ellington (as a wise caution spoken by the same critic will show in a moment), or if it were not partly true of many other of the great jazz composers and "arrangers" like Don Redman, Bennie Carter, Cy Olliver, in their best but often too fragmentary passages. It is quoted as much in praise of jazz and its correct appreciation as in praise of Ellington. Jazz is in constant danger from the commercialization of the money-changers who exploit it and the vulgarization of the immense public that consumes it.

Thus the word of caution, which Darrell offers to Ellington, ought to be stressed for all who come into the dangerous zone of commercially controlled popular music. Darrell says: "He may betray his uniqueness for popularity, be brought down to the level of orthodox dance music, lose his secure footing and intellectual grasp in the delusion of grandeur. Most of his commercial work evidences just such lapses. But he has given us, and I am confident will give us again (Darrell wrote this in 1932), more than a few moments of the purest, the most sensitive revelations of feeling in music today." All this is the common enemy of the jazz musician, white and black. But the artistic loss would be irreparable for the Negro musician, whose spirit-child jazz is, and whose artistic vindication its sound development must be. If these musicians can accomplish what they have, with commercial chains on and hampered by the strait-jacket of popular dance tempo and pattern, they must seek

101

to break through these limitations or else yield the future possibilities of jazz to the modernistic musicians who are trying "symphonic" jazz. There is enough genius, however, in the ranks of the professional jazz musicians to do the job independently.

The present vogue of "swing music," and the development of groups like the "Hot Clubs" for the serious study and support of undiluted jazz, true to the Negro idiom, comes at a strategic time. Already this support has rejuvenated the old guard veterans like Ellington, Armstrong, Fletcher Henderson, Noble Sissle, Wm. ("Fats") Waller, Earl Hines, "Chick" Webb, and Don Redman, who are returning to their original traditions. They must try to minimize the empty tricks of eccentric jazz on the one hand and thus get over the minstrel dangers of the "scat period" of popular jazz, and on the other, avoid the musical shallows of diluted, sentimental "sweet jazz," still popular but by the testimony of every expert neither racially or musically very significant. Behind the "old guard" organizations mentioned stand the promising younger Negro bands: Luis Russell's merger with Louis Armstrong, the Claude Hopkins' Orchestra, the Blue Rhythm group of "Lucky" Millinder, and most especially the band of Jimmie Lunceford, that is composed almost exclusively of musicians of high technical and cultural training. Shoulder to shoulder with these exponents of "real" jazz stand such white musical organizations as the orchestras of "Red" Nichols, "Red" Norvo, the Dorsey Brothers, and the now favorite "swing" group of Bennie Goodman, who, by the way, uses principally Fletcher Henderson's arrangements, and has in his group the sensational young Negro jazz pianist, Teddy Wilson.

102

What is a "jazz classic?" Can jazz or any popular music produce classics? What exceptional recognition and influence did Negro jazz receive between 1926 and 1936? What contributions has jazz made to modernistic music? To modern orchestration and harmony? What is the difference between "sweet jazz" and "hot jazz?" Which is more racial? Which has the widest vogue today? What are the contributions of Duke Ellington, Louis Armstrong and Fletcher Henderson to serious jazz? Which school of jazz did Paul Whiteman follow? Is the influence of the Gershwin-Whiteman school of jazz growing or on the wane? What is the relation of "jazz" and so-called "swing music?" Does the vogue of "swing" represent a come-back for the truly Negro idioms of jazz? What is the present standing of jazz among competent musicians and critics?

READING REFERENCES

Same as Chapter X and
Darrell, R. D.: *Black Beauty* (on Ellington)—"Disques," June, 1932.
Ferguson, Otis: *The Spirit of Jazz*—New Republic, Vol. 89—Dec. 30, 1936.
Knowlton, Don: *The Anatomy of Jazz*—Harpers Magazine, 1926.
Lambert, Constant: *Music Ho!*—*The Spirit of Jazz*—pp. 192-214.
For adverse criticism of Jazz: see Hare: *Negro Musicians and Their Music:* pp. 131-157. Also *Literary Digest*, 105:20—April 12, 1930.

RECORD ILLUSTRATIONS: "JAZZ CLASSICS"

Duke Ellington and Orchestra: *"Awful Sad"*—Brunswick 6805; *"Black and Tan Fantasy"*—Victor 24861; *"Black Beauty"*—Victor 21580 and 21137; *"Creole Love Call"*—Victor 24861; *"Creole Rhapsody"*—Victor 36049; *"East St. Louis Toodle-O"*—Victor 21703; *"Hot and Bothered"*—Okeh 8623; *"It Don't Mean a Thing"*—Brunswick 6265; *"The Mooche"*—Okeh 8623; *"Mood Indigo"*—Victor 24486; *"Rockin' in Rhythm"*—Brunswick 6038; *"Reminiscing in Tempo"*—Brunswick 7546/47; *"Solitude"*—Victor 24755; *"Sophisticated Lady"*—Brunswick 6600; *"Swanee Rhapsody"*—Brunswick 6288; *"Take It Easy"*—Brunswick 6803.

Ellington's Orchestra with Jazz Solos: *"Clarinet Lament"* (Barney Bigard) and *"Echoes of Harlem"* (Cootie Williams)—Brunswick 7750; *"Trumpet in Spades"* (Rex Stewart) and *"Yearning for Love"* (Lawrence Brown)—Brunswick 7752.

103

Louis Armstrong and Orchestra: *"Melancholy Blues"*—Okeh 8519; *"St. James Infirmary Blues"*—Okeh 8657; *"Can't Give You Anything but Love"*—Okeh 8669; *"Ain't Misbehavin'"*—Okeh 8174; *"Chinatown"*—Okeh 41538; *"Mahogany Hall Stomp"* (Spencer Williams)—Victor 24232; *"Body and Soul"* and *"Shine"*—Okeh 41468; *"I Got Rhythm"*—Okeh 41534; *"Star Dust"*—Okeh 41584; *"Sweet Sue"*—Victor 24321; *"I'm in the Mood for Love"*—Decca 579; *"Lazy River"*—Okeh 41541.

Fletcher Henderson and Orchestra: *"Shoe Shine Boy"*—Victor 25375; *"Someone Stole Gabriel's Horn"*—Decca 3563; *"Fidgety Feet"*—Brunswick 500321; *"Riffin'"*—Victor 25339; *"Sugar Foot Stomp"*—Brunswick 500153 and Victor 22721.

Don Redman and Orchestra: *"Chant of the Weeds"*—Brunswick 500160; *"Shuffle your Feet"*—Brunswick 6520; *"I Got Rhythm"*—Brunswick 500194.

Cab Calloway and Orchestra: *"Scat Song"* and *"Cabin in the Cotton"*—Brunswick 6272; *"Minnie the Moocher"*—Brunswick 6321; *"Miracle Man"*—Brunswick 7756; *"St. James Infirmary"*—Brunswick 6105.

Chick Webb and Savoy Orchestra: *"Lonesome Nights"*—Okeh 41567; *"Heebie Jeebies"* and *"Soft and Sweet"*—Brunswick 500324.

"Fats" Waller and Orchestra: *"I Ain't Got Nobody"*—Victor 25026; *"Love Me or Leave Me"*—Victor 22092; *"Sweet Sue"*—25087; *"Christopher Columbus"*—Victor 25295; *"Truckin'"*—Victor 25116; *"Write Myself a Letter"*—Victor 25044.

Claude Hopkins and Orchestra: *"Three Little Words"*—Brunswick 6864; *"Everbody Shuffle"*—Brunswick 6916.

Luis Russell and Orchestra: *"My Sweet"*—Odeon 238287; *"Song of the Swanee"*—Okeh 8780.

Blue Rhythm Boys: *"Blue Rhythm"*—Brunswick 6143; *"Moanin'"*—Victor 22800.

Earl Hines and Orchestra: *"Blue"*—Brunswick 6872; *"Rossetta"*—Brunswick 6541; *"Melancholy"*—Brunswick 500165.

Jimmie Lunceford and Orchestra: *"Rhythm is My Business"*—Decca 369; *"Melody Man"* and *"I'll Take the South"*—Decca 805; *"Runnin' Wild"*—Decca 503.

Coleman Hawkins: *"Rhythm Crazy"*—Parlophone 1743.

Ethel Waters: *"Heat Wave"*—Columbia 2826 D; *"Some of These Days"*—Columbia 14264 D; *"I Got Rhythm"*—Columbia 23460; *Stormy Weather*—Victor 6564.

Adelaide Hall: *"Blues I Love to Sing"*—Victor 22985; *"I Must Have That Man"*—Brunswick 50257.

Mildred Bailey: *"Someday Sweetheart"*—Vocalion 3057.

Jimmy Johnson: *"Riffs"*—Okeh 8770; *"You Got to be Modernistic"*—Brunswick 50023.

Art Tatum: *"Star Dust"*—Decca 306; *"St. Louis Blues"* and *"Tiger Rag"*—Brunswick 500265; *"When a Woman Loves a Man"*—Decca 38389.

Cleo Brown: *"Me and My Wonderful One"*—Decca 486.

Teddy Wilson: *"Every Now and Then"*—Brunswick 7543; *"Breakin' in a New Pair of Shoes"*—Brunswick 7589; *"Blues in C♯ Minor"*—Brunswick 7684.

104

Ben Pollack and Orchestra: *"Song of the Islands"*—Brunswick 7764.

Red Nichols and Orchestra: *"Dinah"*—Brunswick 500404; *"Riverboat Shuffle"*—Brunswick 3627.

Bennie Goodman and Orchestra: *"Moon Glow"* and *"Dinah"*—Victor 25398; *Stompin' at the Savoy"*—Victor 25247; *"Basin St. Blues"* and *"Beale St. Blues"*—Brunswick 7645.

Himber's Ritz Carlton Orchestra: *Midnight Blue*—Victor 25365.

Jerome Kern: *"Old Man River"* (Sung by Robeson)—Victor 21376.

Reginald Foresythe: *"With the Duke"*—Decca B. K. 779; *"St. Louis Blues"*—Columbia 3088 D; *"The Duke Insists"*; *"Serenade for a Wealthy Widow"* and *"Angry Jungle"*—Columbia 2916 D.

Frankie Trumbauer and Orchestra: *I'm Coming Virginia*—Brunswick 7703.

Paul Whiteman and Orchestra: *"Dardenella"*—Victor 25238; *"St. Louis Blues"*—Victor 20092; *"Star Dust"* (Carmichael) and *"Blue Moonlight"* (Dana Suesse)—Victor 36159; *"Southern Holiday"* and *"Serenade for a Wealthy Widow"*—Victor 24852; *"Smoke Gets in Your Eyes"* (Kern)—Victor 24455; *"Love in Bloom"*—Victor 24672.

NOTE.—For comparison of jazz styles several titles like *"St. Louis Blues," "Dinah," "Star Dust," "I Got Rhythm,"* have been cited in a number of versions.

XI

CLASSICAL JAZZ AND MODERN AMERICAN MUSIC

Musical Pathfinding.—Before the onset of classical jazz, there was a half generation of pathfinding experiment seeking a typical idiom for American music. This movement turned in two directions, toward American Indian and toward American Negro themes. The first highly successful use of such thematic material was by the Bohemian or Czeck composer, Anton Dvorak, who was destined to make a step as vital to the development of native American music as it was to the discovery of the serious musical possibilities of American Negro folk-song. He investigated Indian, Negro and other native American materials, but everyone admits that in his epoch-making Symphony "*From the New World,*" produced in 1895, the Negro elements dominate. True, this work is highly composite, there are Indian themes also, with much of Dvorak's own Bohemian style cropping out. And except in the celebrated slow movement and the main theme of the Scherzo, these Negro elements are much diluted; at times heavily enough to be only Negroid, as in the less famous "*American Quartet*" Op. 96, by the same composer. However, in the "*Largo*" of the symphony, we sense the true atmosphere of a Negro spiritual, and in the *Scherzo* or fast third movement, Papa Dvorak, without fully sensing it, was nose close to jazz, for he took his rhythms and tone intervals from the shout type of Negro dance. In this important pioneering, the record stands that Dvorak's guide and musical interpreter was the Negro musician and composer,

106

Harry T. Burleigh, then a graduate student at the National Conservatory, Brooklyn, where Dvorak taught during his American visit.

Once this Negro material had been vindicated so successfully, many native composers turned to it also for serious inspiration. Ernest Kroeger wrote *"Humoresque Negré"* (1899); George Chadwick wrote *"Jubilee,"* No. 1 of his *"Four Symphonic Sketches"* (1895); Henry Hadley titled the third movement of his *"Symphony No. 4,"* *"South"* (1902); Henry Gilbert wrote his *"Comedy Overture on Negro Themes"* in 1907, to be followed 1913 by a *"Humoresque"* (1913) and a *"Negro Rhapsody"* (1915). John Powell, who later tried to discredit the originality of Negro music, used Negro themes throughout his earlier work in *"Suite Sudiste"* (*Elegie Negré*), *"Suite Virginanesque";* and to date his best known composition is perhaps the *"Negro Rhapsody"* (1921). Rubin Goldmark, with even more sympathetic musicianship wrote a *"Negro Rhapsody";* and E. Burlingham Hill wrote numerous studies based on Negro rhythms, notably a *"Scherzo"* and a *"Jazz Study for Two Pianos."*

This was the pre-jazz era, when spirituals for the most part and occasionally Negro dance themes were the accepted models. Along with this group went several talented pioneering Negro composers, whose work will be discussed later;—Samuel Coleridge Taylor, the Anglo-African, and the American Negroes Harry T. Burleigh, R. Nathaniel Dett, whose *"Juba Dance"* is such a favorite, Carl R. Diton, and the early work of Hall Johnson and Edmund Jenkins. The two latter composers eventually broke with the romantic school that followed the footsteps of Dvorak and joined forces with the realistic school that discovered classical jazz by trailing the lowly footpaths of folk jazz.

Classical Jazz.—Then came the second phase of the influence of Negro folk music on the classicists,—the jazz vogue.

As early as 1917, Hiram K. Motherwell took up the critical cudgels for jazz, and suggested a classical jazz concert program as follows:

I

Roll Dem Cotton Bales..................Johnson
Waiting for the Robert E. Lee.............Muir
The Tennessee Blues....................Warner
The Memphis Blues.....................Handy

II

Spirituals:
    You May Bury Me in the East.......Traditional
    Bendin' Knees a-Achin'.............Traditional
    These Dead Bones Shall Rise Again...Traditional
    Play on Your Harp, Little David.....Traditional

III

Nobody's Lookin' But the Owl and the Moon,
                          Rosamund Johnson
Exhortation ....Will Marion Cook
Rain Song........................Marion Cook

IV

Everybody's Doing It...............Irving Berlin
I Love a Piano........................Berlin
When I Get Back to the U.S.A.............Berlin
On the Beach at Wai-ki-ki............Jerome Kern
Ragtime Cowboy Joe....................Muir

No doubt this was designed partly to shock the traditionalists, but the Motherwell's musical heresy has now become unchallenged orthodoxy. He said:

To me ragtime brings a type of musical experience which I can find in no other music. . . . I love the delicacy of its inner rhythms and the largeness of its rhythmic sweeps. I like to think that it is the

108

perfect expression of the American city, with its restless bustle and motion, its multitude of unrelated details, and its underlying rhythmic progress toward a vague Somewhere. Its technical resourcefulness continually surprises me, and its melodies, at their best, delight me. . . . I firmly believe that a ragtime program, well organized and sung, would be delightful and stimulating to the best audience the community could muster. . . .

Goldberg, who quotes this, relates that in six short years, Eva Gauthier gave a concert of "American Music" and, with George Gershwin as accompanist, sang jazz songs to a shocked but receptive high-brow audience. Musical New York, a year later, on February 12, 1924, listened to Paul Whiteman's first concert of "classical jazz," with selections of orchestral complexity and classical form from Zez Confrey, Kern, Ferdinand Grofé, Irving Berlin, Gershwin,—the climax and sensation of the concert being Gershwin's *"Rhapsody in Blue."* By 1926 Whiteman had published his critical analysis of *"Jazz,"* Henry O. Osgood, his *"So This Is Jazz,"* and Abbe Niles, with the collaboration of W. C. Handy, his *"Blues: An Anthology,"* with the famous preface on Negro folk music from which we have frequently quoted. Darius Milhaud, the French modernist composer, made two visits to America to study the new prodigy, wrote enthusiastically of its prospects as "the music of the age" in 1918 and in 1922 wrote his African ballet: *"The Creation of the World."* It was his efforts that introduced jazz to the feverishly experimental younger French musicians who afterwards became famous as *"The Group of Six."*

By coincidence America's entry into the World War took jazz to Europe in the knapsacks of the Negro soldiers, most particularly in the kit of Jim Europe's *Fifteenth New York Regiment Band.* George Antheil says:

Since Wagner, music has had two gigantic blood transfusions; first the Slavic and then the Negro. Two epochal dates in the latter are

109

the *"Ritual of Spring"* of Stravinsky with its revolutionary primitivism in 1913 and the arrival in 1917 of the first Negro jazz band in Paris. By 1919, Stravinsky, a sub-conscious convert to jazz, became a conscious exponent of it in his *"Piano Rag Music"* and his *"Ragtime."* Since then European and American music—popular, semi-classic and classic, have all in various ways reflected an ever-deepening vogue of characteristic Negro rhythm and harmony.

Milhaud wrote enthusiastically about jazz and its future. He also wrote it, beginning with *"Three Rags"* and *"Shimmy for Jazz Band"* but climaxing, in 1923, with an African ballet based on an African legend of creation, *"La Creation du Monde,"* produced by the Swedish Ballet in Paris and only once in America (1933 in New York). This is a work that one critic says is "probably the most perfect of all pieces of symphonic jazz, excelling even Copland's piano *"Concerto,"* which by the way is preferred by most musicians to Gershwin's *"Concerto in F Major."* Then came in quick order, Kurt Weill's semi-jazz opera "Mahogonny Hall," Krenek's jazz opera, given once at the Metropolitan, *"Johnny Spielt Auf"* (Johnny Strikes Up), Ravel's "blues movement" in his *"Violin and Piano Sonata,"* Walton's *"Portsmouth Point,"* Constant Lambert's *"Florida; Tone Poem"* and *"Rio Grande."* Europe's most original younger composers thus paid this instant tribute; and Ravel, Stravinsky, Delius, Rachmaninoff, Milhaud have all made formal acknowledgment, so that in Europe even more than in America, jazz is linked with what is typically modern or modernistic in music.

Meanwhile, the younger Negro musicians were tossing off anonymously impromptu jazz creations that could have established musical fame and fortune, if more deliberately handled. There were one or two exceptions: Edmund Jenkins had the training and foresight to write his *"Charlestonia": a Negro Rhapsody for Full Orchestra,* which was played in Brussels

110

and Paris in 1924; and under the inspiration of Edgar Varesé, Wm. Grant Still began presenting his serious classical compositions on the programs of the International League of Composers. Thus New York heard in 1927 *"From the Land of Dreams,"* for chamber orchestra; in 1929 *"Levee Land,"* a suite for voice and orchestra,—a vehicle, by the way, for Florence Mill's one and only serious concert engagement, *"Africa": a Symphonic Poem* in 1930, and parts of the now completed *"Afro-American Symphony."* The latter and other works in classical form have been presented often under the patronage of Howard Hansen, of the Eastman School of Music, Rochester, where seldom a year passes without some new work by Mr. Still on the annual festival program. Both Jenkins and Still are graduates of the jazz ranks, and while many of their anonymous "arrangements" have made the reputation and fortune of others in commercial jazz, the fruits of that apprenticeship have deepened the skill and racial character of their more formal music.

But on the whole, the Negro musicians of the first jazz decade suffered from musical myopia: too close to jazz, they could not see its far future. Until the day of the composer-conductor in jazz, which began about 1927, many a fine bit of creative composition was cloaked and put down as an "arrangement." But out of these humble ranks, the most original and gifted American composers, Negro and white, have come. The list is worth calling, even in rapid review: Porter Grainger, Spencer Williams, Clarence Williams, Will Vodery, Lovie Austin, Jim Europe, Rosamond Johnson, Fletcher Henderson, Duke Ellington, Don Redman, Bennie Carter, Luis Russell, Cy Olliver, Jimmie Lunceford, Reginald Foresythe, Jenkins and Still. Their musical significance becomes all the more obvious

111

when we mention some of their white colleagues, all of whom served a jazz apprenticeship, Frank Black, Ferde Grofé, Adolph Deutsch, Hoagy Carmichael, Irving Berlin, Jerome Kern, Rodgers and Hart, Cole Porter and George Gershwin. Their mere mention tells the story of the uniquely close relation between the popular and the serious strains of American music. With American music still in the making, it is quite obvious where its main ingredients are coming from. Symphonic jazz, breaking from the shell of dance jazz and popular song ballad, is the present hope of seriously representative American music.

The American School.—Classical jazz, however, is still a somewhat unstable and anaemic hybrid. In many cases, the effort to lift jazz to the level and form of the classics has devitalized it. Often it has been too evident where the jazz idiom left off and the superimposed Lizst, Puccini, Stravinsky or Wagner began. George Gershwin has, of course, been associated in the public mind with this movement, and must be given credit for his bold pioneering and firm faith in the future of "symphonic jazz." From the *"Rhapsody in Blue"* in 1923 up to last year's *American Folk Opera, "Porgy and Bess,"* he has feverishly experimented, with increasing but not fully complete success. Discerning critics detect too much Lizst in the *"Rhapsody"* and too much Puccini and Wagner in *"Porgy";* and it is not yet certain how well such musical oil and water can be made to mix. Oddly enough some of the most recent work in serious jazz, Reginald Foresythe's *"Jazz Toccata and Fugue"* and Van Phillip's jazz canon and fugue *"Thank You, Mister Bach"* suggest that if jazz idioms have any vital classical affinities, they are with the contrapuntal traditions of the old polyphonic music rather than with the more modern classics. Be that as it may, Bach and jazz blend

112

more successfully than Liszt, Wagner and jazz; perhaps the first generation of jazz classicists were too timid about their protege.

The most musically satisfactory compositions of this "super-jazz," American as well as European, have treated jazz contrapuntally, that is in terms of its basic factors, rhythm patterns and kaleidoscopic harmonic sequences. One of the best and earliest compositions of this type was Aaron Copland's *"Piano Concerto"*; John Alden Carpenter's pioneer work for classical jazz similarly tried to link it with the strictest classical tradition and form. In the meantime, Paul Whiteman, guided by Gershwin and Ferde Grofé, was exploiting and popularizing jazz tone color, harmony and rhythm in the larger forms. This was no inconsiderable service: Whiteman has converted the American public to the seriousness of jazz and clinched Dvorak's prophecy that future American music would draw its substance from Negro sources. Louis Gruenberg has taken classical jazz to new heights in his *"Daniel Jazz"* and his setting of one of Weldon Johnson's Negro sermons, *"Creation"*; and recently in his opera, *"Emperor Jones,"* effectively broadening the path that has led from Frank Harling's pioneer opera *"Deep River"* to the latest and revealing success of Gershwin's *"Porgy and Bess."*

A most promising sign is that the latest classical jazz is clearly in a style more fused and closer to the original Negro musical idioms. Constant Lambert's *"Rio Grande,"* Dana Suesse's *"Jazz Nocturne," "Concerto in Three Rhythms,"* and other brilliant compositions, Otto Sesana's *"Negro Heaven,"* Lamar Strigfield's *"Parade"* and symphonic ballet *"The Legend of John Henry"* are beacons of the new style. Unlike the first phase of classical jazz, they are not artificial hybrids, but genuine developments of the intimate na-

113

tive idioms of jazz itself. Thus, with these younger generation efforts, we are considerably nearer to a true union and healthy vigorous fusion of jazz and the classical tradition.

However, much yet remains to be done, and one has a right to expect a large share of it from the Negro composer. The death of Edmund Jenkins, just a week or so before his *"Rhapsody No. 2"* was scheduled for performance in Paris by the Pasdeloup Orchestra, was one of the tragic losses of our racial and national art. Jenkins grew up as a juvenile member of his father's famous Charleston, S. C., Orphanage Band, and never lost his hold on Negro idioms and the jazz accent even after years abroad following his graduation from the London Royal College of Music. No composition of maturity and genius equal to his appeared from Negro sources until the rather recent work of Wm. Grant Still and William Dawson. But with the successful presentation of symphonies based on folk themes from each of these young composers in the last year, the hope for symphonic music in Negro idiom has risen notably. In 1935, ten years after his enthusiastic championing of the serious possibilities of jazz, Leopold Stokowski was able to present with his great Philadelphia Orchestra William Dawson's *"Negro Folk Symphony"*; certainly one of America's major contributions thus far to symphonic literature. This work is a somewhat romantic but unorthodoxly orchestrated treatment of themes from Negro spirituals in a broad and dramatic style in three movements,—*"Bond of Africa," "Hope in the Night,"* and *"O, Let Me Shine."* Mr. Dawson, formerly of Chicago, though born in Anniston, Alabama, and now director of the Tuskegee Institute school of music, demonstrated mastery of the full resources of the modern orchestra, and

114

showed unusual maturity for a first symphony; as even the most skeptical critics admitted. After several performances by the Rochester Symphony Orchestra, under Howard Hanson, Wm. Grant Still's *Afro-American Symphony* had its New York premiere with the Philharmonic under the baton of Hans Lange, in December, 1935. Much of this composer's work, especially his *"Sadjhi: an African Ballet"* and his *"Eben Chronicle"* are ultra-modernistic and too sophisticated for the laity; though startling bits of musicianship. The *"Symphony,"* however, has a moving simplicity and directness of musical speech. It, too, has a folk theme, treated in contrasted moods with corresponding rhythms, making for a combined symphony and tone epic of Negro experience. This work is, however, less programistic than Dawson's, and gains by its nearer approach to pure music. An interesting third contribution from the pen of a Negro composer is the *"Symphony in E Minor"* by Florence E. Price of Chicago, presented several times by the Chicago Orchestra under Frederick Stock, with whom Mrs. Price has also had the honor of playing her own *"Piano Concerto."* In the straight classical idiom and form, Mrs. Price's work vindicates the Negro composer's right, at choice, to go up Parnassus by the broad high road of classicism rather than the narrower, more hazardous, but often more rewarding path of racialism. At the pinnacle, the paths converge, and the attainment becomes, in the last analysis neither racial nor national, but universal music.

DISCUSSION QUESTIONS

What was Dvorak's role in the development of American music and the discovery of the serious possibilities of Negro folk music? What influence did he

115

exert on American composers? Who were the pioneers of "classical jazz?" What contributions has jazz and the jazz apprenticeship made to serious American music? Who are among the important European composers in this field of classical jazz? What American composers and what American Negro composers have followed this school? What are the claims of those Negro musicians who ignore the racial idioms and compose in "straight" classical forms?

READING REFERENCES

Brawley, Benj. G.: *Edmund Jenkins*—Opportunity Magazine—December, 1926.

Hare, Maud Cuney: *Negro Musicians and Their Music*—pp. 178-198.

Lambert, Constant—*Music Ho!*—Scribners, N. Y.—1934—pp. 192-214.

Rosenfeld, Paul: *Discoveries of a Music Critic*—Harcourt Brace, N. Y. —1936. pp. 227-238; 264-272; 286-289.

RECORD ILLUSTRATIONS: CLASSICAL JAZZ AND MUSIC ON NEGRO FOLK THEMES

Carpenter, J. A.—*"Skyscrapers Ballet"*—Nat Shilkret Orchestra—Victor 11250-2.

Carmichael, Hoagy: *"Southern Rhapsody."*

Debussy, Claude: *Golliwog's Cakewalk*—Victor 7148.—*Minstrels*—Columbia 9062M.

Dvorak, Anton: *"Symphony No. 5. From the New World"*—(Phila. Orchestra)—Victor M273.

Ellington, Duke: *"Creole Rhapsody"*—Victor 36049; *"Black and Tan Fantasy"*—Victor 24861; *"Reminiscing in Tempo"*—Brunswick 7546/47; *"Black Beauty"*—Victor 21580.

Foresythe, Reginald: *"Jazz Toccata and Fugue"* and *"Lullaby"*—Columbia 3012 D.

Gershwin, George: *"Rhapsody in Blue"*—Composer & Whiteman Orchestra—Victor 35822; *"Rhapsody in Blue"*—(full version) Sanroma and Boston Orchestra—Victor 11822/23; *"Concerto for Piano in F Major"*—Columbia C 50139-141; *"Porgy and Bess"* (opera excerpts), Lawrence Tibbett and Helen Jephson—Victor 11878-81.

Ferdie Grofé *"Shades of Blue Suite"*—Paul Whiteman Orchestra—Victor 35952; *"Metropolis"* (A Blue Fantasie), (Whiteman)—Victor 35933-34; *"Mississippi Suite"*—(Whiteman)—Victor 35859.

Gruenberg, Louis: *"Emperor Jones—Spiritual Prayer"*—(Tibbett)—Victor 7959.

Lambert, Constant: *"The Rio Grande—Choral Suite"*—Halle Orchestra—Columbia 68370-71.

116

Milhaud, Darius: *"Creation du Monde—An African Ballet"*—Columbia Masterworks Album X 18.

Stravinski, Igor: *"Piano Rag Music"*—Columbia 68300 D.

Villa-Lobos, Hector: *"Brazilian Quartet No. 5"*—Gramophone 2098-99 D. B.

Walton, Wilton: *"Facade Suite"*—Victor 2836-37.

Weill, Kurt: From *"Three Penny Opera"*—Alabama Song Trio and Jazz Orchestra—Ultraphone 956.

Arrangements: *"Negro Spirituals"*: Flonzaley Quartet—Victor 6594; *"Negro Spiritual Melody"*—Dvorak-Kreisler (Kreisler)—Victor 1122.

117

XII

NEGRO MUSICIANS TO-DAY

The Negro's admitted excellence in song has not been an unmixed musical blessing. It has diverted interest from other forms of musical expression, limited musical opportunity by the general impression that this was the Negro's special field, and led to too much emphasis on the interpretative rather than the creative aspect of musical art. Only very gradually is this one-sidedness being corrected. The public still expects the Negro to sing and dance principally. In fact prejudice has seriously handicapped the Negro musically, even through admitting his special musical aptitude.

For this reason the serious Negro musician was driven away from a good deal of his folk music by the prejudiced insistence that this represented his particular musical province. The sensitive, ambitious and well-trained artist saw in this, with some warrant, the threat of a musical Ghetto. Often he reacted too violently to the extreme of ignoring his own folk music and renouncing its rich heritage. So for a painful period there was a feud in the ranks of Negro musicians between those who championed "the classics" and those who defended the folk-forms. And the latter were for a long while in the great minority. Moreover it is still possible for a Negro who has mastered the classic repertory of the world's music, or at least the European half of it, to be artistically insulted by the query: "Why don't you sing spirituals?" To which the really correct answer, however, is not the older generation reaction: "No, I don't particularly care for spirituals," with an inflection on the particularly, but

118

the new generation answer: "I like all great music, particularly the spirituals."

It has been the spectacular victory of Negro musicians, especially a group of master-singers, who have made possible this healthy reversal of attitude. If we trace briefly the careers of some of the notable interpretative artists of the last two decades, it will be all too evident what external and internal obstacles had to be overcome.

It is not an accident that the majority of the trained singers and instrumentalists of two generations of Negro musicians came from either the Oberlin Conservatory of Music or the New England Conservatory, Boston. These were practically the only centers liberal enough to accept them. They received consideration according to their talent, which was often beyond average, but the very circumstances turned their faces away from the folk music and cut them off from it. There still exists a regrettable disinterest in racial music on the part of many conservatory trained Nego musicians, though it is waning fast.

The credit for turning this tide goes principally to a convinced group of Negro musicians in New York City, all of them with formal conservatory background, but a deep faith in the dignity of Negro folk music. Two of them, J. Rosamond Johnson and Will Marion Cook, projected a Negro Conservatory of Music and the other, Harry T. Burleigh, was destined to dignify and popularize the spirituals by winning a place for them in the general repertory of the concert stage. For Mr. Burleigh not only sang the spirituals into favor with a more select audience than they had hitherto reached, but by his refined arrangements of them, made them standard favorites with concert artists and their audiences. This was yeoman service, even though it did entail over-polishing these folk

119

gems. More than any single other person, Mr. Burleigh as arranger, composer and baritone soloist played the role of a path-breaking ambassador of Negro music to the musically elect. In 1894 he became the baritone soloist in the choir of the fashionable St. George's P. E. Church,—not without some protests which the courageous rector, Rev. Rainsford, ignored until Mr. Burleigh's own artistry won its way. In 1900, he joined the choir of Temple Emanu-el Synagogue, and held both posts for many years, one of them up to the present. In thirty years Mr. Burleigh has published nearly a hundred concert arrangements of the "spirituals," most of them for solo voice, and about a hundred original songs, most of them semi-classical ballads, some of which like *"Jean," "Little Mother of Mine," "Just You"* and *"The Young Warrior"* have been stellar successes in their field. In 1917 Mr. Burleigh very appropriately received a Spingarn Award for distinguished achievement in music.

Coleridge-Taylor.—However, the decisive up-swing in the musical recognition of the Negro came about between 1904 and 1907 through a strange combination of forces. During those years, an Anglo-African composer, Samuel Coleridge-Taylor, who had won fame as a composer and conductor in England, was persuaded to visit America and to publish a volume of *"Twenty-Four Negro Melodies"* transcribed for piano. It is almost impossible to realize now what revolutionary effects followed this publication and the composer's public recital and choral festival appearances in the great American music centers. His prestige as then one of England's leading composers and his appearance in the unfamiliar role of composer and conductor of oratorio and classical orchestral music had tremendous effect both on white musical prejudice and black musical aspiration.

120

Coleridge-Taylor was born in London, August 15, 1875, the son of a doctor of medicine, a native of Sierra Leone, and an English mother. Reared by her in Croydon, he entered the Royal College of Music in 1890 as a scholarship student of violin, studied composition under Stanford, and in six years time had written a symphony, a string quartet, a quintet for clarinet and strings and sundry chamber music. It was not apprentice work either, for the *"Quartet"* and *"Quintet"* are valued chamber-music items today. Oddly enough, in complete ignorance of the role each was to play in stimulating Negro music in America, Coleridge-Taylor was an ardent admirer of Dvorak's music. In 1898 the first part of his famous oratorio *"Hiawatha,"* *"The Wedding Feast"* was performed at the Royal College, the second section, *"The Death of Minnehaha"* was sung at the Staffordshire Festival the next year, and the year following *"Hiawatha's Departure"* was sung at Albert Hall by the Royal Choral Society. These successes in what was a favorite English music form made Mr. Taylor a leading musical figure. Requests for new compositions for festivals became numerous and with remarkable facility he produced *"The Blind Girl of Castel-Cuilee"* (Leeds Festival, 1901), *"Meg Blane"* (Sheffield, 1902), *"The Atonement"* (Hereford, 1903), *"Five Choral Ballads,"* (Norwich, 1905), and *"Kubla Khan,"* (Handel Society, 1906). Since 1904 he had been the conductor of the Handel Society. Numerous works for symphony and chamber orchestra were poured forth during these crowded years, many of them on African themes or subjects: *"African Suite,"* *"Songs of Slavery,"* *"Solemn Prelude,"* *"Symphony in A Minor,"* forty songs, anthems, and finally toward the close of his brief life, the operatic oratorio *"Tale of Old Japan"* to a libretto by Alfred Noyes.

121

Coleridge-Taylor died at 37, in 1912, really of over-exertion in his professional duties. His style was romantic and highly colored, too much so for the musical taste of today, but he has his permanent outstanding place in his own musical generation. To what greater stature he would have grown will of course, never be known.

After Coleridge-Taylor's visit, a choral group named for him was founded in Washington, several other choral and orchestral groups were formed at Chicago, Philadelphia, Atlanta, Hampton, New York, and within Negro circles more ambitious music became a general vogue. But the next outstanding step came from a single rare talent,—Roland Hayes.

Roland Hayes.—This was a career of destiny, not only for its spectacular individual success, but for its national and international significance for the Negro musician. For as a result of it the double standard of judgment as so conventionally applied to Negro talent was scotched forever. Born on a farm plantation in Curryville, Ga., in 1887, migrating with an ambitious but uneducated mother to Chattanooga, Tenn., working there with no musical prospect beyond singing in a church choir, and even this ambition choked by hard labor in an iron foundry, this talent was fated to be discovered by a Negro musician of vision, Arthur Calhoun. Hayes was tinder to the Calhoun spark at eighteen and instantly formed the great ambition which was fuel to his genius. For from that point on every move had a single objective,—to be as great an artist as the Caruso he heard sing on a record at the home of a friendly patron to whom Mr. Calhoun introduced him, and by his own efforts, for the sake of independence. From his first self-financed concert on the way to Fisk to study to a venturesome self-managed initial concert in London years later, by which he won

122

his first international hearing, this has been a principle with Roland Hayes and it is not unconnected with the actual realization of that seemingly ridiculous ambition. From the *Fisk Jubilee Singers* to voice study with Arthur Hubbard in Boston, through patient years of limited concert opportunities in Negro churches and schools, to foreign study in London and Vienna on the proceeds, there was a steady progress, so that by 1920 he had mastered voice and interpretation sufficient to challenge absolute musical standards. From then on it was the critical London trial, Paris, finally a command performance at Buckingham, a revealing appearance at Symphony Hall, Boston, in 1923, and a series of European and American tours that by 1925 and '26 comprehended over seventy recital appearances for the season and an itinerary from California to Vienna, Prague, Budapest and Moscow; and by some irony of fate, back even for one triumphant concert at Curryville, Ga.

To the resources and repertory of the international artist, Mr. Hayes added a gift of interpretation which the critics universally hailed as belonging to only a few artists of each generation. Barriers raised for generations against Negro musicians fell like the Walls of Jericho; international acclaim forced American recognition and a great musical personality clinched it. A phenomenal tenor voice would merely have been a sensation, but Roland Hayes vindicated Negro musicianship, especially since every concert program bracketed the Negro spirituals with the older and the modern classics.

This career threaded through and inspired many others, mostly vocalists, Florence Cole Talbert, soprano, Caterina Jarboro, operatic soprano, Charlotte Wallace Murray, contralto, Jules Bledsoe, baritone, Paul Robeson, bass-baritone, Marion Anderson,

123

contralto, Anne Wiggins Brown, mezzo soprano, a score of others of whom these are perhaps the outstanding,—all of them having after this, the easier task of confronting doors that had been known to open, at least to a demonstration of superlative talent. In our small compass, we can only treat two of these younger careers, briefly but typically.

Paul Robeson.—Paul Robeson's versatile career from star athlete to Rutgers' College scholastic honors, and from folk-song singing to recitalist, actor and movie star is a symptom of an ever-widening range of ambition and recognition for Negro talent. But in the three art fields that he has successfully touched, the talisman is a bass-baritone voice of exceptional timbre and a typically racial quality that has won both a popular and an academic following on an international scale. The highest point of Mr. Robeson's art, however, still resides in the ability with which his musical career started at the Greenwich Village Theatre in 1925, when with Taylor Gordon, he sang a program of Negro spirituals and work-songs with a power and virility that was typical and revealing. For Robeson sings the Negro folk songs in their flesh and blood reality; Hayes in their disembodied spirit and mystical inner meaning. Our musical tradition is richer and better understood for both interpretations, however different.

Marion Anderson.—Another career that must be mentioned, all too briefly, is that of Marion Anderson, Philadelphia born, who began as an alto voice in the hometown choir but who has now achieved international fame as "one of the greatest voices of this generation." Hers was a great natural voice endowment, phenomenal in fact, but Miss Anderson profited by the lesson of the Hayes career that musicianship and gradually seasoned artistry over patient years of

124

study were really the pre-requisites of enduring musical success. After years of study under Guiseppe Boghetti, she made a formal debut in December, 1929, and then in spite of assuring success in Philadelphia with the Philharmonic Society and in New York with the prize contests for the Philharmonic Stadium auditions, Miss Anderson retired for several years of European study. Hers is for the moment the outstanding success in vocal achievement by virtue of the exceptional combination of a phenomenal voice with exceptional interpretative power and versatility. After three years of sensational acclaim in Europe from Stockholm and Copenhagen, Finland and Russia to Salzburg, Vienna and Paris, she returned to last season's triumphal success in New York. Miss Anderson has mezzo-soprano, lyric soprano and contralto ranges, all under thorough control, and operatic calibre of voice as well as oratorio and lieder technique. With her career supplementing that of Mr. Hayes, there remains to the Negro singer only one unopened door in American musical recognition, and that the Metropolitan opera. And many critics agree that Miss Anderson is entitled to such recognition.

Behind such pathbreakers are an ever increasing file of younger composers and artists, a great many of them on their way to recognition as great or perhaps in some instances, greater. Fortunately, the day of regarding such success as exceptional, except in the sense that all human genius and talent is exceptional, is waning, and with that a normal career looms ahead for the Negro musician. American artists, a less degree to be sure, have had similar prejudices and barriers to hurdle as compared with the preferred public bias for foreign and foreign-trained singers and musicians. Negro talent is filling an increasing segment in the public ranks of appreciated native-born and native-trained musical talent. Without any attempt to be exhaustive, mention should be made of some outstanding Negro names in these ranks: Rosamond Johnson, Clarence C. White, Nathaniel Dett, Hall Johnson, J. Harold Brown, Florence Bond, Grant Still, William Dawson, Florence Bond, Margaret Bond, Reginald Foresythe among the composers; among the many fine singers: Abbie Mitchell, Florence Cole Talbert, Catherine Jarboro, Madame Evanti, Eva Taylor, Ruby Elzy, Anne Wiggins Brown, who with Todd Duncan created the title roles of *"Porgy and Bess,"* Dorothy Mainor, Edward Matthews, and Clyde Barrie of radio and concert fame. In the lists of the instrumentalists, there is yet a lag, primarily because of limited opportunity as yet for conservatory trained artists to enjoy full access to the recital discipline and incentives of the metropolitan concert stage: only one or two having enjoyed as yet the honor of invitations to play with the larger symphony orchestras. Hazel Harrison, pianist and pupil of Busoni, and Mrs. Price alone have had such opportunity, one with the Minneapolis and the other with the Chicago orchestra, leaving out the well-known symphony appearances of Mr. Hayes and Miss Anderson, here and abroad, but principally abroad. But the Negro instrumentalist is daily nearer such goals. The competence of violinists like Kemper Harreld, the late Joseph Douglass, Cameron White, Gertrude Martin, the promising young Romaine Brown; of organists like Melville Charlton, Roy Wilfred Tibbs, Ernest Hays, Carl Diton, Orrin Suthern; and of pianists like Miss Harrison, the Lawsons (father and son), Tourgee Du Bose, Margaret Bonds, Josephine Harreld, William Lawrence, and Bernard Butcher, the juvenile prodigy, warrant the expectation of full recognition and acclaim when opportunity comes.

126

DISCUSSION QUESTIONS

Is there a real antagonism between "folk-music" and "classical" or art music? What circumstances forced serious Negro musicians to dislike and disown the spirituals? What developments counteracted this? What were the main handicaps of Negro artists in serious musical careers? Assuming that American artists often had to gain European recognition first, what additional factors forced Negro artists into international careers? What eventually happened in American musical circles as a result of Europe's recognition of Negro artists? What constructive services to Negro music were performed by Burleigh? By Coleridge-Taylor? By Roland Hayes, Paul Robeson, Marion Anderson? To what extent are there still obstacles to be overcome by the Negro musician?

READING REFERENCES

Brown, Sterling: Roland Hayes: *An Appreciation*—Opportunity Magazine.

Dett, Nathaniel: *Musical Standards*—Etude, Vol. 15, No. 323, 1920.

Diton, Carl: *Struggle of the Negro Musician*—Etude, March, 1923.

Fisher, Isaac: *Marion Anderson*—Southern Workman, March, 1936.

Hare, Maud C.: *Negro Musicians and Their Music*—Chaps. XIV & XV—pp. 321-85.

Henderson, W. H.: *Negro Musicians*—Musical News—Vol. 67—August, 1924.

Robeson, Eslanda: *Paul Robeson: Negro*—Harper & Bros., N. Y.—1931.

Sayers, Berwick: *Life of Samuel Coleridge-Taylor*—Crowell, N. Y.—1915.

RECORD ILLUSTRATIONS

Roland Hayes: *"Arioso"* from *"Pagliacci"*—Columbia 62281; *"Go Down Moses"* and *"Bye and Bye"*—Vocalion 21002.

Paul Robeson: *"Water Boy"* and *"Lil Gal"*—Victor 19824; *"Weepin' Mary"* and *"Git on Board, Lil Chillun"*—Victor 22225; *"Deep River"*—Victor 20793; *"The Black Emporer"*—Gramophone H. M. V.—8483; *"The Song of Freedom"*—H. M. V.—8482.

127

Marion Anderson: Three Spirituals—*"City Called Heaven"* (Hall Johnson); *"Heaven, Heaven"* (Burleigh); *"Lord, I Can't Stay Away"* (Roland Hayes)—Victor 8958; *"Two Handel Arias"*—Victor 1767; *"Two Songs"*—(Jan Sibelius)—Victor 1766.

Dett, Nathaniel: *"Juba Dance"*—Victor 21750.

White, C. Cameron: *"Nobody Knows the Trouble I've Seen"*—Kreisler —Victor 6482.

Samuel Coleridge-Taylor: *"Othello Suite,"* Op. 79—Gramophone b. 4273/74; *"Songs of Hiawatha"*— Gramophone (H. M. V.) — C 1931/34; *"Death of Minnehaha"* (Royal Choral Society)—Gramophone C 2210/13; *"Onaway, Awake, Beloved"*—H. M. V.—1142 D.

128

XIII

THE FUTURE OF NEGRO MUSIC

Negro Music's Future.—It is of course easier to
see that Negro music has a future of consequence than
to forecast what that future will be. But there are
certain safe predictions that can be made, prolonging
a generation or so trends that are already underway.
It is above all quite obvious that with the fuller recognition of the Negro musician, Negro music of the
genuine sort has a better chance both in sound interpretation and in fuller creative expression. Particularly so since now except in a few conventional conservatory centers there is no longer a feud between
the exponents of folk music and the champions of the
classics. It is also clear that, though late, there is
still some precious time left for the study of the original folk sources of this music before it vanishes in
its original forms. Some primitive communities, some
older links have miraculously survived, but research-
ers must hasten. Then, too, it is clear from the increasing volume of classical music based on Negro folk
idioms that an influential school of this music is well
underway, and that it bids fair to become accepted
as a major variety of American music.

The greatest accomplishment to date, excepting the
joy of the music itself, lies in the fact that there is
now no deep divide between our folk music and the
main stream of world music. That critical transition
between being a half understood musical dialect and
a compelling variety of world speech has been successfully made. But great pains and native genius
are still necessary. For Negro music in gaining universal vogue and significance must not lose its char-

129

acteristic and unique qualities. Within the last century Russian, Hungarian and Bohemian music confronted this same difficulty. But in widening the localisms of Russian, Hungarian and Czech music to a universal speech, their composers were careful, in breaking the dialect, to reflect the characteristic folk spirit and preserve its rare raciness and unique flavor. What Glinka and his successors did for Russian music, Liszt and Brahms, for Hungarian music, Dvorak and Smetana for Czech music, can and must be done for Negro music.

But Negro idioms will never become great music nor representative national music over the least common denominators of popular jazz or popular ballads that are in common circulation today. Even "classical jazz," promising as it is, is perhaps only a transitional form. Eventually the art-music and the folk-music must be fused in a vital but superior product. Neither America nor the Negro can rest content as long as it can be said: "Jazz is America's outstanding contribution, so far, to world music." Yet we must distinguish between a superficial jazz that is superficially Negroid and a deeper jazz that is characteristically Negro. And following the latter still deeper to it folkroots will probably produce the new growth we are anticipating. Deep well-watered roots in its own native soil, open and abundant access to the common air and sun of artistic freedom and nurture, these are the two necessities of a flourishing growth of Negro music,— and lacking one or the other, it cannot be expected to grow.

"Well-Watered Roots."—Can anything more be done with the folk music than merely to preserve it? It seems that there can. We forget that the roots divide as they go deeper. While one strand of our musical heritage leads us back to the plantation and

130

the delta and the few surviving folk-lore deposits of the South, another strand leads to the Negro elements in the West Indies and Central America and still another to the common tap-root source in Africa. Nothing more important could have been undertaken than the research project, since discontinued regrettably, of the African musician, Ballanta Taylor, who, after study of the spirituals at St. Helena Island off the Carolina Coast then went back to his native West Coast Africa to hunt for similarities with the tribal folk music there. He found differences, of course, but also some vital similarities. The Negro musician of the future must study African music, and perhaps African culture generally. It should be remembered that Roland Hayes was on his way to Africa on such a quest when his phenomenal success in London started a new phase of his concert career. Then, too, nearer home there are those rich fields of West Indian native music—and a flourishing school of Afro-Cuban and Brazilian composers fully aware of the possibilities of a new Negro music.

The Afro-Cuban Composers.—In the last few years there has developed a brilliant school of composers, mostly mulatto, though not entirely, who have been using native Antillian and African elements in their music. Though some come from Mexico, Central America and Brazil, they are known as the "Afro-Cuban School." Much is to be expected especially of those two young geniuses of this group,—Amateo Roldan and Garcia Caturla. Caturla says: "The so-called Afro-Cuban native music is our most original type of folk song and is a mixture of African primitive music with early Spanish influences. It employs many percussion instruments which have been developed in Cuba and are to be found nowhere else in the New World, although they have their origin in

131

primitive African instruments." . . . "But indigenous instruments," he continues, "both melodic and percussion, should not be used to obtain an easy local color, but with the purpose of widening their significance beyond the national boundaries. The sound of a banjo must not always bring jazz to our minds, nor should the rhythm of our guiro (the rattle gourd) always recall a rumba." So, Roldan has written a *"Poema Negro"* for string quartet, an Afro-Cuban ballet, a *"Danza Negra"* for voice and seven instruments, and his famous *"Motivos de Son,"* based on native song-motifs, with unusual combinations of native instruments and harmony. Caturla has written *"Three Cuban Dances,"* a suite *"Bembe"* that was performed in 1933 by the Boston Chamber Orchestra, and many other compositions of native inspiration. In fact the serious music of Central and South America, but particularly Cuba, Mexico, Haiti and Brazil, are saturated with African idioms and survivals, which only need further study to stimulate and nourish the Negro elements in the North American musical tradition. In this connection, then, the Negro contribution to American music becomes doubly significant and may in time become doubly effective.

One great advantage resides in these new idioms. They are more strongly racial and are free of the cultural distortions of the plantation tradition; that is, they have no minstrel taint. A healthier primitivism and a more dignified tradition are valuable today when we are trying to develop the deeper possibilities of our music. Fortunately this trek back to the African sources has struck the American Negro composer and the American stage. In 1931, Walter Merrick, a Trinidadian, in collaboration with Wilbur Strickland, wrote *"Black Empire,"* a light opera of the life of Christophe of Haiti, using West Indian

132

motives; and in 1932, C. Cameron White concluded his opera, *"Ouanga,"* based on a voodoo drama in the life story of Dessalines, the Haitian patriot. Wm. Grant Still has written a well accepted West Indian ballet, *"La Guiablesse,"* produced by Ruth Page in Chicago, 1933, and a still more pretentious African ballet, *"Sadjhi,"* for orchestra, ballet and singing chorus, which was performed with sensational success at the Rochester Music Festival in 1932. In addition, the New York season of 1934 saw the startling novelties of Asadata Dafora Horton's African dance opera, *"Kykunkor,"* which was thoroughly native in plot, cast, music, dances and type of orchestra. In fact, the native drum orchestra was a revelation of new musical possibilities, and *"Kykunkor"* represents the beginning of an entirely new and healthy adaptation of the pure African tradition of ritual dance, costume and music, after several generations of mere sentimental dabbling in African local color and cheap pseudo-African effects. Much as we owe to the earlier *"Abyssinia,"* *"In Dahomey"* and kindred productions, they were musical comedy snared, and were dominated by the transposed plantation formula. *"Kykunkor's"* success has had wide influence already, and an African dance unit of the Federal Theatre Project has been organized in Harlem and has just presented its first African "dance drama," *"Bassa Mona,"* under the direction of Momodu Johnson, with a cast of seventy, many of them African born. Nothing could be more significant than this reuniting of severed cultural links, and the artistic collaboration of Negroes of African, West Indian and American descent. Another promising instance is the work of the Hampton Institute *"Creative Dance Unit,"* where under the direction of Charles Williams and Charlotte Moton, African stu-

133

dents with an ensemble of their American Negro cousins present African and other folk dances.

Nor has this vogue been without its complementary influence on the modern dance itself. Martha Graham's repertory includes Mompu's *"Magic Chant,"* Gruenberg's *"Two Jazz Epigrams,"* Toch's *"Jazz Tempo"* and other similar items, Agna Enters has worked out Negro dance motives for her *"American Ballet No. 2,"* Tamaris and her dance group have given an interpretative series of *Negro Spirituals,* Doris Humphrey and Charles Weidman have devised Negro dances of both social significance like *"Lynch Town,"* in *"Atavisms: a Dance Series,"* and of decorative appeal like *Americana.* Before his tragic death, Hemsley Winfield, the young Negro director of the *Negro Dance Unit* that did the choreography for the Metropolitan Opera performances of *"The Emperor Jones"* had attempted to organize a permanent Negro dance troupe with a concert repertoire; Katharine Dunham had attempted the same thing in Chicago, and the first National Dance Congress last year adopted as one of the major items in its program the objective of "encouraging and sponsoring creative Negro dancing."

In sorry contrast, comes the realization that for two generations the American Negro dancer has been in vaudeville chains. His accomplishments within such a narrow compass of routine foot work and acrobatic eccentricity have only been possible through sheer genius; but what Stella Wiley, Ada Overton, Florence Mills, George Stamper, Harland Dixon, Eddie Rector, Earl ("Snakehips") Tucker, Johnny Hudgins, Bessie Dudley, Pete, Peaches and Duke, "Peg Leg" Bates, the Berry Brothers and Bill ("Bojangles") Robinson could have done in a freer medium with more artistic background can only be imagined. As

134

it is, they have captured the hearts and heels of America and the world, not, as is thought, by mere magic of agile, fascinating and often comic feet, but by skill of body pantomime, magnetic drama of facial expression, and above all else, mastery of patter and sound rhythm. A Bojangles performance is excellent vaudeville, but listen with closed eyes, and it becomes an almost symphonic composition of sounds. What the eye sees is the tawdry American convention; what the ear hears is the priceless African heritage, which only needs to be re-welded to a significant and appropriate pantomime to be great ballet, with a symbolism more realistic and suited to modern ideas than the artificial and somewhat outmoded classical ballet. At the proper moment, Hudgin's pomposity, Stamper's laze, the Mills' wistfulness, the trembling shudder of "Snakehips," or even the lascivious lure of Josephine Baker could be climaxes of pantomime description. A most talented young African dancer, Feral Benga, has demonstrated how much of this can be transformed on the more artistic level, because he has a conception of the dignity and purposefulness of the primitive African dance.

Let us sample this, by contrasting a brilliant description of an Ivory Coast fertility dance, given us by Geoffrey Gorer in his book, *"Africa Dances."* There is this fundamental difference between Negro dancing in Africa and America; the African dance is largely ceremonial and is associated with a fixed ritual. It is really primitive ballet with leading and secondary roles, characterization, a dancing chorus and a group of accompanying musicians. Contrary to general belief, African dances are formally stylized and the tradition held for generations; they only appear to be improvised. Gorer says of one dance: "So impressed were we, that we had it repeated. Not a single movement was altered; the pantomime was most exquisitely observed and acted. It seemed spontaneous, but could hardly be so, for the rhythm of the drums and rumba rattles was carefully observed." This particular "fertility dance" dramatizes the ritual by which the earth, actually about to be fertilized by the rains, is symbolically inducted into the new life of the Spring. Pantomime of human and animal courtship was successively mimicked,—even more realistically than the *"Rite of Spring"* made famous by the Russian Ballet, until finally, timed to the very minute of the first rainfall in the dance observed by Mr. Gorer, the climax was thus introduced:

"When all had finished, they made a ring round the drums, and then four little girls, naked except for a necklace of red seeds and a tiny apron, broke through the ring of dancers, approximately from the four quarters of the compass. Very slowly and seriously they danced their way to the centre, keeping exact time with one another. They danced almost squatting on the ground, holding their tiny aprons in one hand, and scattering imaginary seeds with the other; they progressed with a sort of zigzag, a few steps to the right, then as many to the left. They arrived in front of the old men together and knelt on the ground; and each old man (priest) blessed them in turn, laying both hands on their heads. Four of them then picked up the little girls and carried them off on their shoulders out of the ring. During all this time the big ring of dancers had been circling and singing, shouting loudly after each clap of thunder. As the storm got nearer they shouted louder and louder, until suddenly the first drops of rain fell; the dancers broke the ring and rushed to the tomtoms, and with the drummers at the head the whole group returned to the village in a mass."

This is a typical example of a primitive dance in its native setting full of its fine, serious, symbolic meaning and purpose, reverently executed even in its orgiastic movements, hallowed by ancient custom, and performed only at the appropriate season by the authorized professional celebrants like a Catholic mass or a serious patriotic ceremony, though eventually participated in by the whole community.

All this has a direct connection with African music, into which we can go only most briefly. We must

136

never forget that the dance is the cradle of Negro music; and its prominence in the Negro's ancestral culture is the root of his mastery of rhythm.   In Nancy Cunard's Anthology, *"Negro,"* which has by the way some of the best modern material on the Negro arts in Africa and the West Indies, George Antheil says (p. 346):

One thing is certain, the Negro has a rhythmic sense second to none in the world; one can scarcely believe that one has not to do with a highly civilized race, in hearing these choruses from the Congo . . . so intricate in rhythmic pattern, so delicately balanced in counter-rhythms and proportions, and so breathtaking in unisons and choral impact are these extraordinary performances.   One is reminded of a colossal *Noces* fabricated by a single people for ages . . . broader . . . wider . . . infinitely more intricate and at the same time more epic; not accompanied by four pianos in a Parisian ballet, but by the gigantic xylophones of a thousand wooden drums fashioned from the hollow trunks of trees; the sound of the tragxylophone, iron bells, the rattle of baskets of stone, primitive but sonorous harps fashioned from a memory of thousands of years back which long ago came down the Nile, one-stringed zithers on long narrow poles, harps with gourds attached to their middles, violins with zebra-hair strings played by a zebra-hair bow with several gourds attached and sounding like clarinets of the richest quality, palm flutes, wooden trumpets, great horns made of elephant tusk, the twisted horns of antelopes, each one with a stranger sound (a sound which no European orchestra could possibly duplicate).   Imagine added to this the great Negro choirs themselves, and the strange high, vibrant treble of the Negro women, and the special Negro throats of the men, and . . . incredible co-ordination.

African music must be interpreted, however, by scientific study rather than by sentimental admiration for its effects; that type of study is beginning.   It is not merely a case of different instruments, and tonalities, but even quite different principles of structure.   Several African composers, trained in both the European and African music, contest the assertion made by European experts that there is absence of harmony in most African music.   Ballanta and others believe that it is only the extreme subtlety of the African music intervals and patterns that disguises the harmonic modes to European ears.   However, one of the most basic principles of African music is that of antiphony, or

the following out of the same tone scheme in different and contrasting pitch and tone timbre, or often
even just the rhythm pattern itself duplicated and
compounded in varying but formally traditional ways.
When thoroughly understood, African music will have
lessons of great musical originality to teach us.

The African Musical Gulf-Stream.—The more we
trace back to sources, the more evidence we discover
of the wide and distant influence of the gulf-stream
of African musical influence. It has followed the wide
dispersion of the African wherever he has gone. The
nearer to the source, the deeper and more torrid the
idiom. Strongest in the deep American South, the
Carolina coast islands, Haiti, the Bahamas, the eastern provinces of Cuba, Vera Cruz and Yucatan and
Guiana, it tinctures out hybrid in Brazil, the Spanish
West Indies, the Creole area of America and lower
Spain, and finally becomes only a faint tinge in the
American Southwest, in the sophisticated Mexican and
Argentine music and in that widespread dilution of cosmopolitan jazz. Yet it is strong enough to flavor distinctively almost any mixture. It turns up unmistakably
in a Southwestern ballad like the *"St. James Infirmary Blues"* or in the *"Brazilian Quartet"* of the leading Brazilian composer, Hector Villa-Lobos, or in the
carioca of Trinidad, the beguine of Guadeloupe or
the Argentine tango.

Even where the stream divides between two different cultures, as in the case of the basic triple rhythm
characteristic of Creole, Carib and Negro South
American music and the two-four or four-four rhythm
with the displaced beat characteristic of North American Negro music, if we trace both back far enough we
find them side by side in Africa. Similarly, the distinction still made by many critics between the Afro-American and the African music generally fades out at the

138

source. It is said that the harmonic element in American Negro music is "an acquired element mainly due to the religious music of the Anglo-Saxons." Lambert insists that harmony does not exist in primitive African music, and thus that its presence in Afro-American music is a sign of Anglo-Saxon influence. But in comparing Negro sprituals with West African folksong, Ballanta insists that both are sung in harmony, whereas all other folksongs, except those of Hungary, are expressed in unison. If this is so, it is only the strangeness of African musical patterns that has led the European critics astray. Just as the European melodic style was in solution in the polyphonic music of Europe, so a characteristic Negro harmony is latent in the complex antiphonal music of Africa, and needs only simplifying to become obvious. But the obvious connecting link between all styles and varieties of Negro music is of course, the element of rhythm, which though everywhere distinctive enough to be recognized, in Africa reaches a peak of development admittedly unsurpassed.

This racial mastery of rhythm is the one characteristic that seems never to have been lost, whatever else was, and it has made and kept the Negro a musician by nature and a music-maker by instinct. When customs were lost and native cultures cut off in the rude transplantings of slavery, when languages and rituals were forgotten, and nature worship displaced, underneath all, rhythm memories and rhythmic skill persisted to fuse with and transform whatever new mode of expression the Negro took on. For just as music can be carried without words, so rhythm can be carried without the rest of the music system; so intimately and instinctively is it carried. From this mustard-seed the whole structure of music can sprout anew. From a kernel of rhythm, African music has

139

sprouted in strange lands, spread out a rootage of folk-dance and folk song, and then gone through the whole cycle of complete musical expression as far as soil and cultural conditions have permitted.

But after the initial sprouting stage, it is just these favoring conditions that are vital. Folk song is a hardy growth; art music, a sensitive one. As Negro music progresses to its maturer stages, it will require more sun and air than rain and sub-soil. Without favorable nurture and appreciation it can never attain full stature and flowerage. Cultural opportunity and appreciation are just what for the moment the Negro musician critically needs, especially the creative musician, and to the degree that these are extended, the future development of Negro music will be possible, and only to that extent. Certain it is, that with proper encouragement and sober cultivation, Negro music can enrich both our national and our racial culture. We have seen how it already has.

DISCUSSION QUESTIONS

Are the prospects of Negro music linked with its development as "folk-music" or as "art music?" Is there real opposition between them? What further developments are possible after folk music has died out on the natural level of peasant life? What scientific study of Negro folk music origins has been undertaken and what can yet be done? Does the proper understanding of Negro music depend on the study of West Indian and African sources? What differences and similarities have been found between Afro-American and African music? Can any basic connection be traced in the several streams of Negro musical influence? What basic significance has the dance for showing the connections between African and American Negro music? What similarities exist between

them? What differences? What role has Negro
dance played in serious ballet? Can it go further, and
how? Are Creole, Afro-Cuban and American Negro
music related? To what extent is each national? To
what extent racial? Will Negro music lose its racial
character in becoming a basis for native American
music?

READING REFERENCES

A. African Music:

Ballanta, N. J. T.: *Preface to St. Helena Spirituals*—Schirmer,
N. Y.—1925.

Chauvet, Stephen: *La Musique Negre*—Paris, 1929.

Cunard, Nancy: *Negro Anthology*—London, 1934—various
authors: *Section on Negro Music:* Africa, West Indies;
America. pp. 346-422.

Hare: M. C.: *Negro Musicians* (African Musical Instruments)—
pp. 386-432.

Hitchens, W.: *Music: A Triumph of African Art*—Review of
Reviews, Feb. 1932.

Hornbostel, E. M.: *African Music*—Africa: Journal Inter, Institute of African Languages and Cultures, Vol. I, No. 1.

Murphy, J. R.: *The Survival of African Music in America*—
Pop. Science Monthly, 1899.

Roberts, H. H.: *Possible Survivals of African Song in Jamaica*—
Musical Quarterly, July, 1926.

B. Negro Dance:

Gorer, Geoffrey: *Africa Dances*—Alfred Knopf, Inc., N. Y.—1934.

Kirstein, Lincoln: *Kykunkor*—*The Nation,* June 13, 1934.

Levinson, Andre: *The Negro Dance* in *Theatre: Essays on the
Arts of the Theatre*—ed. Edith J. R. Isaacs—Little Brown,
1627. pp. 235-45.

C. The Future of Negro Music:

Gershwin, Geo.: *The Relation of Jazz to American Music*—in
Cowell's *American Composers*—Stanford Univ. Press—1933.
pp. 186-188.

Caturla, G.: *The Development of Cuban Music*—in Cowell—
pp. 173-175.

Curtis, Nathalie. *Negro Contributions to the Music of America*—
Craftsman, Vol. 23; March, 1913.

Kirby, P. R.: *Study of Negro Harmony*—Musical Quarterly 16:
July, 1920.

Locke, Alain: *Toward a Critique of Negro Music*—Opportunity
Magazine, November-December, 1934.

Roldan, A.: *The Artistic Position of the American Composer*—
in Cowell: pp. 175-178.

RECORD ILLUSTRATIONS

Rosenfeld, Paul: *Discoveries of a Music Critic—Emperor Jones* —pp. 293-297; *Four Saints in Three Acts*—pp. 297-301; *Chauvez*—pp. 337-343; Epilogue: *The Land Awaits*—pp. 349-360.

Hanson, Howard: *An American School of Music*—Museum Vol. 39. Dec., 1932.

Dance: Bojangles Robinson: *"Ain't Misbehavin' "*—Brunswick—7706; *"Keep a Song in Your Soul"*—Brunswick 7705. Fred Astaire: *"Bojangles of Harlem"*—Brunswick 7718; *"Let's Face the Music"* Brunswick 7608. *"Tambah"—Rumba Negra*—Columbia 54284; *"Tribal African Dances"* (Yoruba, Haussa, Ibari)—Odeon Album —20140/45; *"Typical Mexican Dances"*—Victor 20384; *'Villa-Lobos,"* Hector (Brazilian): *"Momo Precoce,"* Victor 4223 X; *"Chorus No. 7,"*—Victor 11214 X; *"The Creole Biguine"*: (Stettco and Martinique Orchestra) Columbia: 522881/84.

142

NEGRO ART: PAST AND PRESENT

by
ALAIN LOCKE, Ph.D.
Professor of Philosophy
Howard University

ASSOCIATES in NEGRO FOLK EDUCATION
WASHINGTON, D. C.
1936

PRINTED AND BOUND IN
THE UNITED STATES OF AMERICA
by
THE J. B. LYON PRESS
ALBANY, N. Y.

CONTENTS

NEGRO ART: PAST AND PRESENT

EDITORIAL FOREWORD

The author of "Negro Art: Past and Present" was born in Philadelphia, September 13, 1886, was educated there; and in college, graduate study and teaching has divided his interests between philosophy on the one hand and literature and art on the other. Following the former, after study at Harvard, Oxford and Berlin Universities, he has taught philosophy at Howard University since 1912. But as an avocation, especially since editing "The New Negro" in 1925, he has been active as a literary and art critic and has become a spokesman and interpreter of the Negro's ever-increasing contribution to American culture and art.

I
NEGRO ART: PAST AND PRESENT

The Negro as Artist.—When a few American Negroes, less than three generations ago, began to paint and model and aspire to be "artists," it was not only thought strange and unusually ambitious, but most people, even they themselves, thought it was the Negro's first attempt at art. Art in fact, in those days was thought to be the last word in culture; the topmost rung of the ladder of civilization. For the Negro, it was thought to be a little presumptious, like beginning with poetry instead of a "blue-back speller." The Western world had yet to learn, to its amazement, that primitive civilization not only had its artists but had produced a great art, and that of the many types of primiive art now known but then yet to be discovered, that of the Negro in Africa was by all odds the greatest and the most sophisticated. Yes,—believe it or not, the most sophisticated; at least it is the most sophisticated modern artists and critics of our present generation who say so. And even should they be wrong as to this quality of African art, the fact still remains that there is an artistic tradition and skill in all the major craft arts running back for generations and even centuries, among the principal African tribes, particularly those of the West Coast and Equatorial Africa from which Afro-Americans have descended. These arts are wood and metal sculpture, metal forging, wood carving, ivory and bone carving, weaving, pottery, skillful surface decoration in line and color of all these crafts, in fact everything in the category of the European fine arts except easel painting on canvas, marble sculpture and engraving

1

and etching, and even here the technique of the two latter is represented in the surface carving of much African art. So we must entitle our booklet: *Negro Art, Past and Present.* The pioneer American Negro artists were, really, unbeknown to themselves, starting the Negro's second career in art and unconsciously trying to recapture a lost artistic heritage.

How the Heritage was Lost.—The reader will naturally ask: Why should this be? How was this heritage lost? There is one great historical reason; incidentally one that, tragically enough, explains much about the Negro. Slavery is the answer. Slavery not only physically transplanted the Negro, it cut him off sharply from his cultural roots, and by taking away his languages, abruptly changing his habits, putting him in the context of a strangely different civilization, reduced him, so to speak, to cultural zero. And no matter how divided one may be as to the relative values of human civilizations, no one can intelligently think that the African stood, after centuries of living and a long inter-tribal history, at cultural zero. One of the high points in African civilization, like all primitive cultures, was dexterity of hand and foot and that co-ordination of eye and muscle which constitutes physical skill. This expressed itself in elaborate and fine native crafts, the traditions of which had been built up on generations of trial and error experience. These patterns were lost in the nakedness and horror of the slave-ship, where families, castes, tribes were ruthlessly scrambled. When subsequently slavery substituted the crudest body labor with only the crudest tools, it finally severed this bruised trunk nerve of the Negro's technical skill and manual dexterity. Alexandre Jacovleff, the Russian artist whose drawings of African types are today unsurpassed, has well said of Africa: "It is a continent of beautiful bodies, but

2

above all, of beautiful hands." This fact is really a symbol: life in Africa required a skill of hand and foot and almost perfect co-ordination of nerve and muscle. And as with all nature peoples, this skill that could throw a weapon accurately and weave or tie with accuracy brought with it an art that could carve, scrape or trace to a nicety. Nature had moulded out of the primitive artisan a primitive artist.

We will never know and cannot estimate how much technical African skill was blotted out in America. The hardships of cotton and rice-field labor, the crudities of the hoe, the axe and the plow reduced the typical Negro hand to a gnarled stump, incapable of fine craftmanship even if materials, patterns and artistic incentives had been available. But we may believe there was some memory of beauty; since by way of compensation, some obviously artistic urges flowed even with the peasant Negro toward the only channels of expression left open,—those of song, graceful movement and poetic speech. Stripped of all else, the Negro's own body became his prime and only artistic instrument; dance, pantomime and song were the solace for his pent-up emotions. So it was environment that forced American Negroes away from the craft arts and their old ancestral skills to the emotional arts of song and dance for which they are known and noted in America. When a few Negroes did get contact with the skilled crafts, their work showed that here was some slumbering instinct of the artisan left, for especially in the early colonial days, before plantation slavery had become dominant, the Negro craftsmen were well-known as cabinet-makers, marquetry setters, wood carvers and iron-smiths as the workmanship of many colonial mansions in Charleston, New Orleans and other colonial centers of wealth and luxury will attest.

3

Artistic Reversals.—But even in surviving, the Negro's artistry was turned completely inside out. His taste, skill and artistic interests in America are almost the reverse of his original ones in the African homeland. In Africa the dominant arts were the decorative and the craft arts,—sculpture, metal working, weaving. In America, the Negro's main arts have been song, dance, music and later, poetry. The former, being technical, are rigid, controlled, disciplined; thus characteristic African art expression is sober, heavily conventionalized, restrained. The latter are freely emotional, sentimental and exuberant, so that even the emotional temper of the American Negro represents a reversal of his African temperament. For example, the American Negro is generally credited with a"barbaric love of color,"—which indeed he does seem to possess. But as a matter of fact, African arts are in most instances very sober and subtle in their use of color, representing a very sophisticated taste. The notion of tropical extravagance about color turns out to be one of those myths that the facts do not sustain. Formal decoration and design are much more important than color in typical African art. What we have then thought "primitive" in the American Negro, his naive exuberance, his spontaneity, his sentimentalism are, then, not characteristically African and cannot be explained as an ancestral heritage. They seem the result of his peculiar experience in America and the emotional upheavals of its hardships and their compensatory reactions. True these are now very characteristic traits, but they represent the Negro's acquired rather than his original artistic temperament, his second, not his basic artistic nature. So the experiences which unmade the African as artist made the American Negro over into a different sort of artist, after a painful gap in which he was barely artistic at all.

4

Historical Perspective.—So we need this historical perspective at the very outset to get at the true values of the Negro as artist. After achieving what is today recognized as great art and a tradition of great art in Africa, the Negro artist in America had to make another start from scratch, and has not yet completely recaptured his ancestral gifts or recovered his ancient skills. Of course he must do this in the medium and manner of his adopted civilization and the modern techniques of painting, sculpture and the craft arts. But when this development finally matures, it may be expected to reflect something of the original endowment, if not as a carry-over of instinct then at least as a formal revival of historical memory and the proud inspiration of the reconstructed past. But until we reach the late date at which the world of art and the younger Negro artists rediscovered the art of the Negro past, we will now leave this background out of our picture, and follow first the slow revival of the Negro's formal fine art as it begins in halting and somewhat over-ambitious imitation of the arts of the white man's culture. Even this short foreground progress is romantic and inspiring as we see the Negro, adjudged pretty generally as the man who can sing and dance and play but who was not supposed to paint, draw and sculpt, gradually evolve from the white-wash pail and brush to the painter's brush and palette and from the jack-knife and whittle-stick to the carver and the graver's tools.

DISCUSSION QUESTIONS

Did the Negro make his first acquaintance with art in America? What previous achievements in the arts had he made? Are the skills of the craft arts similar to those of the fine arts? Is there much difference between them in primitive civilization? What can be said for primitive art? What was the main basis and principal types of African primitive art? How is this art now regarded by Western artists? What are the main artistic interests of the African Negro? Of the American Negro? What historical circumstances explain the difference? Why this reversal of skills and interests? When did the world discover African art? When did the American Negro rediscover his artistic past? What may happen when he completely recaptures it? Will the Negro's art then be African or American, primitive or modern? Or will it be a composite of all these?

READING REFERENCES

Goldenweiser, A.: *Early Civilizations.*
Locke, Alain: *The Legacy of the Ancestral Arts* in *The New Negro.—* pp. 254 267.

6

THE NEGRO ARTIST AND NEGRO ART

Somehow, too, in this dislocating process of being transplanted from Africa to America, Negro art and the Negro artist got separated. It was generations before they got together again. Meanwhile, we had African art forgotten and discredited; the Negro theme and subject matter neglected by American artists generally, and many Negro artists who themselves regarded Negro art as a Ghetto restriction from which they fled in protest and indignation. All this has changed and today the exact opposite is largely true. African art today is widely recognized and highly prized; in fact for the last twenty years has been a great inspiration for the best and most original modern painters and sculptors. Gradually American artists have come to treat the Negro subject as something more than a passing and condescending side-interest; the portrayal of Negro types with serious dignity and understanding has become a major theme in the program for developing a "native American art." And still more importantly, the younger generation Negro artists now regard it as one of their main objectives and opportunities to interpret the Negro and to develop what is now called "Negro art." For although the Negro as a vital part of the American scene is the common property of American artists, black and white, he is certainly the special property and a particular artistic interest and asset of the Negro artist. However, this could come about only after African art and the Negro theme had acquired artistic dignity through the recognition of master artists and world critics. Before that the shadow of prejudice clouded the Negro in the mirror of art almost as darkly as prejudice and social discrimination hampered and clouded his real life.

Art, in fact, always mirrors social ideals and values. If the history books were all lost or destroyed, we could almost rewrite history from art. A keen eye could tell from the way in which art painted him just what the Eighteenth, Nineteenth and Twentieth Centuries thought of the Negro,—or for that matter any other class, race or type. And whenever there has been a significant change of social attitude, it has either been reflected in the mirror of art or sometimes even, this sensitive medium has registered the change before it has become generally apparent in the conventional attitudes of society at large. By this token, for example, we may reliably judge that for the Seventeenth Century, the Negro was an unfamiliar figure exciting curiosity and romantic interest, and that this attitude shown first in the blackamoor figures of the Negro king in the three legendary magi who came to Bethlehem with their gold, myrrh and frankincense continued into the tradition of the Eighteenth Century, when most Negroes painted, though personal attendants of notables, were fancy dress favorites obviously as personally intimate as court jesters, only more prized and petted because of their rarity. Few portraits of the courtesans of the Empire and Pompadour period were complete without this traditional figure of the black page or personal attendant, dressed elegantly as a pet possession. And of course, we must not forget the occasional black notable or scholar, whose idealized portrait reflected the admiration and sentimental interest of the Eighteenth Century in the Negro. As literary examples, characters like *"Oronooko"* by Mrs. Aphra Behn, or *"Rasselas, Prince of Ethiopia"* by Voltaire, are typical. These

8

men, like Juan Latino, the Spanish Negro scholar, Gomez Parera, the apprentice disciple of Velasquez, Capitein, the black Dutch theologian, down to Samuel Brown, the learned servant of Samuel Johnson, sat for the best painters and engravers of their day, and thus from this tradition we have the occasional but important Negro figure portrait of a Velasquez, Rembrandt, Rubens, Goya, Reynolds or a Hogarth.

Such a tradition even carried over into early colonial America, wherever the aristocratic tradition was strong. We see it unmistakably in the portrait of George Washington's family, where the dark brown, elegantly groomed Lee is a prominent figure in the group. In fact, there is scarcely a grotesque or carelessly painted Negro figure in art before the beginning of the Nineteenth Century, which coincides exactly with the Negro's lapse into chattel slavery and plantation bondage. Then it was, that the social stigma was branded from which it has taken more than a century to free him; and from which he is only now slowly emerging. For a time, the Negro completely disappears from the canvas of art, and when he makes his reappearance it is in the background corner as a clownish, grotesque object setting off the glory of his master or as the comic subject of his amused condescension. The "old faithful uncle," — later Uncle Tom, Uncle Ned and Uncle Remus, the broad expansive "mammy" from Aunt Chloe to Aunt Jemima, the jigging plantation hands in tattered jeans and the sprawling pickaninnies all became typical stereotypes, and scarcely any Nineteenth Century art show was without its genre portrait study of one or more of these types or its realistically painted or sketched portrayal of *"The Plantation Quarters"* or *"Ole Virginia Life"* or some such glorification of the slave system. The tradition was so strong that it lasted forty years at least after the nominal fall of chattel slavery; and it has been and still is one of the mainstays of the literary and artistic defense of the "lost cause" of the Confederacy. In fact the cleverest argument for the slave system was this misrepresentation of the Negro as happy, content and "naturally in place" in such a romanticized presentment of the patriarchal régime of the Southern plantation. It was from this that American art had to react in the latter decades of the Nineteenth Century, and it was this tradition that made the Negro artist, during all that period dread and avoid the Negro subject like the black plague itself.

Few were able to remember that the Negro subject had been treated with dignity and even romantic touch in the previous century; and no one dared to resume it against so strong and flourishing a stereotype of Nordic pride and prejudice. A Negro figure not obviously a peasant or servant, decently clad, with decent clothes and without a counterfoil of his overlord to show his inferior social status was a rarity; a book in a Negro hand instead of a serving tray would have been an intolerable heresy. Oddly enough, the few Negro painters and sculptors did not realize that at this juncture it was their duty and opportunity to furnish the antidote to this social poison. For the most part, instead of counteracting it, they, too, shunned the Negro subject. Gradually this fixed tradition began to lapse. It was undermined for artistic rather than social reasons, and for the most part by pioneering white artists. As we shall see in more detail later on, while a few Negro painters were proving that Negroes could become competent and recognized artists, pioneering realists and "Americanists," were developing a realistic art of native types including a new and almost revolutionizing portrayal

10

of the Negro subject. Some of them began, like Winslow Homer, with sketches of the exotic Negro of the West Indies, less familiar and therefore less subject to the American stereotype; others started with one foot in the plantation school, like Wayman Adams, but the other rather firmly in the advance ground of true type portraiture. Finally, with the great American realists, like Robert Henri and George Luks at the turn of the Twentieth Century, Negro types took on the technical thoroughness of a major artistic problem, and finally reflected the dignity of an entirely changed artistic approach and social attitude. Now with contemporary artists like George Bellows, John Stewart Curry, James Chapin, Julius Bloch, Thomas Benton, and many others, the Negro subject has become a matter of a major interest and reached dignified, sympathetic portrayal even, at times, spiritual interpretation.

But this is just a favorable beginning. Now that the Negro subject has become artistically respectable and important again, it is the duty and opportunity of the Negro artist to develop this province of American art as perhaps only he can. Certainly from the point of view of spiritual values and interpretation, the Negro painter and sculptor and graphic artist ought to be able to advance an additional message, if not add the last word. Although one-tenth of the population, one trembles to think what posterity would have thought of us had some Vesuvius buried us under or tidal wave washed us out in 1920. The archeologists of the next age of civilization, digging out the evidences of American art, would not only have had a sorry idea of the Negro but no clue as to his factual bulk or cultural character. By only the narrow margin of a little over a decade, then, are we safe from such a serious misrepresentation.

11

There is a double duty and function to Negro art,—and by that we mean the proper development of the Negro subject as an artistic theme—the role of interpreting the Negro in the American scene to America at large is important, but more important still is the interpretation of the Negro to himself. Frankness compels the admission and constructive self-criticism dictates the wisdom of pointing out that the Negro's own conception of himself has been warped by prejudice and the common American stereotypes. To these there is no better or effective antidote than a more representative Negro art of wider range and deeper penetration. Not an art artificially corrective or self-pluming; but at least one that aims to tell the whole truth, as the artist sees it, and tells it, as all good art must, with an accent of understanding or beauty, or both.

Negro art, then, is an important province of American art, and a vital challenge to the Negro artist.

DISCUSSION QUESTIONS

How does the portrayal of the Negro subject show the general principle that art mirrors the social status of a class or race? What, according to such evidence, was the Seventeenth Century conception of the Negro? The Eighteenth Century? The Nineteenth Century? How did slavery affect the portrayal of the Negro? How long after emancipation did this effect continue in American art? What reactions did it cause in the attitude of Negro artists toward the Negro subject? What trends in American art broke these stereotypes? In this connection what contributions did the following artists make to the portrayal of the Negro: Winslow Homer, Wayman Adams, George Luks, Robert Henri, George Bellows, Stewart Curry, James Chapin,

12

Thomas Benton, Julius Bloch? Is the development in the direction of more adequate portrayal for the Negro yet complete? What is the special role, if any, of the Negro artist in such a development? What are the present prospects of Negro art as a province of American art? As a field of special interest and contribution by the Negro artist?

READING REFERENCES

Barker, Virgil: *A Critical Introduction to American Painting*—Whitney Museum Publication, N. Y.—1931.

Cahill, Holger and Alfred H. Barr, Jr.: *Art in America in Modern Times*—Reynal & Hitchcock, N. Y.—1934, pp. 10-13; 30-33.

Guthrie, A. L.: *American Art: A Study Outline*—H. W. Wilson Co., N. Y.—1917.

La Follette, Suzanne: *Art in America*—Harper & Bros., N. Y.—1929.

Facsimilies of paintings of Negro subjects by Rubens, Van Dyck, Reynolds, Gainsborough, and four paintings by Sebastian Gomez: *Ebony and Topaz: an Anthology*—published by Opportunity Magazine, N. Y.—1927, pp. 68-79.

13

III

EARLY NEGRO ARTISTS

The Pioneers.—The task of the early Negro artist was to prove to a skeptical world that the Negro could be an artist. That world did not know that the African had been a capable artist in his native culture, and that independently of European culture he had built up his own art techniques and traditions. It thus had the notion that it was ridiculous for a Negro to aspire to the fine arts. Before 1885 or even 1890, any Negro man or woman with artistic talent and ambitions confronted this almost impassable barrier. Yet in this long period of trying apprenticeship, quite a few Negro artists surmounted both the natural and the artificial obstacles involved with sufficient success to disprove the prevailing prejudice, but not enough significant success or volume to dispel it. That task, however, was successfully accomplished by the next generation of Negro artists whom we shall treat in the next chapter *"The Negro Artist Wins His Spurs."* So the progress of the Negro artist very clearly divides itself into a three-stage development of apprenticeship, journeyman's test and master's maturity,—the latter scarcely yet attained but so well-indicated as to be regarded inevitable in less than another generation.

The Artist Craftsmen. — In fact, the very first Negro artists in America can never be known by name, but only by their craft work, which in many cases reached the level of the best craft art. They were the wood-carvers, cabinet-makers whose skillful work went into many a colonial mansion of the hand-craft period. The most authentic tracing of any consider-

14

able school of master Negro craftsmen has been in connection with the famous Negro blacksmiths of New Orleans who furnished the hand-wrought iron grills that ornamented the balconies and step-balustrades of the more pretentious homes. Strangely enough they were working in an original African skill without knowing it, for metal forging is one of Africa's oldest and greatest arts. However, this was retaught them in the new home, and the probable reason for their almost complete monopoly of the trade was their ability to endure the extreme heat. Only with the greatest skill and energy, however, can a smith work quickly enough in wrought iron before the white heat has faded to red; and before the horribly inartistic period of cast iron, this hand-wrought product was one of real beauty and true decorative value. The vanishing relics of this brief period are now highly treasured, although much of the very best has undoubtedly disappeared before taste for handicraft revived after a period of debased taste incident upon the mechanizing of our industries.

There would be little need to mention these nameless craft artisans but for two important points; that it proves the artistic capacity of the group to be more broadly rooted than just an occasional flowering talent of formal art at the top, and calls attention to the point, just as important today as ever, that a sound art should have a handicraft basis, and that the development of isolated "fine art" is not a profitable way of starting the artistic education of a group. When curves were beaten out free-hand by the eye, when ornament was improvised in a quick turn of mechanical skill, when the designs were wrought from memory instead of blue-prints and callipers, there was and always will be that original creative skill out of which the best art inevitably and naturally comes.

15

Formal Art.—Of the first formal painter of this early period we have only indirect evidence; Phillis Wheatley's poem written before 1773 to "S. M." (Scipio Morehead), "a Young African Painter, on Seeing His Works." We have the testimony of her dedicatory poem that at that time there was this young talent, evidently academically trained, painting allegorical landscapes from the classics fashionable in that artificial day. Phillis in her poem describes one as symbolic of dawn, *Aurora,* and another of the legend of *Damon and Pythias,* sufficient evidence of sophisticated taste even though we shall never know of what degree of technical ability. Like his contemporary, Morehead was simply early evidence of capacity in an age that regarded any such talent on the part of a Negro as too exceptional to be a serious example. Yet in the perspective of history we can see it as a reliable forecast of what was to be.

Our Pioneer Painter.—Edward M. Bannister, of Providence, R. I., is entitled to the great honor of being the first Negro in America to achieve distinction as a painter. For he was not only a competent artist, but sufficiently a leader as to pioneer for art organization. He founded the Providence Art Club, which today is still the leading art organization of that city. Bannister was not a great artist, but American art was not out of its journeyman's stage at that time and he was among the most competent of his generation. His interest was marine paintings and landscapes; one of the latter *"Under the Oaks"* was awarded a medal at the Centennial Exposition in Philadelphia in 1876, which of course was an outstanding assemblage of the best contemporary American art. Few Bannister canvases are left, so the range of his work cannot be judged except from the high standing which he occupied in art circles of his day. The fact

16

that he was a professional painter, with professional standing and associations is certainly of great significance and undoubtedly had much to do with breaking a path for the subsequent recognition of Negro artists. So far as known, Bannister painted no Negro types, which was perfectly proper since his field was not figure or portrait painting. But even had he been so interested, it is likely that their disfavor in general art circles would have acted as an artistic taboo. For artists are, generally speaking, at the mercy of the taste and ruling ideas of their generation. Not only the style of the times, but often more directly the taste of the patron class influences all but the revolutionary few who are incurable Bohemians or "geniuses." American artists were highly imitative and over-conventional during the first generations of our national art; Negro artists were doubly so, and for obvious reasons. Only recently have Negro artists broken through to artistic originality and independence.

Our Pioneer Sculptor.—The next career represented pioneering in three directions. Edmonia Lewis, born of mixed Negro and Indian parentage in Boston in 1845 was, so far as we know, not only our first sculptor and our first woman artist of note, but also first to enjoy the advantage of European study and contact. She was introduced by Wm. Lloyd Garrison to a sculptor whose work she admired and by the time she was twenty (1865), she was modelling portrait busts of distinction. Her bust of Robert Gould Shaw, then famous as the colonel of the first Negro Civil War regiment, attracted favorable public and artistic attention, and under the patronage of the famous Story family of Boston, she was sent to Italy, where for years she studied and worked. In fact, she returned only for occasional visits in connection with portrait commissions and exhibits of her work; hav-

17

ing her most notable display, like her contemporary Bannister, at the Philadelphia Centennial in 1876.

By that time she had mastered the hard technique of sculpture, working direct to the marble block, and had executed many whole figure and figure groups. Among these was a *"Death of Cleopatra," "The Marriage of Hiawatha"* (probably the outcome of her Indian loyalty), a *"Madonna with the Infant,"* and an emancipation group, still in the possession of the Glover family of Boston, called *"Forever Free."* Done in 1867, it is not one of her best technical works, but sentimentally is of great interest. It is a portrayal of a muscular, scantily clad Negro freedman greeting freedom with uplifted arm and clenched fist, half in confident defiance, half in doubt as he shelters with his right arm the half kneeling figure of his frail mulatto wife. Artistically Miss Lewis' best work was in her portrait busts, in the Roman classical style so popular during this period, of men like Charles Sumner, John Brown, Lincoln, Longfellow, William Story. It is known that the Story and the Sumner busts were posed for, and the latter, still in a private collection in Chicago, is probably the best example of her mature style. Contemporary with Miss Lewis was another sculptor from New Orleans, Eugene Warburg, about whom little is known except that he was successful and talented though no genius, and died in Italy after a long residence there. His bust of *"Victor Sejour,"* the tragedian, is his only known work in America.

Robert Duncanson.—Another interesting Negro art pioneer was Robert S. Duncanson of Cincinnati, of mixed Scotch, Canadian and Negro parentage. The limitations of art education in his home town undoubtedly led to his going first to Canada and finally to England and Scotland. In Canada, his first painting of note, an allegorical interpretation of Ten-

18

nyson's "*Lotus Eaters,*" led to his opportunity to go abroad for further training. In Glasgow he retouched his "*Lotus Eaters*" and graduated from several years' apprenticeship a talented and technically well-equipped artist. By 1857 he had returned to Cincinnati to execute several portrait commissions, and a few canvases of this period survive. A Duncanson portrait of "*William Cary*" still hangs at the Ohio Military Institute and one of "*Nicholas Longworth*" at the Ohio Mechanics' Institute.

In Glasgow and in London, Duncanson exhibited with much success, and Moncure D. Conway is authority for the statement that he was one of the popular personages of London art circles at the time, enjoying the patronage of the Duchesses of Sutherland and of Essex, and Lord Tennyson, the latter, no doubt, because of his several allegorical paintings on subjects inspired by his romantic poems. The *London Art Journal* in 1866 credited Duncanson with being one of the outstanding landscapists of his day. However, he was also a good figure painter, somewhat known for his historical paintings illustrative of life in the American West, and a good mural painter. This versatility was Duncanson's chief claim to fame, for he, too, did not possess great originality. His superior technical equipment won him commissions for portraits and mural paintings from many of the patrician families of Cincinnati, in spite of prejudice, and he was accordingly given recognition in the small art circles of this Southern city, which though small, contained recognized artists like Hiram Powers, the sculptor, and James H. and Thos. Buchanan Read, prominent painters of their day. Unfortunately most of these murals of Duncanson have disappeared with the mansions they decorated; a few of his portraits

19

and historical paintings survive. The titles indicate the range of his interest: *"Shylock and Jessica," "The Ruins of Carthage," "The Lotus Eaters," "The Trial of Shakespeare," "The Battleground of the River Raisin," "The Western Hunters' Encampment,"* the latter in the possession of Wendell P. Dabney, book and art collector of Cincinnati, to whom is largely due the revival of the memory of this almost forgotten pioneer talent.

Net Results.—The period covered by these path-breakers is obviously an apprenticeship period; imitative and not reflecting any organized art movement among Negroes generally. But it does mark the beginning of the Negro artist's slowly developing career. After a few outstanding colonial painters, mostly trained abroad, American art had no great figures; no master painters came until after 1870 with Whistler and Winslow Homer. So while American art generally was in its journeyman period, Negro artists were in a rather advanced apprenticeship stage, scarcely more than a half-step behind. A competent critic, Holger Cahill, says in *"Art In America,"* "Up to the period of the Civil War, European critics had considered American art no more than a tasteful resumé of certain European tendencies." So in following the European and cosmopolitan tradition, these Negro artists were merely following the art trends of their time. It was doubly necessary for them, because recognition and even opportunities for training were denied at home. To them Europe represented not only the fountain source of art but the only open door of opportunity. Bannister, Edmonia Lewis, Duncanson are thus names worthy of remembrance and, though half-forgotten, they will be appreciated more and more as the Negro artist comes to the fore in America's art progress.

20

What were some of the handicaps of the early Negro artists? Who was the first American Negro painter? Sculptor? Mural Painter? What opportunities for formal study were available for Negro artists? What significant contribution did any of them make to general art progress in their communities? Did any who went abroad for training remain abroad? What recognition came to those who returned? What type of style and subject matter did these pioneer talents generally follow? Why were they so conventional and "imitative"? Could they have promoted Negro art and painted Negro subjects? Who among them did do Negro subjects? Were they behind the general development of American art and their fellow American artists, and if so, about how far and for what reasons? Did their success change the general American public opinion about the capacity of the Negro in art? What role did the Philadelphia Centennial Exposition play in the recognition of pioneer Negro artists?

READING REFERENCES

Brawley, Benjamin: *The Negro in Literature and Art.*—pp. 138-142.
Dabney, W. P.: *Duncanson*—in *Ebony and Topaz*—pp. 128-130.

THE NEGRO ARTIST WINS HIS SPURS

Periods in the cultural life of people do not always run to either the almanac or the historical calendar. Yet it is interesting to note that the Reconstruction period (1865-1890), was almost precisely the apprenticeship phase of Negro artists. And later we shall see that beginning with the date of the World War or thereabouts was the dawn of the contemporary period of Negro art. In between,—that is 1890 to 1914, was the journeyman period as we have called it, in which the Negro artist won world-wide recognition, won his freedom in the world of art or, so to speak, his artistic spurs. After proving his prowess and right to be an artist in the fullest sense of the word, he was next to start to conquer a province of his own.

Henry Ossawa Tanner.—The leading talent of this intermediate generation was Henry Tanner, whose career may be truthfully said to have vindicated the Negro artist beyond question of shadow of doubt or a double standard of artistic judgment. It was in 1891 that Tanner sailed for Rome to make a career of international fame and influence. Born in Pittsburgh in 1859, son of a bishop in the African Methodist Church, Tanner was by family plans destined for a professional career, preferably the ministry. From the age of thirteen, however, he wanted to be an artist, meeting constant opposition from the immediate family and relatives. He finally managed to enter the Pennsylvania Academy of Fine Arts where the sound basis of his technique was laid by a group of master instructors, particularly Thomas Eakins and William Chase. After graduation, embittered by the struggle against family opposition and lack of immediate opportunity to go abroad which he should have had as an outstanding student of the academy, Tanner was forced South to Atlanta where a brother was head of a prominent Atlanta church. There he tried to earn a semi-artistic living by selling drawings, making photographs and teaching art classes for two years at Clark University. Many of Tanner's early sketches and paintings are still scattered around in Southern school circles; a few of them prized, like those at Atlanta University and Hampton Institute, as the early work of a coming master. His general surroundings were uncongenial and unsympathetic, and but for the patronage of Bishop and Mrs. Hartzell, this great talent would probably have been snuffed out into a mediocre art instructor.

But after a summer of feverish sketching of folk types in the North Carolina mountains, the Hartzells arranged an exhibition of Tanner's work in Cincinnati. It was financially most unsuccessful; except to the Hartzells, nothing was sold. They decided nevertheless to back his ambitions for foreign study and, with friends they canvassed, raised the necessary funds. So if one Bishop nearly blocked Tanner's art career, another made it possible. Tanner never went on to Rome; in Paris, he found what he wanted in the friendship and criticism of the famous French academician, Benjamin Constant. Afterwards he enrolled at the Julien Academy and put in five years arduous study. At home folk types had interested him; and some of his early work like *"The Banjo Lesson"* now at Hampton, showed a possibility that, had it developed, would have made Tanner the founder of a racial school of American Negro art. But in Paris he took feverishly to one interest after the other, first animal sketches, then landscape, then peasant types,

23

and finally through his interest in Jewish peasant types, religious Biblical subjects for which perhaps he is best known since this was the interest of his mature period. However later as we shall see, he shifted back to landscape painting, exotic North African scenes and types, and later still, technical studies and still life. So with the exception of portrait painting, Tanner has ranged through every major province of painting.

By 1896, Tanner had found an interest that made his fame, which, although apparently remote from any racial association, was spiritually close after all. For in the Paris Salon of 1896 he received honorable mention for a religious painting, *"Daniel in the Lions' Den,"* with a curious combination of realism in the figure drawings and of mystical symbolism in other features, as the light of the presence of holiness at which the lions are portrayed blinking in stunned bewilderment. This seems a Negro note, even though the folk realism is a cosmopolitan one from another racial tradition. With the assistance of Rodman Wanamaker, who still owns some of the best work of this period, Tanner went to Palestine, and from these experiences grew the great Biblical series that was to found his fame and fortune. It was the *"Resurrection of Lazarus"* exhibited in 1897 that the French government purchased for the Louxembourg Gallery Collection, the hall-mark of contemporary fame. There followed *"Christ on the Road to Bethany," "Christ at the Home of Mary and Martha,"* particularly notable for its plain human realism, the *"Return of the Holy Women,"* and then with a striking shift from a dark sombre palette to an opalescent light-green and blue color scheme, such canvases as *"Christ and Nicodemus on the Housetop," "The Five Virgins"* and *"The Annunciation."* Many of the above

24

are in prominent American museums, the Carnegie Institute, the Wilstach Collection, Philadelphia, the Pennsylvania Academy, Chicago Art Institute, Los Angeles Art Gallery; so that in addition to building up a solid reputation for the artist, the recognition of the Negro artist as an artist pure and simple became an accomplished fact. And as one medal award after the other recognized competitively the superior technique of a master painter,—the Lippincott prize in 1900, the silver medal of the Paris Exposition, 1900, similar awards at the Buffalo Exposition, the St. Louis Exposition, and finally the gold medal at San Francisco, and then the French Legion of Honor, Tanner became a magic symbol of the Negro's artistic aspiration and achievement.

Tragically the more this was emphasized, the more embittered Mr. Tanner became. He resented the sensational publicity of this emphasis on his race instead of on his art; rightfully,—but with little appreciation of how inevitable it was. Except for occasional family and business visits, he shunned returning to America, in spite of its now being an excellent market for his work. He became more and more the studio recluse even in Paris, painting away with increasing technical interest until finally he became dry and academic. His masters, Thomas Eakins, Jean Paul Laurens and Benjamin Constant were great academicians to start with, and the one thing that would have vitalized Tanner's art more than anything else would have been to head up a new and experimental school of racial expression, but that was lacking. American art was still an expatriated art centered in Paris and the cosmopolitan tradition, and the reaction to early prejudice and the sensationalism of public opinion about his race once he was so successful combined to antagonize a sensitive and cynical soul. So that the

25

only direct art influence directed toward his own race was occasional advice and criticism given to a few young Negro painters who sought his help, and to them he was always careful to explain that he was interested in them as painters not as Negroes.

Two of these younger talents who came under Tanner's influence were Wm. A. Harper of Chicago and Wm. Edouard Scott of Indianapolis. Both were students of the Chicago Art Institute, and about a decade apart contacted Tanner in Paris and found him ready with artistic advice and help. Both show marked influence of his style without either his deep mastery of technique or versatility. Harper's early death in 1910 was a great loss, as he was just approaching maturity after much promise. His work was favorably received at several Chicago Art Institute shows, after his return from an all too brief stay in Paris. Many thought one of the great landscape painters of his day was in the making. The titles: *"The Avenue of Poplars," "The Last Gleam," "The Hillside," "The Grey Dawn"* cannot convey the meaning or promise of this man's work, for he was more than a blind follower of the romantic school of landscape painting then in favor. Composition and color and light were all judiciously balanced in his work, with an unusual control of light for a man who was so capable a draughtsman. Here undoubtedly was the talent that should have carried on to a younger generation the tradition of Tanner.

Wm. Edouard Scott.—Mr. Scott, still living, has had an artistic career of considerable success and variety. After study in Indianapolis, Chicago and Paris, he exhibited in 1912 and 1913 in the Paris Salon; *"The Poor Neighbor"* (La Pauvre Voisine) and *"The Unfortunate"* (La Misere) and *"The Art Collector"* (La Connoisseure) ; all under the influence

26

of Tanner's carefully studied style. To this period belongs also a fine bit of landscape, *"Rainy Night at Etaples,"* the latter by the way, being Tanner's summer studio retreat in Normandy. However, on his return to America, Mr. Scott was successful in receiving a series of commissions for mural paintings, in the City Hospital at Indianapolis, the Illinois State House, the Fort Wayne Court House and much later, several Negro colleges and Y.M.C.A.'s. The broad style of mural painting is hard to combine with the smaller scale technique of easel painting and few but the great old masters have been successful in combining great proficiency in both. All through his later career, the conflict of these styles has affected Mr. Scott's work, giving his easel paintings a handicapping looseness of composition and an undesirable flatness except in a few happy instances. Thus this pioneer in the important field of mural painting and the more immediately profitable type of applied painting has somewhat paid the artistic price of that commercial contact until recently, when after a period in the West Indies on a Rosenwald grant, he has recovered some of the lost artistic ground and brought out in a somewhat new and tighter style an interesting series of tropical sketches and Negro peasant Haitian types. This latter work really belongs to another period and will be discussed later; for Mr. Scott's longer career has carried him over to a new generation to whose new points of view he has responded creditably. The roots of his style are, however, in the academic, realistic tradition of which, in painting, Tanner was by far our most outstandng representative.

Meta Vaux Warrick.—The next artistic career of note was that of a woman artist and a sculptor. Sculpture has been strangely prominent in the work of Negro artists, for painting usually claims in modern

times far the greater share of attention. But sculpture
has been unusually popular with Negro artists, in spite
of its technical difficulties and expensive processes.
Certainly we have to deal with a more direct and
vivid sense for form, unless we try to explain it by
some doubtful carry-over of the African preference
for three-dimensional form. Another odd fact,—the
majority of the outstanding Negro sculptors have
been women; the first three in fact were, and two
among the five most prominent contemporary ones.
Three moreover, have worked in the old arduous way
with chisel and mallet; in addition, of course, to the
more modern indirect process of plaster and clay
modelling. Meta Warrick's career as a sculptor was
next to Mr. Tanner's the great vindicating example
in the American Negro's conquest of the fine arts.

Miss Warrick, now Mrs. Solomon Fuller, was
born in Philadelphia, June 9, 1877, and after attend-
ing the Pennsylvania School of Industrial Art, was
graduated with honors in 1898. In 1899 she went
to Paris for further study and spent three years at
Colarossi's Academy there. Her diploma pieces,—
"The Medusa" and *"Christ in Agony"* had already
attracted favorable attention, but *"The Wretched,"*
exhibited at the Paris Salon in 1903, stamped her as
a sculptor of power and originality. This and other
pieces drew the commendation and interest of Auguste
Rodin, then the greatest figure of the French art
world, a recognition peculiarly appropriate since Miss
Warrick had absorbed much from a deep study of
this master's strong and revolutionary style. In fact,
the work of this period was of the Rodin type in both
form and subject; the modelling was strong, dynamic
and definitely symbolic, and the themes, as many titles
showed, were tragic and philosophical. *"Secret Sorrow," "Oedipus," "Death on the Wing," "The Man*

Who Laughed," "John the Baptist," the "Three Gray Women," a modern group of the *"Fates."* Thus, *"Falstaff"* and *"The Comedian,"* the latter modelled after George Walker, must have been a relieving contrast, for most of the work of this frail young woman was sombre and almost too serious for popular taste and favor.

In 1907, a commission for a series of commemorative figures illustrating the history of the Negro for the *Jamestown Tercentennial Exposition* turned her interest definitely to Negro types and a more realistic style. In 1909 the artist became the wife of Dr. Solomon Fuller and settled to a pleasant home life in Framingham, Mass. In 1910 a disastrous studio fire destroyed most of the work of her Paris period, and active work was not resumed until another commission for a series of Negro historical groups for the *New York Semi-Centennial of Emancipation.* From this point on, there has been a decided change of style in Mrs. Fuller's work. Her subjects and moods have become more placid and optimistic. *"Mother and Child," "Life in Quest for Peace," "Watching for Dawn,"* the *"Immigrant in America," "Peace Halting the Ruthlessness of War,"* characteristic subjects since 1914, clearly show this change. It provides an interesting contrast to the somber despair and melancholy of earlier work like *"The Impenitent Thief"* and the symbolic group,—*"The Wretched."* However, some idea of the vigor and powerful imagination of this first period may be gathered from Professor Brawley's description of *"The Wretched"*: "Seven figures, representing as many forms of human anguish, greet the eye. A mother yearns for the loved ones she has lost. An old man, wasted by hunger and disease, waits for death. Another, bowed by shame, hides his face from the sun. A sick child is suffering from some

29

terrible hereditary trouble; a youth realizes with despair that the task before him is too great for his strength; and a woman stands afflicted with madness. Crowning all is the Philosopher, who suffering through sympathy with the others, realizes his powerlessness to relieve them, and bows his head in stony despair." One wonders what the full maturity of this message would have brought had the sculptor continued in this vein; certainly no such work could have the taunt of conventionalism or imitativeness cast at it.

The later works are pleasanter to contemplate, but do not have the powerful originality of the earlier period. Lately, religious subjects and symbolism have come to the fore and mystical peace and resignation are the dominant moods. One of Mrs. Fuller's most significant works is a life-size *"Awakening of Ethiopia,"* a semi-Egyptian female figure emerging from a casing of swathing bands like an awakening mummy. It is a happy blend of the artist's somber and optimistic styles. Fortunately Mrs. Fuller, although she belongs to the middle period we are discussing, still continues to model.

May Howard Jackson.—Another Philadelphian, born May Howard, was the third Negro woman sculptor of note. Trained at the Pennsylvania Academy of Fine Arts, she was graduated from there in 1899 and began a long, quiet career as a sculptor in her own home studio in Washington where she moved, shortly afterward, as the wife of Sherman Jackson. At first it seemed that her lack of European training and experience was a handicap, perhaps it was in technical respects and for contact with the great traditions of cosmopolitan art. However, it was because of her more American experience, no doubt, that she was the first to break away from academic cosmopolitanism to frank and deliberate racialism. May Howard

Jackson was always intrigued by Negro types, their puzzling variety and their distinctive traits. In her portrait busts of *"Paul Laurence Dunbar," "Kelly Miller," "Dr. Du Bois"* and *"Archibald"* and *"Francis Grimke,"* she tried to convey more than the individual personality of the subject. They were to her studies in a new field of human types. A critic commenting on her work aptly says:

Here is a woman who has achieved in a field untouched by any sculptor. Shunning the easier role, she has elected to give her life to this work, unpopular though it be. Where else can one find studies of the American Negro types? It is the African in his primitive beauty that one finds in the art galleries of the world. The composite group of American Negroes has not yet been rcognized as a people in whom intellect as well as sensuality exists is a variety of interesting forms. This is the new field to which she has dedicated an original and experimenting talent.

Other subjects of Mrs. Jackson's were even more definitely social and symbolic. *"The Mulatto Mother and her Child"* was an attempt to portray the dilemma of the half-caste and as well, the power of the double heritage; the *"Head of a Child"* was more than a study of the charm of adolescence, it was in her view, the prophecy of a new emerging composite humanity. Yet this social philosophy was neither sentimentally presented nor too emphasized for the directness of individuality and the impression, at least, of a personal subject. When a school of Negro sculpture fully emerges, Mrs. Jackson's work will be seen in a new perspective as noteworthy pioneering. Yet a painfully restricted career, because of the isolations of prejudice in a Southern center, prevented the full maturity and freedom of her talent. She died, with only occasional recognition, in 1930.

But except for prophetic gleams, the Negro artists of this generation worked as individuals not as a school of Negro artists, with race hovering over them as something of a handicap and shadow rather than as

31

a warming sun of inspiration. For instead of being the challenging theme and special interest which it is for the Negro artist of today, race was for them a ghetto of isolation and neglect, from which they must escape if they were to gain artistic freedom and recognition. And so, except for occasional gestures of sentimental loyalty, they avoided race as a motive or theme in their art.

We have already mentioned the exceptions, but the career of Mr. Tanner is in this respect typical of the tragedy of this generation of Negro artists and shows clearly why, for all their technical competence and their professional achievement, they must be considered a transitional generation. Under the influence of his American teacher, Thomas Eakins, Tanner's early realism turned him with marked interest toward the portrayal of Negro peasant types. As it was, this interest eventually turned away, first to the study of Jewish types for his Biblical pictures and finally faded out in the half-romantic, half-realistic symbolism of his mature period. But for his enforced exile and the warrantable resentment of race as an imposed limitation, Tanner would have undoubtedly added a strong chapter to American regional art, in treating Negro types with as much mastery and more intimate understanding than came from white American contemporaries like Winslow Homer, Wayman Adams, Robert Henri, who did do Negro types occasionally as we shall see later.

Yet this group, Tanner especially, did have, after all, a constructive influence upon the American Negro artist, even though they did not develop in the direction of a special province of Negro art. They were inspiring examples to the younger generation and gave convincing demonstration to a sceptical public opinion of the artistic capacity of the Negro in the fine arts.

This capacity to absorb the best traditions and to re-express them with competence and creative originality is now taken for granted, but largely as a result of their pioneer effort and achievement. Through their genius the Negro artist won his spurs.

DISCUSSION QUESTIONS

Who were the main artists of the middle period of the American Negro's art career? How were the advantages of formal academic training and European contacts somewhat offset by certain other disadvantages involved? In what ways could Tanner's art career have been more closely associated with Negro life? What accounts for the unusual interest in sculpture among Negro artists? What unusual prominence have women had among Negro artists? What differences were there in interest in racial types between Tanner, Mrs. Fuller and Mrs. Jackson? What were the positive group achievements of this generation of Negro artists? Have the younger contemporary Negro artists another angle on Negro types and racial expression in art?

READING REFERENCES

Brawley, B. G.: *The Negro in Literature and Art*—pp. 142-161.
Henry Tanner: *Story of Artist's Life*—World's Work—July, 1909; *Tanner: Negro Painter*—Current Literature Vol. 45, October, 1908; *Poet Painter of Palestine*—International Studio—Vol. 50, July, 1913.
O'Donnell, W. F.. *Meta Warrick Fuller: Sculptor of Horrors*—World Today Vol. 13, 1907. *Meta Warrick*—B. G. Brawley—Southern Workman, January, 1918.

V

EUROPE DISCOVERS NEGRO ART

Negro Art Revives.—Up to now we have had the strange phenomenon of the rise of the Negro artist, but the continued eclipse of Negro art. The possibilities of Negroes in art, however, were now conceded; but the achievements of Negro art, past and future, were as yet unknown. Moreover there were no forces in America capable of discovering them; there was too much obscured and distorted vision before the eyes of black and white artists alike with the smoke cloud of slavery still on the horizon. In Europe the atmosphere was clearer, although Europe for a long while had neglected any fair study of Africa and its native productions. But shortly after the turn of the Twentieth Century European artists began to discover Negro art. The results were destined to revolutionize European art itself and to bring about an entirely new cultural evaluation of Africa and the Negro.

This spiritual discovery of Africa began with artists, and was caused by their discovery of the powerful originality and beauty of African art. It was of course known that Africans made curious things with odd shape and strange primitive purposes. The missionaries had saved a few, primarily to show the state of degredation and idolatry from which Christianity was trying to save the poor, benighted heathen. Everyone was singing in Sunday school how "The heathen in his ignorance,—bowed down to wood and stone;" and what we now prize and cherish as African art was pious exhibit A,—at least that small remnant saved from the pious bonfire which had already consumed so much of it. And then, too, traders, colonial officials and soldiers had to have their souvenirs, and museums and private collections gradually began to fill with these tagged and labelled, and eventually dusty, trophies of imperialism. By the turn of the century, twenty years after the great modern imperialistic penetration of the African interior, a scientific interest in things African had sprung up and elaborate museum collections were in the main capitals of the European powers, the *British Museum* at London, the *Trocadero Museum* Paris, the Ethnographic museums of Berlin, Brussels and Vienna. The Germans especially, interested in their new African colonial ventures, were feverishly collecting materials and, as might be expected, in a more methodical and scientific way. Not only were there great collections being built up at Berlin, but at Hamburg, Bremen, Leipsig, Frankfort, Munich, Dresden and even smaller centers like Cologne, Lubeck and Darmstadt. This was the situation about 1900. But all this was as yet mere trophy collecting and scientific curiosity at best.

Finally two things happened in the next decade to open European eyes to the art values in these African curios which had been almost completely overlooked. In 1897, a British military expedition had sacked and burned the ancient native city of Benin in West Africa as punishment for tribal raids and resistance to colonial penetration of the interior of that region. Although much was destroyed by fire and careless handling, cartloads of cast bronze and carved ivory from the temples and the palaces were carried to England, and accidentally came to the auction block. Discerning critics recognized them to be of extraordinary workmanship in carving and casting, and that the bronze casting especially had been done by an ancient process by which the finest bronze masterpieces have been made. Acting without official orders, a young curator of the Berlin Museum bought up nearly half of this unsuspected art treasure and founded a reputation and a career. For his auction bargain has turned out to be the most prized and valuable collection of African art in existence, the Benin collection of the Berlin Ethnographic Museum, duplicates were traded to form the basis of the famous collection at Vienna, and the young scholar, Felix von Luschan, by a four-volume folio publication on this art and its historical background easily became the outstanding authority of his generation on primitive African art. The British Museum secured its share of this material, and what was sold for little more than its junk value as old bronze and block ivory was secured as a cornerstone treasure of African art in its best classical period, now considered artistically priceless and on the commercial market today actually worth nearly its own weight in gold.

The Paris Group.—At about the same time, a group of young painters and art critics in Paris, coming into contact with some fine specimens of native African fetish carvings from the French West Coast colonies, prized them for their fine finish and workmanship and started to study them out of the atmosphere of dusty museum cabinets and glass cases. Their interest was at first purely technical, but as they became more familiar with these odd objects, their representation of forms,—human, animal and in abstract design, was seen not to be a crude attempt at realism, an unsuccessful attempt to copy nature, but a very skillful and reworking of these forms in simplified abstractions and deliberately emphasized symbolisms. For instance, an animal or human form would be purposely distorted to fit into an element of design as a decorative pattern or the anatomy would be distorted to emphasize an idea and convey an impression of terror, strength,

36

ferocity, fertility, virility or any idea or mood of which the object was a symbol or which was back of the particular cult connected with it. It was then realized that a difference of stylistic patterns had stood between us and the correct interpretation of this art. Moreover, it was seen that the breaking down of such conventional barriers was just as necessary for the appreciation of African art as for understanding the arts of the Orient, which until a half generation before this had been similarly misunderstood. As a result, a New Africa was discovered,—the new continent of the black man's mind. With art as a key, the secrets of African civilization were about to be opened and revealed.

This discovery of the new values of African art came at a time when the younger artists were restlessly experimenting for a new style and a new philosophy of art. European art by generations of inbreeding had become sterile, especially sculpture. In painting, impressionism, the older generation style, had about exhausted all the possibilities of an emphasis on color, and by a natural reaction the problem of form and design was due for a new emphasis. Cubism, expressing this new emphasis on form and abstract design was just about crystallizing. The young genius destined to lead this movement, the Spanish born but Paris trained Pablo Picasso, was knocking about in art circles dissatisfied with the trends in post-impressionist art looking for new inspiration. He met Paul Guillaume, an art collector, and Guillaume Appollonaire, an art critic, who were pioneers in the serious appreciation of African art or "L'Art Nègre" as it was beginning to be called.

What happened can best be told in the words of a member of the group:

What formerly appeared meaningless took on meaning in the latest experimental strivings of plastic art. We came to the realization that hardly anywhere else had certain problems of form and

37

certain technical ways of solving them presented itself in greater clarity or success than in the art of the Negro. It then became apparent that previous judgments about the Negro and his arts characterized the critic more than the object of criticism. The new appreciation developed instantly a new passion, we began to collect Negro art as art, became passionately interested in corrective reappraisal of it, and made out of the old material a newly evaluated thing.

The "newly evaluated thing" was that much discussed, much misunderstood but powerfully original and influential something called "modernist art." Negro art is, thus, one of the great original ingredients of that radical change in art styles that characterizes the present generation of artists, and that has come to be the characteristic and representative art of our times. So, just as Negro musical forms have been the basis of much modernism in music, Negro or African art has been the most powerful force in modernism in art. Dr. Albert C. Barnes, whose celebrated Barnes Foundation at Merion, Pa., holds one of the most valuable collections of modern art and of African Negro art, said (Opportunity: May, 1928): "It is no exaggeration to claim that the best of what has been developed in contemporary art during the last twenty years owes its origin to the inspiration of primitive Negro sculpture. In the painting and sculpture of the leaders of our age—Picasso, Matisse, Modigliani, Lipchitz, Soutine and others—any trained observer can recognize the Negro motive." While Lewis Mumford testifies: "As an example of the current extension of aesthetic sympathies, arising out of world-wide communication, Negro sculpture is historically significant; as a means of helping the Western artist to step outside the dead convention of literalism and superficial representation, and as the authors say, to afford a compromise between representation and design."

Modernism and Negro Art.—Of course, this could not happen overnight, but the quick conversion of these young French artists to this new interest and point of

38

view was an art revolution in the making. A rapid succession of new styles and schools arose, one after the other: Cubism, Expressionism, Futurism, down even to the contemporary Super-realism (Surrealisme); but all have the common denominator of the new revolutionary cult of form for symbolism or design rather than for realistic representation. As their work began to have public influence, the older tradition in art was radically changed. By 1925, when the famous Paris *Exposition of Decorative Art* was organized, modernism had triumphed over traditionalism. The new principles of unrealistic and abstractly conventionalized design swept not only the formal arts of painting and sculpture, but the applied arts of architectural decoration, home decoration, modern furniture and, eventually, even modern dress and beauty culture. From the portraits of the modernistic painters who followed Picasso, imitating the rigid stylizations of African sculptures, women, from Paris, France, to Paris, Illinois, and Tennessee, began blocking their lip contours in intensified outline and plucking their eyebrows to narrow, severely outlined thin ridges. The flowers and animals on curtain chintzes and dress designs began to be so conventionalized that only the designer could tell from what nature form they originally came. Eventually every primitive art, from Africa, Polynesia or Aztec or Peruvian Indian, was ransacked for design motives and stylistic suggestions. Any primitive would today find plenty to recognize and admire in the decoration patterns and principles of our latest art; he would be artistically at home in the modernistic art gallery or the decoration schemes of most of the prevailing modes. And should he need to know why,—the explanation would be merely this: that modernistic art has been built up on the basis supplied by the discovery and experimental

39

imitation of primitive art, and especially, primitive African art.

If the historical record of this influence was lost, there would still remain the evidence of the striking similarities between primitive art and modernistic art to prove this. Fortunately, however, the founders of modernistic art themselves make formal acknowledgment of their indebtedness. The first converts were the French modernist painters, Picasso, Matisse, Modigliani, of the latter of whom a critic has recently said: "The only influence in his painting was that of primitive African sculpture, and his arrangement of forms, his rhythms in patterns and composition were absolutely original." The latter, of course, in terms of European eyes. From the work of Picasso and Modigliani, both of whom were sculptors as well as painters, the new style spread; in sculpture to Lehmbruck, Archipenko, Lipchitz, Georg Kolbe, Epstein, Brancusi, in short the great names in modern sculpture; and in painting to innumerable followers, of whom it is only necessary to mention an outstanding few: Fernand Leger, Bracque, Rousseau (le Douanier), Juan Gris, Soutine, de Chirico, Kisling, Derain, Salvador Dali.

Eventually every younger modern talent was indirectly affected by these innovators in modernism. Many of them, affected at second or third remove, are not aware of the original sources of this inspiration: they copy from some modernist master who, in turn, however, has derived his style and mannerisms from some primitive art source. Summing up, one may say that while it was the French painters who, generally speaking, pioneered in this direction, every other national modernist art has in turn felt the influence and expressed it in its own characteristic way. The Germans, in addition to much creative art, have pioneered in the critical interpretation of primitive art.

40

Finally English, American and even American Negro artists have followed the trend, usually at second remove through being influenced by French and German modernism, though sometimes by the direct study and inspiration of African art.

One important by-product of this whole movement has been to enlarge the scope of European art and throw under it a common denominator; since the style idioms of the arts of China, India, Persia, Egyptian and Ethiopian art, Mexican and the American Indian of both North and South America, are all, in spite of their many periods of style and national differences, closer to this general art style of abstract design and symbolic form than to the special style idioms of traditional European painting and sculpture. Strangely, too, the primitive or archaic periods even of our European styles,—Early Greek, Early Gothic also are. Both modernist art and African art are, thus, nearer the common denominators of world art, and whoever understands them has a master key to the art expressions of humanity at large.

DISCUSSION QUESTIONS

What attitudes and conventional beliefs obscured for a long time the proper understanding of African art? When did these attitudes begin to change? Through what art influences and conditions? Why were the French pioneers in such changes? What role did Picasso, Paul Guillaume, Guillaume Appolonaire play in this, and what art movement was started? Why were these artists and critics interested in a radically new style? How did the element of abstract design, heavy stylized and symbolic representation spread in modernist art from painting and sculpture to the applied arts? What was the eventual influence on modern architecture, interior decoration, modern furniture

41

and modern dress? Does "style" in this sense come from nature or from art? What evidence is there to show that we imitate our favorite art modes? What proofs are there, direct and indirect, of the indebtedness of "modernist art" to African art and Negro sculpture? What common denominator now prevails for world art as the result of the spread of modernist style?

READING REFERENCES

Barnes, A. C.: *The Temple*—Opportunity Magazine, May—1924; *Primitive Negro Sculpture and its Influence on Modern Civilization*—Opportunity Magazine—May, 1928.

Barr, Alfred H., Jr.: *Cubism and Abstract Art*—Museum of Modern Art,—1933.

Guillaume, Paul & Thos. Munro: *Primitive Negro Sculpture*—Harcourt, Brace, N. Y.—1926.

Fry, Roger: *Negro Sculpture in Vision and Design*—London, 1920.

42

VI
AMERICAN ART RE-DISCOVERS THE NEGRO

American Art and the Negro.—While European artists were discovering Negro art, American art was rediscovering the Negro. For worse than completely ignoring him, American art, as we have seen, had treated the Negro subject with a distorting and condescending disdain. Whether in the foreground or the background of its canvas, he was but a foil to the highlights of a philosophy of Nordic superiority. In the presence of the white man, he was invariably relegated to an inferior and servile status, corresponding with the conventional social notion of his "proper place;" alone, his role was invariably cast as a semi-comic type without that individualty or depth that could only come from a more serious human attitude toward him on the part, first of the artist and then, of the observing public. It is this superficiality of view that was the main handicap in the way of the development of any artistically worthwhile portraiture of the Negro. How it changed in a decade and a half is the interesting story of this chapter; doubly interesting in fact, because such a changed attitude has social and cultural as well as merely limited artistic significance and influence.

One might have expected the moral sympathies of Abolitionism and Emancipation to have worked some profound change in the public mind with regard to the Negro. However, the attention drawn to his plight only accentuated this status in the public mind, which forgot the types and considerable groups of Negroes whose position was far from the common lot. Recon-

43

struction literature and art prolonged the values of slavery and the slave status unduly. The shadow of the plantation was dreadfully elongated in the lurid twilight of the slave system. We heard and saw more of "uncles" and "aunties" and "plantation darkeys" in the decades when they were actually fast disappearing; and the newer more modernly representative types were seldom, if ever, presented in fiction, drama or pictorial art.

Nor, when a changed attitude eventually came, did any moral or reform interest bring it about. It was primarily a new technical interest that did so. And it began within the shell of the plantation tradition and the peasant stereotype. A few artists wanted to make their "Uncle Remuses" something more than sketchy generalized types. Slowly, the romantic type sketch and the melodramatic genre or situation picture changed to a more serious study of character or local color scene. The same change occurred in the portrayal of the Indian, and realism is to be credited with the obvious advance and gain. Our grandmothers thrilled to badly painted pictures of Indians on horseback in which the horses, war feathers and tomahawks or the blankets and "peace pipes" had more character than the Indians. Similarly with the Negro bandannas and banjos and the other paraphernalia of the low-genre or situation appeal. They still hang over somewhat today as relics of this period of limited artistic taste and narrow social vision. However, even the old-fashioned academicians began to be ashamed of these productions as paintings and felt their artistic inadequacy. As an example of growth within the shell of the plantation tradition and the Southern attitude one can cite the creditable change in a painter like Wayman Adams. In the beginning of his career, it was the "big porch" and the "quar-

44

ters" that were important, later in pictures like *"At Church,"* the Negro types and their local color atmosphere, finally as in *"Foster Johnson and His Family"* the individuals, in definitely well-studied character and personality. *"Foster Johnson"* is a Negro peasant farmer, sitting with his wife, daughter or daughter-in-law and her child on a broken-down cabin porch, but artistically the important thing is what a critic remarked as "the utmost reading of character in the physiognomies of the two seated Negroes." Starting, then, in more careful and serious realism, the portrayal of the Negro began its steady rise to the point at which it now is in American art. And that is a point of considerable dignity and importance, verging on spiritual insight and appreciation in a few contemporary cases.

The Realists.—Winslow Homer (1836-1910) was in many respects the father of this movement without intending to be. He was a skillful realist, fond of the sea, ships and fishing, and in his sketches in Florida, Bermuda and the Bahamas, — later in all the length of the Carribean, he did many sketches of the native Negro types. These types were painted as Negroes had never been painted before by an American artist. As early as 1885 he had sketched "a Negro in a straw hat and white shirt sprawled on the deck of a dismantled sailboat drifting out to sea in a tropical squall, as a white-bellied shark swam hungrily about." This was the original sketch for his best known painting *"The Gulf Stream,"* which has hung for years in the Metropolitan Museum as a landmark in American realistic painting. It had a great deal to do with breaking artistic stereotypes about the Negro, especially as in the oil painting the Negro is half nude, modelled with a musculature and physical power that was revealing and in a situation of com-

45

mon human appeal. It broke the cotton-patch and back-porch tradition; not all at once, but inevitably. There are many later and better Winslow Homer sketches of Negroes; like *"Rum Kay, Bermuda," "The Turtle Pound," "After the Tornado,"* and his more mature West Indian sketches; but *"The Gulf Stream"* began the artistic emancipation of the Negro subject in American art.

Since then the portrayal of Negro types by American artists, black and white, has become an ever-broadening and deepening phase of realism and localism in American painting and sculpture. Reaching a still more deliberate point in the work and influence of Robert Henri (1865–1929), it has spread among most of the prominent "Americanists" especially since 1908, when the Henri group organized in New York to fight academic and cosmopolitan tendencies in the American art of their generation.

Henri's *"Pickaninny"* harks back only in title to the old stereotypes; it is a revealing character sketch entirely on a par with Henri's other studies of American city types, and his portrait of a Negro boy, entitled *"Portrait of Willie G.,"* is as far in advance of any work that preceded it in human sympathy and understanding as Homer's *"Gulf Stream"* was over its contemporaries. George Bellows, Henri's pupil, continued by including Negroes frequently in his famous boxing and sporting paintings and lithographs, and then George Luks, Boardman Robinson, Thomas Benton, Henry McFee and Winold Reiss took up the Negro theme with ever-increasing interest and emphasis. Finally we have arrived at the deeply interpretative work of the younger American artists of today, notably the work of James Chapin, Jules Pascin, Maurice Sterne, Eugene Speicher, John Steuart Curry, Charles Locke, Reginald Marsh, Miguel Covarrubias

46

and Julius Bloch, who have added, so to speak, another dimension to the portrayal of Negro character and life. The Negro artists paralleling this development, we will treat in the next chapter.

Beyond a certain point the race of the painter or sculptor is not the significant thing. In the last analysis it is the adequacy of the interpretation that counts. However, the revolution in the attitude of the white American artist toward the Negro theme and subject is in certain respects highly significant. First, because it rests upon some subtly and slowly changing social attitude which it reflects. Then, because it re-enforces that liberalization of public opinion in a subtle and powerful way. Finally, because as long as the Negro theme is taboo among white artists or cultivated in a derogatory way, a pardonable reaction tends to drive the Negro artist away from an otherwise natural interest in depicting the life of his own group. What might in a healthy atmosphere become a prized specialization and a favorite artistic pasture becomes instead, for fear of a fence, a pound or pen to be avoided at all costs. So the vindication of Negro art in the work of the best and most representative of today's American artists has a significance and influence of great moment and greater potential power.

The Americanists.—Directly after Henri came the two talented and vigorous realists, George Luks (1867–1933) and George Bellows (1882–1925), the latter a pupil of Henri's. Both went in for American types and American life in the raw, with democratic disregard for social caste and artistic convention. The daring which took Luks to the immigrant street urchins led him with consistent logic to do a few strong and appealing Negro types that in their day had revolutionary influence. It was Luks who, when

47

a talented young Negro painter had been done out of his due for a foreign scholarship, gave him six hundred dollars of his own and sent him off with his blessings. That incident gave us the most daring of the young Negro modernists, William H. Johnson, who though born in Florence, South Carolina, lived three years in Southern France and now lives and works in Copenhagen, Denmark. The unconventionality that made Bellows do bar-rooms and prize-rings, brought him occasionally to the Negro subject, and he painted us entirely out of the "plantation tradition." No more Uncle Remuses, Aunt Chloe's or Jemimas or pickaninnies for Bellows, or through his influence, for progressive American art. After this Negroes were individuals, not mere types. If their Negro subjects lacked dignity it was because their other subjects also did; the intention was personality and fidelity to fact. Thus the double standard was thrown overboard by the realists. In addition, we learn from Bellows' graphic indictment of lynching,— "The Law is Too Slow" and his "Benediction in Georgia" that he dared carry this theme through to social criticism and even propagandist protest.

But then came a still younger generation of painters who went deeper, with an interest in the Negro mainly as social subject matter rather than as unusual technical study. For often the earlier men stopped, when in a few half experimental sketches, they had satisfied their artistic curiosity in this new province. But for an artist like Thomas Benton, (b. 1889 in Neosho, Missouri), the Negro subject was more than part of the search for local American color; he was spiritually representative of some things in American civilization. Mr. Benton's specialty is historical murals, although he does many fine easel paintings. His ambition since 1924 has been to paint the "epic of America." In 1925 Benton did a startling mural in oil entitled *"The Slaves,"* that for all its broad sculpture-like treatment, says the vital things about slavery in a way never painted before. The horror, cruelty, exploitation and bigotry of it are there almost as though blood, pain, shrieks and curses were in the canvas. Yet there is no melodramatic realism; postures, gestures tell the whole story; the painter has absorbed the essence of the matter and needs no petty pictorial details. In a single figure, one of Benton's finest works is his *"Negro Boy,"* chosen for the Wanamaker Prize purchase in the 1934 show of American regional art. In group figures, his best work is the series depicting American life done for the murals of the *Whitney Museum* in New York, which in 1933 received the gold medal for decorative painting. The significance of this work is basically national, but it has a revolutionary racial significance in that the Negro appears as an integral part of American activity, with full justice as to his share and relative position. In the panel representing "salvation and ecstasy" it is the Negro that is to the fore in conformity with the facts rather than the Nordic theories of American life. But the Billy Sunday type of preacher in the pine-wood pulpit, under the sign "Get Next to God" and the woman before him on the "mourners' bench" happen to be white. It is obvious that Mr. Benton has observed American life with an unprejudiced eye; that as he himself says: "I know what camp meetings are and political rallies of the backwoods, barbecues, school house dances (with the jug in the bush)." Here obviously we have common denominators of American life presented; the white peasant with the black peasant, instead of the traditional white aristocrat and black servant.

The emphasis on the social viewpoint may seem out of place, but when painting is technically good and artistically satisfying, social significance is certainly not fatal to art values. Thus, after discovering that in spite of older social taboos, the Negro subject offered the most untouched available field of human subject portraiture, with difficult and intriguing technical problems of subtle color variety and "values," American painters had gradually to discover the deeper integration of the Negro with the general American life. Thomas Benton was one of the pioneers of this latter discovery.

New Negro Portraiture.—Another pioneer in the field of Negro type portraiture was Winold Reiss, of Norwegian birth and training. Reiss's influence happened to exert itself particularly upon Negro artists and Negro opinion because of his selection in 1925 to illustrate the Harlem number of the Survey Graphic, and subsequently *"The New Negro"* which grew out of it. There were a few competent Negro artists available at this time, but in all frankness, it must be recorded that they were not only victims of the academy tradition but of artistic lily-whitism. In defensive reaction to Nordic color prejudice they either avoided Negro types or gave them in Nordicized transcriptions to off-set what they genuinely felt to be a prevailing over-emphasis of racial traits. Really they often shared the blindness of the Caucasian eye and saw little or no beauty where there was beauty of another kind. It was like the "official Germans" of today stressing "Aryan" blondes and ignoring their own brunettes.

Under such conditions,—especially as it was the program of the movement of which this book was an early expression to lead a campaign of healthy-minded racialism, it was particularly necessary to have the

50

whole interesting gamut of Negro types portrayed with even-handed objectivity, and yet not photographically. (Unless we could have had the kind of careful folk portraiture which the art photography of the late Doris Ullmann later proved was possible.) So Mr. Reiss was chosen; he was a folk painter of skill and experience, had served an apprenticeship on several other folk types, Norwegians, Laplanders, Mexicans and the Crow and Sioux Indians. In fact, it was the Indians who had lured him to America. Besides, he was a Scandinavian, neutral as far as color prejudice was concerned. At another point we will discuss Negro professional and lay reactions to these skillful color-drawings of Reiss's.

Artistically the series, only half of which could be published in the then expensive process of color reproduction, was a great and effective revelation not only of the range but the expressiveness of Negro types. Some younger Negro artists fortunately followed the bold lead; particularly the young Western art teacher, Aaron Douglass, who came to New York to become a professional painter and exponent of "Negro art" under this influence. It also did much to create a considerable body of vogue and appreciation for the painting of the Negro subject. The scales of color prejudice fell from some eyes, and many Americans, black as well as white, saw more understandingly. The psychological bleach that was threatening the development of a truly racial art began to fade in a strong sunlight of artistic common sense and impartiality.

Yet there were adverse reactions, particularly in "cultured" Negro circles, to the Reiss drawings and their art creed. It is safe to say that some of this was artistic conservatism, partiality for older more "pretty-fied" styles of portraiture, and some other, just Philistine misunderstanding of modernistic technique;

51

but more than two-thirds of this negative criticism was repressed "lily-whiteism" masquerading as an artistic objection. It is a fact that instead of our art mirroring what we see, we see what our art teaches us to see. So art has to pioneer in the discovery of new interests and new beauty. But we must remember that eyes artistically opened rarely contract again; one is not less appreciative of the Greek statue after having learned to find beauty in the utterly different idiom of African sculpture. Italian madonnas will be no less beautiful because we can see and appreciate the varied beauty and human interest of Negro physiognomy and Negro types. Or of any and all diverse human types, for that matter. True, it is hard to discover beauty in the familiar—although one phase of modern art development has taught us that; and it was doubly hard with the Negro types which in America had the combined handicap of familiarity and social contempt.

Mr. Reiss began with the young poets, writers, artists and scholars of the so-styled "Negro Renaissance," but he eventually did another revealing series of Southern types on a commission visit for the *Survey Graphic* to Penn School on St. Helena Island off the Carolina coast. To date, the two series are among the most thorough and extensive artistic portrayals of the American Negro. In both cases, care was taken to treat the whole gamut of class and color, from the artist and the professional man to the peasant, and from the quadroon and "high-yellow" to the pure-blood black. Only in such a level handed way is a sound school of American Negro art possible. Mr. Reiss's medium of pastel and crayon drawing handicapped his results somewhat, but such a series in a more tedious and permanent medium would have been the work of half a lifetime. Alexandre Jacovleff, who similarly has made the most magnificent documentary type portraiture of African types, when he was artist with the Citroen Trans-African auto caravan, did a few oil paintings, but because of limitations of time and climate had also to resort to chalk, crayon and pastel drawings. The Jacovleff series is of greater artistic value, perhaps, but the progress of Negro art in America holds a debt of gratitude to Winold Reiss.

There are other artists of the younger school who carry either technical or social interpretation a step or so further, and two who combine a rare double interest in the Negro theme. On the technical side, there is Henry Lee McFee with some very powerful Negro subject portraits, especially his *"Negro Girl,"* a brilliantly painted brown-skin girl with picture hat and white stole collar. Or again, Eugene Speicher's admirably painted *"Tennessee Negro"* and Jules Pascin's *"Negro Family"* and *"Charleston Crowd."* Also Maurice Sterne, who incidentally has a promising Negro student, Lillian Dorsey, whose portrait he has painted along with other colorful canvases of Negro subjects. But the really interesting work of the last five years has been an increased output of social art dealing with the Negro as theme and subject. James Chapin, John Steuart Curry, Peggy Bacon, Charles Locke, Paul Travis, Jose Orozsco, Miguel Covarrubias and Julis Bloch treat the Negro variously, but all with an interpretative power unknown to the elder American painters. The same can be said for sculptors like Jacob Epstein, Mahonri Young, Malvina Hoffman, Harold Cash, Maurice Glickman, and others too numerous to mention,—for the Negro subject now has great popularity in contemporary sculpture; after having been limited for generations to a tedious repetition of slave subjects, fugitive, suppliant, or rising from chains.

53

A few of these more modern interpretations call for detailed comment. James Chapin began in the Chicago show of 1928 with a strongly painted *"Negro Boxer,"* not an action sketch like Bellows' work, but a well and sympathetically painted still study as the fine specimen sits in his corner waiting for the gong. From then on, Chapin has matured in his grasp of the difficult Negro subject and has reached one of the high-water marks of technical and spiritual interpretation in his painting of *"Ruby Green Singing."* Against a gold-yellow background, with up-tilted countenance and half-opened lips, this slim dark-brown skin girl is as much a beautiful racial symbol as a well-done portrait study. It is really a notable picture; outstanding even when compared with Glenn Philpott's sensitive portrait of *"Roland Hayes"* or Julius Bloch's more symbolic *"The Singer of Spirituals."* Of course there is a direct connection between the spectacular success and the prestige of Negro singers on the concert stage and the appearance of these notes in the mirror of art.

John Steuart Curry, Charles Locke and Reginald Marsh still stick to the peasant subject for the most part, but with a revolutionized attitude. A drawing like Curry's *"Mississippi Noah,"* — a Negro family afloat a housetop in the devastating flood or a painting like his *"The Fugitive"* are full of a realistic understanding of the Negro's social fate, and echo with social protest. In the latter, a tattered, breathless Negro in the fork of a swamp-oak tree, flattens himself out against the tree trunk as dim figures of the cruel man-hunt pass by unawares in their frenzy of mad hate; it is one of the path-breaking instances of a new art approach. Similarly, Thomas Benton's *"The Lynching"* and Reginald Marsh's ironical drawing *"Her First Lynching,"* —a little girl held shoulder

54

high on the fringe of a lynch crowd to see the spectacle. Or the irony of Ernest Fiene's shivering Southern migrant on the snowy steps of Lincoln's monument in a northern city square. Five years ago such notes would never have appeared in art, or if so, in purely melodramatic values.

Perhaps we should say, in art of native sources, for it must be acknowledged, that painters with foreign backgrounds were the first to be sensitive to the broadest social implications of the Negro subject and theme. For example, there was the Mexican Jose Orozco's famed mural for the New School of Social Research called *"The Table of Brotherhood,"*—eleven races and nationalities grouped fraternally around a table bare except for a symbolic open book, with obvious logic in its prominent inclusion of an African and a Negro-American. Or Diego Rivera's significant inclusions in his Workers School murals called *"The Portrait of America."* Another instance in a more conservative style is to be found in the Spanish painter, Jean Sert's murals in Rockefeller Center on the *"Emancipation of Labor."* This is no narrow emancipation of the black slave, but a pictorial review of the chattel, labor and wage slavery of all mankind, from which machinery and justice bring eventually a new freedom. This is clearly emphasized in the alternate rows of black, white and yellow peasants broken on the labor rack and then, in a companion panel, participating in a common emancipation and escape. In such wide perspective and common denominator human significance, the Negro subject promises to achieve its latest and deepest social and artistic interpretations.

But the Negro subject can be universalized even in specialized or particular treatment, provided there is human sympathy and understanding of the deeper

55

kind. Many younger painters, too many for short mention, are no longer painting Negroes as "wooden shoes," but as living documents, sometimes as living indictments. Special mention must be made of the Negro subjects of Julius Bloch of Philadelphia and of the brilliant young Mexican artist, Miguel Covarrubias,—for each in a different way shows penetration of an unusual kind. In neither is the approach of a dry technical sort, nor is it sentimental or condescending. In fact in the work of the latter, the sympathetic understanding can only be detected beneath the surface of a crisp humor and a surgical kind of characterization. Bloch has specialized so deeply that nearly half his artistic output is of Negro subjects. They range from the tragic agony of *"The Prisoner"* and the bitter irony of *"Crucifixion"* (The Lynching) to penetrating portrait and character studies like *"The Singer of Spirituals"* and *"Mrs. Williams,"* in black velvet gown and gray toque against a Pompeian red background. Bloch's insight comes from long study and deep social understanding; he has brought the same spiritual touch to the Negro ghetto that modern Jewish artists have to their's. In that sense, Bloch is one of the pioneer discoverers of the gold that lies beneath the dross of Negro low life, which has until recently repelled the too sensitive Negro artists. Few Negro artists have yet attained this revealing insight; there is a flash of it in the young Negro artist, Elton Fax, and it was swiftly maturing in the last work of Malvin Gray Johnson. But it is a rare thing, because it requires a combination of detachment with intimate understanding. That, in addition to experienced technical mastery of the Negro physiognomy, the work of Julius Bloch eminently has.

In quite another style and approach, Miguel Covarrubias has this same combination of qualities. Start-

56

ing out with a clever grasp of Negro traits from his caricatures of New York types, Covarrubias has deepened his understanding of Negro types until he is now one of their outstanding interpreters. This comes both from his close knowledge of Mexican folk types and from his deep understanding of primitive life of no matter what race or clime. He has seized on a new and elusive phase of Negro character,—its rhythm of movement and has thus caught a new and important angle of interpretation. We might expect sculpture to have seized on this, but in spite of some very fine sculptural treatment, American sculptors on the whole have not yet advanced beyond careful studies of types. Yet as we shall see later, the deepest interpretation of the Negro may warrantably be expected in this branch of the arts.

In less than twenty years, however, the Negro subject has matured significantly in American art. Oddly enough, Negro art has come into its own by the very development most vital in contemporary American art,—namely the desire to build an art freer from European influences and imitation and to root American art in the materials and themes of the native scene. We must always remember that at one time, the American scene was as unpopular with American artists as the Negro subject was both with him and the academically minded Negro artist. But the startling changes of the last ten years have proved that the Negro artist has as much or more to gain by coming home spiritually as the American artist in general. So after a long detour, Negro art has come to the fore as part of the vigorous contemporary movement to found native American art; and progressive artists, black and white, have, at last, common grounds for promoting a fuller and more representative portrayal of Negro life.

DISCUSSION QUESTIONS

On what note did the portraiture of the Negro begin in American art? Was there a connection between this and the Negro's social history? How was the "Plantation convention" first broken in American art? By whom and by what school of painting? What were the outstanding contributions to the treatment of the Negro theme by Wayland Adams? Winslow Homer? Robert Henri? George Luks? George Bellows? Thomas Benton? John Steuart Curry? Malvina Hoffman? Jacob Epstein? Miguel Covarrubias? Julius Bloch? Jose Orozco? Did realism alone free the Negro subject from its artistic stigmas and taboos? Has socialism and radical social doctrine had an influence on the depiction of Negroes in art? Is the socialistic viewpoint more congenial to the treatment of the Negro as an isolated subject or a part of a common theme? Is the Negro theme likely to expand or diminish in contemporary American art? What is the historical relation of the Negro artist to this movement? What common interests now work toward the development of Negro art?

READING REFERENCES

(1) Agard, Walter: *Cleveland's Artistic Appreciation of Africa*— American Magazine of Art—September, 1931.
(2) Barker, Virgil: *A Critical Introduction to American Painting*— Whitney Museum, N. Y.—1931.
(3) Barr, Alfred H. and Holger Cahill: *Art in America in Modern Times*—Reynal & Hitchcock, New York—1934.
(4) Pach, Walter: *Modern Art in America*, New York—1928.

VII
THE NEGRO TAKES HIS PLACE IN AMERICAN ART

Negro Art to the Fore.—In the last decade, all of the factors involved in the relation of the Negro to art have been drawing closer together in a sounder and more normal relationship. There are three such factors or objectives involved. One is the promotion of the Negro artist; another, the development of Negro art; and a third is the promotion of the Negro theme and subject as a vital phase of the artistic expression of American life. Until recently as we have seen, the share of Negro subject matter in the field of American fine art was negligible and unsatisfactory. Little, if anything was being done for the encouragement of the Negro artist as such; and many thought, as some still think, that there was some implied restriction and arbitrary limitation of the Negro artist in the program for Negro art as "racial self-expession." Now not only is the Negro and his art more definitely on the artistic map but the Negro artist has come to the fore in sudden gains of numbers, technical skill and maturity of artistic viewpoint.

No one is today so foolish as to want to restrict the Negro artist to racial subject-matter or to being merely an exponent of Negro art. Yet as late as 1928 when the Harmon foundation started its series of exhibits of the work of Negro artists with the aim "of creating a wider interest in the work of the Negro artist as a contribution to American culture" many artists thought that was either the motive or would be the practical result. But the first Harmon award for achievement of a Negro artist in 1926 went to a

59

marine painting of *"The Schooners,"* racing toward shore in a spanking breeze by Palmer C. Hayden, while the 1927 award went to Laura Wheeler Waring for her portrait sketch of a kind-faced, dignified middle-aged Negro woman, *"Ann Washington Derry."* Obviously the criterion was good art, whatever the subject. In that exhibition Hale Woodruff, now one of the leading younger Negro painters, had canvases from Paris of *"St. Servan,"* the *"Pont Neuf"* and the *"Quai de Montebello"* while Albert A. Smith had landscape and figure paintings from Southern France and Spain. But there were still some who thought that promoting the Negro artist involved developing Negro art as well, and that he had as much to gain by coming home spiritually as the American artist in general. It was recalled that only within short memory had the white American artist been moved to come home from generations of cosmopolitan exile, physical and spiritual, by the movement to develop native American art.

In 1929, a young Negro painter, with a creditable prize record from one of the great national schools of art, refused a Harmon Foundation invitation to exhibit in a special showing of Negro artists. He very seriously, and at that time pardonably, preferred to try for recognition "as a painter, not as a Negro painter." But after an award of a Guggenheim Fellowship for foreign study on his technical merits and promise, he was in two years' time exhibiting in the successor of the show he first refused to join, six paintings, five of them studies of racial types; one of them a striking study of a pure blood Martiniquian youth against a background of emerald green, striking both as a technical study and a human document. By 1931, there had been a decided change of attitude on the part of younger Negro artists, if the Harmon show of

60

that year was typical. Negro subjects and native materials predominated, and it was amazing to see how the technical quality and vitality of the work had improved as these artists came to closer grips with familiar and well-understood subject matter.

Prejudice had made the Negro half-ashamed of himself, and racial subjects used to be avoided or treated gingerly in soft-pedalled Nordic transcriptions. The full race theme in its own native raciness was seldom attempted. As long as the Negro artist was in this general frame of mind, his whole expression was bound to be weak and apologetic, or self-conscious and falsely sophisticated. Now it was in a fair way toward strength, vitality and originality. It is of great significance though, that this conversion of attitude seems to have occurred primarily on artistic and technical rather than sentimental or propagandist grounds. A real and vital racialism in art is a sign of artistic objectivity and independence and gives evidence of a double emancipation from apologetic timidity and academic imitativeness. In fact, except for closer psychological contact and understanding, the relation of the Negro artist to racial subject matter is not so very different from that of his white fellow artist to the same material. To both it is important local color material, racial to the one, national to the other. We are now able to see that a white artist can be a notable exponent of Negro art if he portrays this material with power and insight, and also to realize that Negro art does not restrict the Negro artist to a ghetto province, but only urges him to sustain his share in its interpretation, with no obligation but the universal one of a duty to express himself in originality and unhampered sincerity. On the whole the Negro subject has come into its own as an integral part of the development of the native element in American art.

61

Thus the younger generation of Negro artists since 1920 have a new artistic background, and most of them another art creed than their forerunners. Not all the contemporary Negro artists are deliberate racialists in art,—far from it. Nor should they be. But they all benefit, whether they choose to be racially expressive or not, from the freedom and new dignity that Negro life has attained in the world of contemporary art. On the whole, freedom from cultural stigma and a healthier attitude of race pride has led to more racially expressive work.

This did not happen of itself. In 1920, the 135th Street Branch of the New York Public Library, through the initiative of its librarian, Miss Ernestine Rose and other associates, especially an enthusiastic Negro painter, Winfred J. Russell, began special exhibits of the work of Negro artists, which have continued to date. The comparative isolation of Negro artists began to break down as they thus discovered each other. In the first shows of this kind, there was a decided emphasis on general themes; so that a *Survey* review remarked: "If the exhibition demonstrated any one thing, it was that all the influences which make an average collection of contemporary paintings a medley of styles and experiments have a corresponding effect on aspiring Negro artists." But even so early, artists like Otto Farrill, John Urquhart, Samuel Blount, Charles Keene and Albert Smith, although immature at the time, showed some trend toward Negro subjects. A few years later, perhaps under the influence of this cultivated group consciousness, these trends had grown to representative proportions. In 1927, public spirited citizens of Chicago, under the leadership of Miss Zonia Baber, chairman of the Race Relations Committee of the Chicago Woman's Club, pioneered with a special *"Negro in*

62

Art Week," a series of talks on Negro art and its contributions in connection with a specially representative exhibit at the *Chicago Art Institute.* This program, signally successful, encouraged several of the younger Negro art students now leading the field of Negro art. It was repeated with modifications, as far south as Nashville and Atlanta, as far north as Boston and Rochester, and as far west as San Diego and Los Angeles.

In 1926, the Harmon Foundation began its stimulating series of prize awards for achievement in art, and a year later started its still more influential series of exhibitions of the work of Negro artists. Five such general exhibits and a number of special smaller ones have been held in New York, and travel exhibits have been sent out extensively. These exhibits have given such publicity to the work of Negro artists that, even assuming it would have been exhibited in general shows, could not possibly have attracted the same attention or exerted a special stimulating influence for the encouragement and recognition of the Negro artist. It is safe to say that, more than any other single factor, this continuing activity has stimulated a new public interest in the Negro artist and has incubated much talent that would otherwise never have been developed. Many artists who started out as fledglings under its encouragement have survived to maturity and independence, and the program has encouraged their eventual affiliation with the galleries, museums, exhibits and contests of the general art world. From a meagre handful of talent registered in 1926,—some score of artists, the registry of the foundation now records 381; and a typical list today shows nearly two score of these Negro artists with regular gallery connections and regular inclusions in standard art shows and museum collections. That is

63

why it can be said that "The public consciousness of Negro art and recognition of the Negro artist has become nation-wide and practically world-wide in the last decade."

And so, at present, the Negro artist confronts an interested, sympathetic public, and that public confronts an interesting array of productive talent. Without undue violence to individualities, these contemporary Negro artists may be grouped in three schools or artistic trends: the Traditionalists, the Modernists, and the Africanists or deliberate Racialists, with the latter carrying the burden of the crusade for a so-called "Negro Art."

The Traditionalists.—Noteworthy among the traditionalists, which is the conservative wing of our Negro artists, are William Edouard Scott, portrait and mural painter, whose work has been already referred to; William Farrow, of Chicago, landscapist and etcher; Laura Wheeler Waring, of Philadelphia, type portraitist of considerable distinction; Allan R. Freelon of Philadelphia, landscapist and marine painter, and the late Edwin A. Harleston of Charleston, South Carolina, whose genre studies of Southern Negro types have competently filled an important niche in Negro painting. His prize canvases of *"The Bible Student"* and *"The Old Servant"* are permanent documents by reason of a double artistic and social significance, and it is much to be regretted that his talent expired just at the point of maturity and success.

Of this group undoubtedly the most competent painter technically is Laura Waring, former prize scholarship winner of the *Pennsylvania Academy of Fine Arts* and for years instructor of art at *Cheney State Teachers College.* Mrs. Waring is particularly successful in careful type studies, in which her competent skill presents the individuality of the subject

64

without the distortion of a highly individualized style. One of the best of these canvases is a double profile painting of a mulatto mother and almost quadroon daughter, an illuminating and thought-provoking symbol of the blending of races so taboo to art in the days of social intolerance. It is in such respects that the full documentation of race has so much to say and add to the interpretation of life, as our artists more fully grasp the unique things that can be said out of the heart of Negro life and experience. Occasionally, with more intuition than deliberate analysis, we are given revealing hints as in this work of Laura Waring's, or in the still more socially penetrating work of her contemporary, the sculptor, May Howard Jackson.

In contrast to the attempt to convey a message, the younger painters have emphasized, perhaps over-emphasized technique. In putting painting first, they have undoubtedly managed to make vast technical gains. With professional opinion against them, this emphasis was natural and wise; although many, it now seems, are still beating the thin air of art for art's sake long after the art of our time has passed to a creed of social analysis and criticism. Negro art, more logically, falls in with an art of social interpretation and criticism. Of course, if our younger technicians, more seasoned than most of their elders, ever come to the place where they have something of social significance to say, it will without doubt be effectively said. But we pass on to brief thumb sketches of some of the more prominent contemporary Negro artists.

Palmer Hayden.—This artist, who won the Harmon Gold Medal award in 1926, went abroad immediately after for further study. Born in Virginia, he had had little or no formal art training up to that time, but a year after going to Paris, was recognized by a

65

one-man show at the Bernheim Jeune Galleries there. He still pursued mainly his early interest in marines, adding a fine series of Normandy coast subjects. In his five years abroad, Mr. Hayden's style matured considerably as shown by his exhibits in the Harmon shows of 1929, 1930, 1931 and 1933. Still favoring marine subjects, of which *"The Schooners," "Port Locmalo,"* and *"Quai at Concarneau"* are among the best examples, Hayden has gradually extended his interests both to other subjects and a more modernistic style; more decorative, high-keyed and in broken color, as shown by such canvases as a brilliant New York skyscraper landscape,—*"Theatre Alley"* or *"Fetiche et Fleurs,"*—an African idol on a table beside a vase of exotic wild orchids. Hayden has also done some interesting sketches of colonial types at the Paris *Colonial Exposition,* and plans to visit the West Indies on a sketching tour. Not ultra-modern in style, but yet far from the purely academic, Mr. Hayden's present work proves him to be one of the soundest technicians among the younger Negro painters.

A much more academic vein includes the work of most of the younger traditionalists, among whom may be mentioned Arthur Diggs, Charles Dawson, and Wm. Farrow of Chicago, W. J. Hardrick of Indianapolis, W. A. Cooper, a portrait type painter of Charlotte, N. C., who is by vocation a pastor, Richard Reid, Robert Pious, portraitists, of New York, Henry Boseman Jones and Allan Freelon of Philadelphia, and Dan Terry Reid and James A. Porter of Washington, D. C. All of these, with differing degrees of success, stress the orthodox academic canons and virtues, and demonstrate a sound technical interest in traditional values and subject matter. Except in our school and college art departments, however, the academic school and its philosophy is very much on the defensive under a heavy and somewhat belated tide of modernism.

The Modernists.—The first Negro modernists were swallows before the proper spring. They died tragically early: Gamaliel Derrick of Philadelphia, painter and etcher of extraordinary talent, a suicide in the face of poverty and lack of recognition; Lenwood Morris of Philadelphia, also, brilliant student of the *Pennsylvania Academy,* victim of frail health and disappointment, missed and probably merited scholarship opportunity for foreign study; painter of what for that time were unusually advanced styles of landscape and strong, high key portrait studies, and finally Richard Lonsdale Brown of Richmond, Va. Brown achieved some recognition in New York art circles through an exhibition in 1919 at the Ovington Galleries, under Miss Mary White Ovington's and N.A.A.C.P. auspices. From sheer intuition, he anticipated the sharp Oriental sketch-line inset details on highkeyed, geometrically simplified flat backgrounds which, fifteen or twenty years later were the high mode among American modernists. But after a brief flare of popularity as a "promising young genius," Brown died, a victim as much of fitful public interest as of tuberculosis. It is safe to say that in the narrow circles to which prejudice confined these young men, born prematurely in the cultural sense, they could not find a baker's half dozen to share their ambitions or their modernistic ideas of art. Their scattered fragmentary work and brief careers are most important, however, in our racial art history. A decade later, the young Nego painters had at least a fighting chance.

Aaron Douglass.—Notably individual, but developed out of the academy tradition, is the work of Aaron Douglass, also one of the pioneer Africanists. Born in Topeka, Kansas, educated at the University of

67

Nebraska, he was attracted from his position as art teacher in the Kansas City High School to New York, where he studied under Winold Reiss, whose work strongly influenced his first period of style. This contact and many commissions to do book illustration on Negro subjects and themes re-enforced a desire to interpret Negro form and spirit. In turning successfully to a modernized version of African patterns, Mr. Douglass has taken his place beside Covarrubias as an outstanding exponent of Negro types and design motives. The beautiful cover jackets, plates and decoration of *"Caroling Dusk"* by Countee Cullen, *"Plays of Negro Life,"* by Locke and Gregory, *"Not Without Laughter"* by Langston Hughes, and most especially of *"God's Trombones"* by James Weldon Johnson are all examples of his decorative genius. A very versatile talent, Douglass has done extensive large scale decoration in murals, usually on the Negro or African subject: the Jungle and Jazz panels of *Club Ebony*, New York, now regrettably lost, the cabaret panels of the *Hotel Sherman*, Chicago, the symbolic Negro History series for the *Fisk University Library*, a later panel series for the auditorium of the *135th St. Harlem Branch Library*, illustrating Negro life in *Africa* (a festival dance), *Slavery*, *Reconstruction* and *Metropolis*, the background of Harlem. In his easel work, Mr. Douglass has a quite more academic style than the very decorative broad effects of his murals and black and white all-over designs; it is largely the result of the influences of his Paris study, on a *Barnes Foundation* fellowship, under de Waroquier and Despiau, a brilliant series of these still life and portrait studies was exhibited at the *Cas Delbos Gallery* in 1933.

Archibald Motley.—Born in New Orleans (1891), son of a dining car chef, confronted with the double

68

struggle against lack of opportunity and prejudice, Mr. Motley finally became a mature artist by way of the *Chicago Art Institute*, where, in 1925, he won the Francis Logan Medal award with *"A Mulatress."* His earlier work centered in somber, quite realistic character types,—like *"My Grandmother," "The Octoroon,"* and *"Old Snuff Dipper,"*—a peasant, older generation type which won the Harmon 1929 Gold Award as much for characterization as fine technical painting. In 1928, Motley held a one-man exhibition at the *New Galleries,* New York and revealed several trends other than his severe, realistic style. One was toward fantastic compositions of African tribal and voodoo ceremonials,—which he has not followed extensively since; the other, to a broad, higher-keyed and somewhat lurid color scheme, with an emphasis on the grotesque and genre side of modern Negro life, in subjects like *"The Picnic in the Grove."* Shortly after, he went to Paris for two years on a *Guggenheim Fellowship,* and concentrated on perfecting his realistic style; from this period some of his technically best compositions have come, among them portrait study types like *"The Young Martiniquian."* But on his return, Motley seems more and more fascinated by the grotesqueries and oddities of Negro life, which he sometimes satirically, sometimes sympathetically, depicts. His style, once curiously restrained, is now highly imaginative, free in rhythm, riotous in color, a combination of Dutch realism with American humor and tempo: from 1933 to 1936, canvases like *"The Barbecue," "Blues," "The Stomp," "Surprise in Store," "Night Club," "The Liars," "The Plotters,"* and the recent P.W.A. Chicago State Street sketch,— *"The Chicken Shack"*—are now typical. Very little of the humor and swashbuckle of Negro life has found its way into Negro art work, although white

69

painters like Irwin Hoffman, Stella Bloch and Covarrubias have been hammering away cleverly and significantly on this note; so Motley's Rabelaisian turn is a promising departure. Lately, Motley has been engaged in two P.W.A. projects: a series of murals on the life of Frederick Douglass for *Douglass Memorial Hall*, Howard University and another for public buildings in Chicago.

The extreme modernists of this generation of Negro painters are William H. Johnson, Hale Woodruff, Malvin Gray Johnson and Lesesne Wells. Short sketches of their careers will not only bring to the reader's attention their individual merits, but a typical cross-section of the evolution Negro artists have passed through between 1929 and the present. Diverse as their temperaments are, there are certain common features, first of all, the strong influence of modernism or abstract art, that is,—art with the shorthand emphasis on generalized forms rather than pictorial realism or photographic detail. This art mode, which has dominated younger American artists for over a decade, began, as we have seen, through European art being influenced by African art. It is, thus, an African influence at second remove upon our younger Negro modernistic painters and sculptors; in being modernistic, they are indirectly being African. Then, in the second place, has come the more direct influence from the ever-increasingly popularity of the Negro theme and subject in contemporary art toward a school of art trying not only to interpret Negro form but, back of that, the Negro spirit. Those who share this are conscious disciples or exponents of "Negro art." Aaron Douglass was one of its first converts; many, indeed most younger modernists have agreed; however, certain exceptions will, in time, be discussed.

70

Wm. H. Johnson.—This artist was born 1902 in Florence, S. C., and finally came unaided to New York to study art at the *National Academy of Design* under Charles Hawthorne and George Luks. At times during his years of art study he worked as longshoreman; but won both the *Cannon* and *Hall Garten Prizes* at the Academy. When he lost the foreign fellowship award, he was sent to Europe by his instructors who believed in his talent. He was in France 1926 to 1929, was strongly influenced by Cezanne, Rouault and Soutine, and returned in the year he received the *Harmon Gold Medal* award, with a series of French and Danish landscape scenes and brilliant still life studies, the latter, of flowers especially, evidently a Van Gogh influence. But though the Danish canvases recall Van Gogh and the French ones Cezanne, they have their own individuality and marked a painter of power and modern accent. Johnson cannot be accused of art snobbery, however. For he returned with enthusiasm to his home town of Florence to paint local scenes and Negro types; and it is far from his fault that after doing so, he returned to the more congenial art circles of Copenhagen, where he has resided since. He did paint a series of Southern landscapes and portrait studies that may eventually put his birthplace upon the artistic map. They are full of Southern atmosphere seen through an eye of piercing realism and satire. His ironic picture of the *"Town Hotel,"* frying in the heat of early summer, paints boldly the decadence of the old Southern régime. His quizzical but nevertheless loving portraits, one of *"Sonny,"* posed by a younger brother, are a revelation of unsentimental analysis. They have a right to their tragic irony (Johnson once aspired to be a caricaturist) for one day when he set up his easel, the town constable arrested him on charges of trespass and vagrancy,

71

outraged that a Negro should paint more than a fence or a barn-door. Yet the South needs the leaven of art and the Negro artist needs the inspiration of his native materials. In Copenhagen, where he is esteemed as an important young "American" artist, Mr. Johnson will, doubtless, have to paint Negroes from memory; but Danish landscapes by his hand are drifting from the important commercial galleries to the museum collections of North and Central Europe.

Hale A. Woodruff.—Hale Woodruff, another important modernist painter, happened to have a luckier introduction to the South and the chance to exert to a more educative influence. Born in Cairo, Illinois, in 1900, Woodruff, after study at the *Herron Institute* in Indianapolis, went to France, through the efforts of Indianapolis art lovers, absorbed modernistic technique and views and then returned to become art insrtuctor at Atlanta University. Mr. Woodruff paints landscapes and abstract formal compositions for the most part. In spite of the formalism though, his color and color harmonies have a daring warmth that seems characteristically racial. Latterly he has taken to local Georgia scenes, in oils and black and white, which are brimming with local color and crisp ironical observation. He has lately done extensive mural work for the *Howard Junior High School,* the living room of the *Atlanta School of Social Work* and a *P.W.A.* project series. In this latter there are two panels of Negro neighborhoods entitled *"Shantytown"* and *"Mudhill Row."* This time, the *"Atlanta Constitution,"* voicing liberal Southern opinion on the Negro artist, makes generous acknowledgment and catches the social as well as the artistic point. For it said, reviewing their exhibition: "This young Negro artist is one of the modern masters. This exhibition is really one of the finest that will be shown anywhere.

72

Hale Woodruff is not a recent discovery, except in Atlanta, where he has been for four years." And continuing, the article says, "There are two paintings there which speak out in rebuke. They are worth more, they say more than all the studies on economics and the need for slum clearance and better housing. *"Shantytown"* and *"Mudhill Row"* hurt with their garish poverty and their stark bleakness. Yet he has not exaggerated a single line nor forced a point." Of course, Woodruff's main interest and significance is as a painter, but it is interesting to see the modern note of social criticism and protest creeping into the late work of this Negro artist.

Ever since winning the Bronze Harmon award in 1926, however, Woodruff has been a ceaseless technical experimenter, with his primary interest technical. Still life, landscapes, portrait studies in a rapid change of styles have characterized his career; first a rather luxuriant period of autumnal scenes and colors; then broadly drawn Negro types like *"The Banjo Player"* and *"Washday";* after that, French landscapes in the then prevailing modernist mode, then formalistic still life, his most extreme phase, and then with his Atlanta residence and teaching experience, a return to more native themes: Georgia landscapes of great originality like *"Summer Landscape," "Autumn in Georgia," "Tree Forms,"* etching and wood-cuts of Georgia town life,—*"The Teamster's Place," "Shacks,"* and the finely interpretative series of which *"Shantytown"* is typical. Mr. Woodruff has several younger pupils and followers, of whom Wilmer Jennings is the most talented and promising: an Atlanta group or "school" is almost on the horizon.

Malvin Gray Johnson.—In the Harmon show of 1928, the Otto Kahn special prize award went to Malvin Gray Johnson for his somewhat technically unsatisfactory picture,—"*Swing Low, Sweet Chariot,*" chiefly as encouraging the idea toward which the young painter was fumbling. Subsequent developments proved the wisdom of that. In the picture in question, over the heads of a praying group of slaves, in a cloud phantasy which he was not yet mature enough to fully deliver, the young artist, in his own words, "tried to depict the escape of emotions which the plantation slaves felt after being held down all day by the grind of labor and the consciousness of being bound out. Set free from their tasks by the end of the day and the darkness, they had gone from their cabins to the river's edge and are calling upon their God for the freedom for which they long." This young talent, born in Greensboro, N. C., in 1896, was a student of the *National Academy* and had already reached a good academy stage of competence in water scenes, life sketches. But the new path was destined in the few short years before his premature death in 1934 to lead to originality and to substantial contribution to Negro art. J. A. Porter, a fellow artist, in an obituary notice, credits him with having been "a restless experimentalist, changing styles feverishly and racing from one art creed to another, first impressionism, then cubism, then a style more directly influenced by African idioms, finally a painting of folk types and Virginia landscapes with a combination of sardonic humor and mystical pathos." In passing, we may notice that these are the two major folk moods of the Negro, but the Brightwood Virginia paintings and water colors, which he poured out rapidly on vacation just before his death, are among the most significant art commentary we yet have of the contemporary American Negro scene. There is a Southern landscape series, numbered one to five, full of vibrant color and vivid Southern local atmosphere, *"Red*

74

Road" and *"Convict Labor,"* lurid with Southern oppression, *"Brothers," "Ezekiel," "Henderson," "Dixie Madonna," "Uncle Joe"*—a gallery of peasant types, and a series of swiftly executed activity scenes in water color that critics regard as a talent that in a few years would have gone to the very forefront of contemporary American art in this difficult medium. Gray Johnson's loss, just as he was approaching maturity and had within grasp the technical means of expressing his earlier concept of "folk-soul interpretations," is a very great loss. But what he has left is also for his generation a very great inspiration, as the younger artists have opportunity to study his canvases and the growth of his message.

James Lesesne Wells.—This artist, now teacher of design in the art department of Howard University, was born in Georgia (1902), son of a minister, was educated in Florida, Lincoln University, the art department of Columbia University and the National Academy of Design. He has not only been an ultra-modern, but a successful pioneer of modernist methods of teaching art to children and college students, especially in the *Harlem Art Workshop* courses of the Harlem Library project for adult education. The exhibit of the work of the latter demonstrated that, in a few months, talent, where it exists, can be brought rapidly to a point of maturity impossible through carefully graded and analytic academic procedures. Mr. Wells, who has had one-man shows at the *Weyhe Galleries,* the *Delphic Studios* and the *Brooklyn Museum,* is primarily interested in design and composition. As a black and white artist in wood block, etching and lithography, he already has an outstanding reputation, in which his African prints on pure design motives represent his earliest mature work; his city and industrial town prints an intermediate

75

period, his Biblical series and his C.C.C. camp sketches his third and fourth. It is the African series, of which *"African Phantasy"* and *"Primitive Girl"* are typical, which established Mr. Wells as a force in the sane, non-melodramatic use of African motives and rhythms in design; while the Biblical series, somewhat in the style of Franz Mazareel, will establish his reputation as a technician of high talent.

Yet Mr. Wells is equally known as a painter: his *"Flight into Egypt,"* now in the Hampton Collection, received the Harmon Gold award in 1931; and several later paintings, including *"The Entry into Jerusalem"* and *"The Ox-Cart,"* have been purchased and exhibited at the *Phillips Memorial Gallery,* Washington. His inclusion in the latter, one of the most authoritatively chosen collections of modernist art in the country, ranks Wells as an ultra-modernist and a successful one. But while ultra-modern in composition and color scheme, many of his paintings have also an unusual mystical quality like *"The Wanderers,"* which reveal to some eyes a typical Negro note; which in his own words, he attempts to express "not in that sensational gusto so very often typified as Negroid, but as that which possesses the quality of serenity, has sentiment without sentimentality and rhythmic flow of lines and tones in pure and simple forms."

The Younger Sculptors.—Turning to sculpture, we have already noticed its unusual importance in contemporary Negro art. For the younger generation, Miss Augusta Savage opened this phase over a decade ago with singular promise, and has since worked in sculpture, wood carving, modelling, painting, applied design and pottery. At Cooper Institute, she began her deep interest in Negro types, which has followed her through years of study and change of style. Whether from the early shock of disappointment

76

when she was denied participation in the American summer school for talented artists at Fontainebleau, in 1928, or from extreme versatility, Miss Savage's sculptural technique has not entirely fulfilled her early promise. Her conceptions are often beyond her actual technical control, especially when on her favorite subject of primitive African types. However, work like her *"African Savage," "The Tom Tom,"* etc., have stimulated popular interest and had constructive effect upon younger artists. Indeed, it is as a teacher that Miss Savage has been most effective; she has organized an art-studio workshop in Harlem, recently affiliated with the W.P.A. art projects and has developed several younger talents, notably the young sculptor, Wm. Artis. She studied two years in Paris on a Rosenwald Fund grant, and *"The Negro Urchin,"* a genre study of this period, is one of her technically most satisfying works.

Miss Elisabeth Prophet.—Miss Elisabeth Prophet, of Providence, R. I., is another contemporary sculptor of significance, with more cosmopolitan style and experience. She commands the attention with strong mass modelling and finely restrained surface treatment. She has frequently exhibited in the *Paris Salon* and in American art shows, and her *"Congo Head"* is in the Whitney Museum permanent collection.

Sargent Johnson.—Judged both by awards and creative output, Sargent Johnson and Richmond Barthe are the two outstanding contemporary Negro sculptors. Mr. Johnson, born in Boston, 1888, but for years now a resident of Berkeley, California, has exhibited with the *San Francisco Art Association* almost continuously since 1925, and with the Harmon Foundation exhibits from 1928 to 1935. In both the former and the latter, he has been prize-man thrice. *"Sammy,"* his black porcelain bust of a Negro juvenile,

77

showed him already committed in 1928 to a strongly simplified style; and his work has grown in the direction of increased simplicity and heavy stylizing until he has come to reflect more than any other contemporary Negro sculptor the modernist mode and the African influence. He has also gone in for experimentation with other than traditional materials; including metal appliqué, wrought metal and various composite materials. Lately, particularly in guoache drawings, he has registered Mexican and other primitive influences; but his most representative work still remains American Negro types, busts like *"Ester,"* purchased by the *San Diego Gallery, "Chester,"* *"Anderson,"*—an adolescent youth, and *"Pearl,"* a Chinese baby done in green porcelain. For purely sculptural qualities Johnson's simplified surfaces are admirably adapted; the African quality is shown very suitable for racial characterization. He has, however, done little or no group figure compositions.

Richmond Barthe.—Mr. Richmond Barthe, on the other hand, has shown particular preoccupation, after an apprenticeship stage on busts, with the full figure, and on occasion, group figure compositions. He is also very disposed to racial subjects done in a less abstract, and therefore, less modernistic style. Yet he is far from academic classicism or old-fashioned realism. In fact, he may be said to owe much of his great popularity to this middle ground position in the matter of style. Born in Bay St. Louis, of mixed Creole stock, his talent was discovered in New Orleans by Lyle Saxon and a Catholic priest. He was assisted to Chicago, where largely by his own efforts thereafter, he studied four years at the *Chicago Art Institute.* On a Rosenwald grant, he took up studies in New York in 1929, after having gone in for sculpture suddenly in 1928, after years of training and preoccupation with paint-

78

ing.   Pinch-hitting for a lack of sculpture in the Chicago *"Negro in Art Week"* exhibit, Barthe revealed
his great talent for modelling when his experimental
attempts were drafted for exhibit at that time.
Since then, he has had a meteoric career, climaxed
so far by the purchase of his *"Blackberry Woman,"*
"Comedian" and *"African Dancer"* in successive years
since 1933 by the *Whitney Museum.*   He has had six
one-man shows, one of them at the *Caz-Delbos Gallery,* and has shown increasing command of figure and
figure group technique.   His work ranges from portrait busts of distinction to Negro types like *"Mask
of Black Boy," "Filipino Head," "The Blackberry
Woman," "West Indian Girl"* and African tribal types.
Then comes his larger figure work like *"Torso of
an Adolescent," "African Dancer,"* the full figure
study of *"Rose Mc Clendon"* in the role of Selena in
"Porgy," "Chorale,"—a figure study of the dancer,
Harald Kreutzberg, *"The Archer"* (also an African
figure), and *"Mother and Son,"* a yet uncompleted
lynching group.   The range of this work, with mural
auditorium decorations and friezes for the *Harlem
River Houses,* a P.W.A. project, has given Mr. Barthe
great versatility of style and a rapidly maturing
experience.   With his continued talented expression
in painting and pastel sketches, in which his style is
much more realistic than in his sculpture, the creative
bulk of his work has given him an outstanding position among the younger Negro artists.   Occasionally,
he has done deft genre sketches like *"The Harmonica
Player," "The Devilled Crab Man"* from *"Porgy,"*
"The Breakaway" (dance motive), and *Negro
Comedian,* after the late "Garbage" Rogers; but on
the whole his is a talent with an undertone of romanti-
cism and a feeling for suave poise and dignity; a trend
not unconnected, we think, with the New Orleans

79

background and his part Creole ancestry. In 1935, Xavier University conferred on Mr. Barthe an honorary Master of Art's degree.

The Youngest Generation.—Among the younger artists, there is talent too numerous even for thumbsketch treatment. It is safe to predict from its present volume and skill a sharp rise in the quality and quantity of the Negro's art output. Among them, one promising talent, Earle Richardson, has been cut off already by death. He was a promising muralist and had won a prize for portraiture in *"Profile of a Negro Girl"* in 1933. Charles H. Alston of New York is a young modernist whose oil studies of Negro types are most promising and who now is in charge of the P.W.A. project decoration of the *Harlem Hospital.* His modernistic panels, "Mystery and Magic Contrasted with Modern Science and Medicine" were chosen for the national W.P.A. show New Horizons in American Art, as were also canvases by Allan Crite and Samuel Brown. Rex Gorleigh, also of New York, has done some exceptional canvases,—*"Baptist Prayer," "Finnish Market Place,"* and a recent *"Self Portrait,"* that shows maturer accent and technical originality than any single canvas of the younger set. Another promising portraitist and folk type painter is Beaufort De Laney; and the group includes prominently Allan Crite of Boston, Grayson Walker, Bruce Nugent, Henry Bannarn, Samuel Countee, Georgette Seabrook, Sara Murrell of New York and Jas. A. Porter, Henry Hudson and Lois M. Jones of Washington. Two strongly original talents deserve brief special mention; Elton C. Fax of Baltimore and Samuel Brown of Philadelphia. Mr. Fax has a promising grasp on the social and regional significance of Negro themes; as instanced in his historical Mississippi panels and his *"Carolina Chain Gang."* Samuel Brown,

80

in some respects the most modernistic of all the group, has a startling power of direct expression, especially in water color, as his P.W.A. canvases *"The Scrub-woman"* and *"Lazy Bones"* attest. He also has a deep feeling for racial values, as in his series of P.W.A. school murals; *"The Music Lesson," "The Writing Lesson"* and *"Children at Play"* have that naive Negro quality so many have sought, but that is so difficult to catch. Obviously, the future of the American Negro painting and sculpture is bright.

One of the most helpful new forces in the life of the younger generation artists has come from the Federal Art projects of the W.P.A. administration; and the generous inclusion of young Negro artists has been one of its noteworthy features. Few of these projects have reached the stage of completion, but the showing of Negro artists in the recent W.P.A. regional and national exhibitions has been striking evidence of the greater productivity of our artists under such sound, liberal patronage. Harlem Projects that have already attracted favorable attention are the series of murals on *"Negro Achievement,"* the last work of the late Earle W. Richardson; the sculptural friezes on motives from *"The Green Pastures"* by Richmond Barthe for the auditorium of the Harlem River Housing project, and an elaborate series of murals for the Harlem hospital by a group of younger artists, among which is a very outstanding epic of Negro life series by Vertis Hayes, called *"The Pursuit of Happiness."* Other projects in other parts of the country promise a great lift forward for the younger Negro artist and vital Negro art.

DISCUSSION QUESTIONS

What dilemma confronted the younger Negro artists in their choice of subject matter? What trends in

81

general American art helped overcome the artificial disinterest in Negro types? Is "Negro art" a matter of an artistic ghetto or a special province of Americanism in art? Can a white artist be an exponent of "Negro art"? What signs are there of an assumption of racial expression as a goal of American Negro artists? Has the public reception of the Negro artist broadened or narrowed with this trend? What was the role of such agencies as the Harmon Foundation prizes, awards and exhibits, the Harlem Library Shows, the Chicago Negro in Art Week program in this movement? What general schools of technical and artistic grouping prevail among the contemporary Negro artists? As between the "Traditionalists" and the "Modernists," what is the present trend? Who were some of the more competent members of each of these schools? What promising younger talent has appeared in the last ten years? In the last five years? What are, in general, the status and prospects of the present generation of Negro artists? If there has been improvement, to what forces do you trace most of the change?

READING REFERENCES

Catalogues of the Harmon Foundation *"Exhibits of the Works of Negro Artists"* for the years 1928; 1929; 1930; 1931; 1933; 1935. Obtainable singly and bound from the Foundation.

Photographs of works of Negro artists, selected from the Harmon exhibits of 1928, 1929, 1930, 1931, 1933, and 1935 are available from the Foundation; and the 1935 Catalogue has a Directory Negro artists, with addresses and biographical notes. There is also available a one reel film on *The Negro and Art;* and a later four reel film on *Negro Artists at Work:* Harmon Foundation, 140 Nassau Street, New York City.

Henderson, Rose: *Exhibits of Painting and Sculpture by Negro Artists*—The Southern Workman—1929.

Locke, Alain: *The American Negro as Artist*—The American Magazine of Art—September, 1931.

Locke, Alain: *Negro Art* in the Encyclopedia Britannica—XIV edition.

Porter, J. A.: *Malvin Gray Johnson:* An Appreciation—Opportunity, 1935.

VIII
THE NEGRO THROUGH EUROPEAN EYES

While the American artists were removing the bean of prejudice from their artistic eyes, and Negro artists were winking out the anti-racial mote, European art, too, in its own way was discovering a new angle of sight on the Negro. It was not that the European eye had ever been subject to the myopia of color prejudice, for color fascinated rather than repelled European artists. But even with that novelty interest of color, their conception of the Negro was limited in most cases to an exotic romantic interest, which caught only the surface and did not penetrate the depths either of the collective soul or the individual personality. The latter achievements were left for Twentieth Century European art.

Before this development, the Negro in painting and sculpture was an occasional exotic novelty, usually treated romantically, but sometimes realistically as in the case of Rembrandt's famous *"Two Negroes"* in the Hague Museum, or Rubens' striking sketches of possibly the same Negro male subject in different poses and moods called *"Tetes de Negrè,"* in the Brussels National Gallery. But the brilliant suggestions of these great canvases are just flashes that lit no continuous fire of artistic interest. Later there was a flicker here and there as in Gainsborough or Hogarth, and later still, Feurbach's *"Negro Sketch,"* now in the Hamburg Museum. But after that, the Negro type, especially the pure-blood type fell from artistic grace as the curiosity of early colonial days gave way to the familiarity and racial contempt of mature colonial mastery and deliberate exploitation.

Wherever this attitude was most marked, the eclipse of the Negro in letters and art was darkest. Understandably, there was never a total eclipse in French art and the interest it reflected. Especially did the French Romantic painters following Delacroix take up again the Negro theme, but usually according to their North African contacts and interest. It was therefore, the exotic and mixed-blood Eastern and North African types that first came into artistic vogue. The work of this period is legion; but its artistic significance is not of great consequence. The painting is superficial type portraiture; lacking much racial character or even profundity of human interest. But it was a path-breaker and a forerunner of something better.

One thing that caused the artistic treatment of Negro types to stop short was the entirely new scheme of color values with relation to the keynotes of the background. Until modern realism confronted painters with more varied and difficult contrasts in these values, only the master painter could dare the unusual difficulties of the dark browns and subtle purple blacks of the real African and pure Negro types. But when modern realism confronted this challenge, it took it up as an intriguing technical problem. One of the first to do this was Manet, whose *"Olympia"* offered a striking contrast between the Caucasian nude in the foreground and the dark serving woman in the background, which he must have taken as a technical challenge. Then, too, about this time, the fad started to go to the colonies on sketching trips, and the new problems of tropical landscapes and tropical types were worked out together in a way that they never could be in the metropolitan studio. This craze for the tropics has brought first the Polynesian and Malay types and finally the African types into high favor

84

with contemporary artists, beginning with the great vogue for the dark brown Tahitians started by the exotic painter, Paul Gauguin.

Today, each European tradition and nationality has some painter who has been intrigued by the Negro subject and treated it with some distinction of technical or psychological understanding. German art has in this category, the painters, Julius Huether, Max Slevogt, Max Pechstein, Elaine Stern, Walther von Reuckteschell, and Georg Kolbe and Rene Sintenis, sculptors. English art circles have furnished a distinguished group in Neville Lewis, F. C. Gadell, Glyn Philpotts, Edith Cheeseman, John A. Wells, Frank Potter, Laura Knight, Erick Berry, Dora Gourdine, and the American exile, Jacob Epstein. French artists with considerable interest in this province are almost too numerous for detailed mention; but Dimnet, Lucie Costurier, Germaine Casse, Bonnard, Rouault, Emile Compard, Foujita, and Allard L'Olivier would have to be mentioned, along with the Belgians, —Jeannot and Auguste Mambour. Kees van Dongen, of Dutch origin is also a noteworthy exponent of the Negro subject, and Russia, though furnishing a small quota, has given two of the most brilliant and masterful of all the European depictors of Negro types,— Vladimir Perfielieff and Alexandre Jacovleff. As might be expected from grouping artists in terms of one isolated interest of subject, an artificial medley of styles and schools has been lumped together. But this special accounting does indicate what has happened in the last twenty years with respect to the Negro theme among European artists and the extent to which they are now interested in the tropics and tropical man. Nor is all of this interest connected with the well-known cult of primitivism, which has for about the same length of time swept European

85

art; although some of it is, undoubtedly. For that would not account for obvious interest in the Europeanized Negro types such as Van Dongen's famous *"Portrait of Doctor Cassadeus"* or Glyn Philpott's symbolic portrait of *"Roland Hayes."*

As an example of this particular trend, let us take the Munich seccessionist painter, Julius Huether. Here we have a front rank artist so enamoured of the Negro subject that it claims nearly a third of his total artistic output. At first, this interest was purely technical; Huether worked hard on it long before he was able to visit Africa or see any considerable number of Negro models. His approach was that of a color romanticist, captivated by the new bronze tones and warm browns of his subject. Later, as his work matures, we see a growing interest in capturing what one must call "the Negro spirit" for there is a careful, sensitive emphasis on the traits of body and physiognomy that are racially distinctive. Huether revels in this field, like a modern Rubens; he might almost be called the Rubens of Somaliland, his favorite artistic stamping ground when he did get to visit Africa.

Huether, with men like Walter von Reuckteschell and the sculptor, Georg Kolbe, stand as pioneers in opening up African types and the Negro subject to the grand tradition and style. Prior to them, in spite of a good deal of work in this field, what we may characterize as the museum study approach was typical and dominant. Kolbe made frequent trips to Africa, and not only sketched industriously, but took the African youth who became the model for his best Negro statues as his constant companion till the lad's tragic death. Rene Sintenis, with her *"Somali Negro"* and *"Negress"* has brilliantly followed Kolbe's lead. Von Reuckteschell's drawings represent careful studies made in German East Africa, half-realistic, half-

86

romantic, but with irresistible human interest. Apart from the technical beauty of the work, there is peculiar success in evoking what one must call, for lack of more adequate phrase, the "race soul." Only familiarity with this art can be convincing on this point, but there has arisen in modern art a feeling for the dignity and beauty of native types which amounts to just this, and nothing short of it. When Mrs. Herrick Wall, interviewing von Reuckteschell, congratulated him "on penetrating the mask of an unfamiliar physiognomy," she quotes him as saying: "Mask! It is we who wear it." Whatever else may be said of the German colonial record, it must in all fairness be admitted that their literary and artistic approach to the African has been thorough, sympathetic and understanding. In work such as we have mentioned, there is revealing interpretation of the deepest human values; it is there in the mellow, sleepy but mystic eyes, the sensuous but genial lips, the grotesque, mask-like simplicity of countenance, the velvety tones and textures of the African skin, the strength, vitality and structural beauty of body, so common to African types, despite their otherwise great diversity. New dimensions and canons of beauty have unmistakably been revealed.

I do not believe that there are many Negroes, even Negro artists as yet, who understand the underlying race temperament, even its American variations, as deeply as the intuitive vision of these artists. But gradually both Negro and other American artists are here and there glimpsing these values, groping through the fog of prejudice and the distorting mists of Nordic conventions. French and German artists have had less of that sort of thing to overcome; hence their early and pioneering success. When the race awakens consciously to its own spiritual selfhood, such work

87

will be prized beyond measure. It is, in fact, the forerunner and necessary first step of such an awakening.

French artistic understanding of African Negro types is more explicit than the German, if not so deep. Of the majority it can be said that the charm of the exotic and primitive has been the dominating lure of interest. Much fine painting and interpretation has resulted. But it requires social as well as artistic vision to get the deeper values. Madame Cousturier's work represents such painstaking absorption of Negro life. She belongs to that school who believe that Negro types cannot be fully interpreted until their cultural background has been thoroughly studied, absorbed and re-expressed. On this basis, the work of artists like Dimnet, Rouault, Compard, Bonnard, Germaine Casse is on another level from that of Cousturier, Foujita, L'Olivier, Jeannot and Mambour. For the latter group have sought to know native life deeply and sympathetically as part of their art project; they add a humane sociology to their artistic equipment. As their example spreads, the local color and exotic cult groups will pass from first line attention merely as pathbreaking overtures, and a more solid school of interpretative art take the fore.

Even English art is outgrowing its limitations in these matters; and we have already seen (Chapter VI), how contemporary American art is enlarging its angle of vision on the Negro. English painters like Frank Potter, Glyn Philpotts, Alfred Wollmark, John A. Wells, Laura Knight, and the London sculptors, Dora Gourdine and Jacob Epstein, are far beyond the narrow blinkers of the colonial type school, and are gradually off-setting the slant and squint of social snobbery in their approach to Negro subjects. Almost invariably now, it is the individual personality which

88

sets the artistic cue, although with warrant, the racial factor can be symbolically associated, and when it is, often enhances the interpretation. Laura Knight, an English woman academician, has been particularly interested in Negro subjects over a long period, and has made some fine paintings and sketches, especially of Negro women and children. She has come several times to America to extend her knowledge of Negro types. Erick Berry, another woman artist, has made in modernist water-color an extended gallery of West Indian, North African and Nigerian types from intensive travel study. Similarly the Baldridge-Singers,— husband and wife, have made their study pilgrimages. Indeed from the influence of such pioneers, it has now become indispensable even for illustrators of travel books and local color novels to know their regions intimately, and to approach it without superficiality, and more important yet, without condescension.

In both the English and the American field, the increasing volume of this more scientifically competent art expression of the Negro theme has become too large for detailed mention in our limits of time and space. But special mention must be made of the masterful Haitian sketches of Vladimir Perfilieff, the artist of the Wm. Beebe expeditions, of the decorative panels of African types by Allard L'Olivier, which with Jeannot's sculptural friezes were the high points of the *Paris Colonial Exposition's* rich array of African art, of Malvina Hoffman's combined scientific and artistic world tour, with a wide series of race types from life for the Field Museum's *Hall of Mankind* and the *Museum of Natural History's* collections. Mention of the rising art level of illustrative museum sculpture makes it interesting to note that the pioneer example in America was the early work of the English explorer, Herbert Ward, whose *"Voice of Africa"* statues were presented to the *Smithsonian Institution Museum* of Washington, along with his great collection of Congo Negro sculpture and arms. Two masterful talents must be briefly mentioned in conclusion: Auguste Mambour, the Belgian painter, and Alexandre Jacovleff, for they represent the apex of this development to date.

Auguste Mambour.—This young Belgian painter insisted on special permission to substitute the Belgian Congo for the usual government art fellowship to Rome. From the beginning of his career, then, he was a conscious exponent of Negro art. As a result, he is at home psychologically with his subject matter; there is small wonder that his paintings of the tribal ceremonies, like *"Kivi Dancers"* or his *"Funeral Dance,"* should breathe the very essence of the jungle. Some of Mambour's work has been acquired by the *Museum of the Congo* at Tervueren, but most of it circulates as the major art expression of one of the leaders of contemporary Belgian painting. His rendering of the characteristic atmosphere, his introduction into painting of the modelling of planes and mass surfaces as in the native sculptures, his use of tropical idioms of color, all lead to a singularly consistent interpretation of the native and his life.

Alexandre Jacovleff.—Jacovleff has a special position among those who are now revealing the real Africa to the world through art. He is a folklorist of the brush and pencil, and has given us the best art documentation we have up to the present of Africa's great diversity of native types. As staff artist for the *Citroen Trans-Sahara Expedition,* which traversed Africa north to south and east to west, he had capital opportunity to see the native interior in its undisturbed purity. Selecting his models with an obvious care as to tribal type, he has made us sense the delicate, fragile

90

elegance of the Mangbetu, the cruel forceful features of the Songhai, the gnome-like animality of the Ulua, the heavy sensuousness of the Banda, and what not. In fact, the Meynial Press portfolio, with only a fraction of these canvases in color reproduction, smashes through all the popular stereotypes about the African, and in a revealing way, documents both their common and their special humanity. The same interpretive accuracy is to be seen in Jacovleff's illustrations to the Mornay Press special edition of Rene Maran's *Batouala* (1928). Such artistry is a high-water mark in the artistic rediscovery of Africa which we have been tracing.

Oddly enough, in this new chapter of art, African types have advanced to a stage of interpretation superior to that attained at present by American art for the American Negro. But since the influence has already begun to spread, the new values of Negro Africa as seen through European art must exert an important effect on the portraiture of the American Negro, as this generation of American artists follow their present interest and work it through to its logical conclusions.

DISCUSSION QUESTIONS

What was the basis of the interest of European artists in the Negro subject in the Eighteenth Century? In the Nineteenth Century? How did colonial attitudes and policies change this interest? When did romantic exoticism again change this art interest? Why were German and French artists first exponents of a more serious attitude? Who are some of the outstanding modern artists who have extensively painted Negro and African subjects? To what extent have they needed to go to Africa? Is social vision as necessary to full interpretation of this subject material as artistic insight? What part of this movement is con-

91

nected with the modern cult of "primitivism" and the lure of the exotic? Are all the values in the African field primitive? How has modern art pioneered in a new understanding of alien cultures and diverse racial types? How has this understanding spread from Continental artists to English and American art? Will American and Negro art eventually be affected by this movement?

READING REFERENCES

Agard, Walter: *Cleveland's Artistic Appreciation of Africa*—Amer. Magazine of Art—September, 1931.

Hoffman, Malvina: *Heads and Tales*—Scribners, N. Y.—1936.

Knight, Laura: *Art Paint and Grease Paint*—Macmillan Co., N. Y.— 1935; also article in Literary Digest, December 17, 1927.

Locke, Alain: *More of the Negro in Art*—Opportunity Magazine— December, 1925; *The Art of Auguste Mambour*—Opportunity— August, 1925.

Mille, Pierre: *The African Work of Jacovleff*—Art & Decoration— June, 1926.

Wall, Louise Herrick: *Walter von Reuckteschell*—Opportunity—May, 1924.

Portfolio of the Citroen Expedition: *"Desseins et Peintures d'Afrique,"* by Alexandre Jacovleff—Jules Meynial Press, Paris—1927.

92

IX

AFRICAN NEGRO ART

It now remains to analyze African Negro art, which, in addition to being the historic art of the African homeland, is the source of the Negro's distinctive art tradition. This ancestral legacy, which but for its revival through European modernism would have been hopelessly lost as an active art influence, is variously called African art, Negro art and Primitive Negro art. None of these terms is quite accurate. African art is a loose generalization: art in Africa really goes by tribes and regions, and has many distinctive and different styles. Negro art, also, is no closer to fact, since Mohammedan, Hamitic and Egyptian zones of influence importantly dot Africa here and there, and in certain cases interpenetrate with the more definitely Negro art tradition that dominates the greater part of the Continent. So the arts of Africa are predominantly Negro, though not all African art is Negro art.

As to calling this art "primitive," there is an increasing division of opinion among the experts. For the most part, the newest studies are advancing the idea that it is by no means a primitive art, even though the cultural product of types of tribal civilization that by comparison with European culture must be classed as primitive. Much of the civilization that originally produced African art was really barbaric feudalism, extending in most cases to large inter-tribal federations or empires. There have been a number of such African empires, some part Islamic, some entirely Negro, —Bantu and non-Bantu Negro. Not all of them have themselves had a strong native art tradition, but like

93

most military feudalisms, have co-opted a conquered tribe or imported a clan of artisans to express the glory and the wealth of the dynasty. In some of the East African groups, there still remain restricted hereditary clans of artisans of different ethnic stock from the majority of the population, still traditionally carrying on the craft of metal working, wood carving, weaving or some other dominant art interest and craft need of the community. The peak of almost every well-known strain of African art is definitely associated with the heyday of some feudal African dynasty that became rich and powerful through conquest of other African peoples, and concentrated their wealth and sometimes their religion on the patronage of some art style and tradition. The famous Benin art thus centers in the rise of the great alliance of the Benin warlords with the priests of the Ifa or Yoruba serpent-cult religion on the West Coast, an empire that was at its height in the Sixteenth Century but lasted in its interior stronghold till Benin's downfall in 1897 at the hands of a British punitive expedition. Another branch of this art is associated with the rise and long dominance of the Gold Coast kingdoms of the Ashanti in Dahomey. Still another great strain of African art is that of the Bakuba branch of the Bushongo, a Bantu dynasty who dominated the Congo lake basin in the late Seventeenth and early Eighteenth Centuries.

So really, speaking of African art is like speaking of European art, when we should and in our own case, really do speak of French art, German art, Italian art. Yet European art in the mass has certain common characteristics, certainly when contrasted with Oriental art traditions. In this sense, then, using the term as a common denominator for these characteristics is warranted; but the experts prefer to speak of Benin art, Yoruba art, Ashanti art, Pahouin and Gabon art,

94

Bushongo or Bakuba art, Bushman art, Zulu or Arosha art, and the like. But again, just as the religious cults of Europe spread a characteristic art expression, like the influence of Byzantine Christian art and later, Italian Renaissance art, so certain African religious cults, achieving wide vogue, have spread their influence, like that of the Yoruban religion spreading from the old religious capitol, Ifa or Ifé; or the Bundu and the Bapende secret societies that spread certain art influences over a great area through their masks, talismans, priest costumes, ceremonial dances and initiation regalia.

Most African art, thus, is by no means a primitive art, especially those phases of it which have so profoundly influenced European art. For only a peasant art or primary craft art is a primitive art. Africa has plenty of that; so has Europe. But much African art is not only the work of expert artisans, with their special and often generation-old traditions of skill and style, but is cultivated in that tradition as a "fine" or sophisticated art style, associated with a culture that spreads over the top of the native peasant culture, as Christian art overlaid the barbaric peasant cultures which it conquered. Of course, African Negro art, especially in sculpture, does represent one of the oldest art traditions in the world. In idiom it is kin to much pre-historic art, like the drawings in the Grimaldi Cave in Southern France,—supposedly the relics of Cro-Magnon culture,—an early prehistoric type that anthropologists think may have come from Northern Africa across the Mediterranean into Europe at a time as remote as 10,000 or 12,000 B.C. Or again, the art of the Altamira Caves of Spain has great similarities with the prehistoric rock drawings of the South African Bushmen. But in African sculpture this basic primitive style is developed to a much more mature expression. It is only as representing an early tradition of style and as associated with primitive or simple types of social institutions like nature worship, fetichism and the like, that African art is in any strictly scientific sense "primitive."

Some authorities today go to the extreme of repudiating the term primitive altogether. John D. Graham says:

African art is by no means a primitive art, in the sense that a peasant art (whether ancient or contemporary) is a primitive art. It is an art that, like Egyptian, Greek, Chinese and Gothic art, it has taken thousands of years of fastidious civilization to evolve and set. It is, furthermore, an art resulting from a highly developed aesthetic viewpoint; from logical "argumentation" and consummate craftsmanship. "Primitive" art, on the contrary, is any art that derives—whatever the date of its creation—from a low state of civilization; an art making its first faulty and undetermined steps toward the formulation, by its artists, of an aesthetic viewpoint. An art that has finally formulated and realized its plastic aspirations, an art, in short, that is definitely poised, is a classical art. The art of Africa is classic, in the same sense that the Egyptian, Greek, Chinese and Gothic arts are classic.

And continuing his analysis, Mr. Graham says:

The art of Africa has served as a liberator for sculptors and painters. It has shown them that, in the plastic arts, proportions can be rearranged, so long as the aesthetic impulse involved in their rearrangement is inspired and noble.

African sculptures have unshackled the modern artist from the tyranny of the camera—the slavery of the seven-heads-to-the-figure rule. Without this liberation, Picasso, Matisse, Braque, Modigliani, Brancusi, Epstein and other modern masters would not have reached their goals.

Negro Art at Home.—But African art must be judged in terms of its native objectives, even when it also takes high rank in terms of our modern and Western super-imposed ones. African art belongs in two native categories:—ritualistic art and craft art, both of which are more primitive and basic than our idea of "fine art." African masks are part of tribal ceremonial, used directly to evoke a mood, sometimes terror or fear, sometimes dignity of priest and witch-doctor or of chieftain, and sometimes even to symbolize the supernatural attributes or the ancestral lineage of the gods. As talismans or fetiches, they often serve to control the supernatural spirits by sympathetic magic. Their primary meaning, thus, is symbolic, or as we would say ecclesiastical and ceremonial. But closely allied is the technical appreciation for their skill and beauty. However, there is always this important difference between African art and our fine art, unless one goes back to the archaic periods of European art. The European artist, typically, works with the idea of self-expression; authorship is important, often too important, in his approach to art. The African artist, though often a great craftsman or technician, is forgetful of self and fully projects himself into the function and tradition of the article he is working on. The secret of the power, vitality, directness and simplicity of African art lies there; it is untainted with egotism and personal affectation. It is by age-long tradition anonymous; you can only praise the artist by admiring the art product.

Furthermore, the obvious craft basis of much African art leads us to mis-judge it under our subordinate category of "applied art." In this we fail to see how irrelevant such a distinction is for a culture where "fine" art and "decorative" art and "craft" art have never been separated from their original unit stalk. In Africa things can be superlatively beautiful and objects of utility at the same time. Indeed it is at this point that African art offers our art its greatest challenge and possible inspiration. As an art that has never been divorced from the vital context of everyday life, it embodies and vindicates one of the soundest and most basic of aesthetic principles,—beauty in use.

Types of African Art.—We find this vital organic connection with the tribal life throughout all the areas

97

and all of the periods of African art. In fact, although African art is very perishable, because of the rapid disintegration of wood, even the hardwoods of the tropics, in the damp hot climate, the styles of African art are very old, and are handed down from generation to generation. So a comparatively recent object may represent a very antique or archaic style. However, most of the best examples of African art are not of very recent workmanship, for especially in the last two generations, the contacts with European civilization, with their double discouragement of missionary propaganda and competition with cheap imported machine-made articles, have almost destroyed the old African arts and the native appreciation for them.

Characteristic of the old African cultures is this sort of art work: large and small-scale carving in ivory, horn and wood of various kinds, hand-forged and decorated work in iron and other metals, metal inlay work, carved and appliqué decorated ritual masks in a great variety of materials, pottery, woven and decorated textiles, and bronze and brass castings, sometimes by the direct mould process, sometimes the more difficult lost-art process of *cire perdue* or melted wax casting. It was in this latter form that the great classical Benin bronzes were cast, which adds both to their artistry and rarity.

' The art styles of Africa are very numerous, in fact each race or tribe having its own. Some tribes have multiple styles, each with its own symbolisms. The form traditions are generations old, but by purity of style and technical excellence of workmanship a classical period can be traced by experts for each particular style. Invariably the two, excellence of workmanship and purity of style have been found to be closely associated. A hybrid style rarely, if ever, yields good specimens. The fact that a level of high development

98

has in several cases been maintained over a span of two or three centuries, with stability of types and patterns, and without perceptible signs of decadence until the recent break-up of the native culture under European influences, gives convincing evidence of an artistic tradition and skill of great strength and vigor. Not all tribes are equally artistic, however. But among the artistic tribes, ethnologists report that every design motif has its proper name and symbolic association, and every pattern variation a meaning. They report also that there is such a widespread appreciation of their art by the people that the average child is taught to draw the basic patterns repeatedly and to name them. We can understand, then, the great general skill of hand and eye upon which the artistry of the tribe is based, and which gives it a few master artists. Other tribes, as we have seen, maintain special family groups as privileged art clans.

Its Antiquity.—Many of us must radically readjust our ideas to get used to the now accepted theories of the antiquity of various strains of African art. The most important thing about this is not the dating of the particular piece but the dating of the type. However, even individual pieces can in some instances be dated; for example, certain changes in the Benin bronzes and the sudden appearance of Portuguese figures with fire-arm muskets definitely dates some specimens as before the middle of the Sixteenth Century. Or again, the Bushongo chronicles of the succession of a hundred and twenty-odd chieftains makes it necessary and reasonable to date back the beginnings of Congo Bakuba art some four or five hundred years, with the portrait statue of one of these kings, now in the British Museum, definitely around 1760. Louis Carré, in his article on *The Art of Benin,* following the German ethnologists, Struck and Baumann

99

in their careful comparative study of this art, places its ancient period, about 1360-1500 A.D.; its classical period, 1500-1691; a late period 1701-1820; and the modern period, 1830-1897. The fine bronze castings and ivory tusk carvings of the ancestral cult of the Benin kings that are in the Vienna, Berlin and British Museums, with a few in this country at the Field Museum and that of the University of Pennsylvania, belong at the latest to the classical period. In fact after 1700 A.D., this work is hardly considered worthy of museum standing. Dutch travellers described the city,—De Bry in 1600 and Dapper in 1668, and their descriptions tally with these findings worked out in highly technical comparative study of the art itself. Portuguese records show contacts with the Benin territory as far back as 1486, but highly developed art, it has been established, was flourishing even before this. Although, at first, Portuguese influences were credited with the development of its technical achievements, it is now definitely proved that the castings showing the earlier styles before Portuguese figures appear are in quality of workmanship superior to those that do register the European contacts.

General Qualities.—The general qualities of African art can be described, although such description represents only a composite view of this art. First, or at least most noticeable, is a great skill of surface ornamentation and mastery of design patterns. Like the Indian, Peruvian and Aztec art, these designs are highly stylized or conventionalized. However, experts consider some African decorative art superior to any other known primitive art in design spacing and the technical skill of its carving. In African weaving, both design and workmanship reach a high level, although except Bushongo raphia cloth, African weaving does not stand out in such superiority over all other tra-

100

ditions of weaving. More important artistically, is the style and technique of block or three-dimensional sculpture, as seen in the statues and statuettes of the African tribes. This is what Roger Fry had in mind when he said: "They have the special qualities of sculpture in a higher degree. They have, indeed, complete plastic freedom; that is to say these African artists really conceive form in three dimensions." Guillaume and Munro put it this way: "Every part in a typical, fully realized Negro statue functions as an element in plastic design; an embodiment, a repetition in rhythmic sequence, of some theme in mass line or surface. . . . Most schools of sculpture have confined themselves to a few favorite themes of line and surface, repeated endlessly, with little feeling for masses. To secure interest, they often rely upon the associative power of the subject represented,—a confusing and precarious appeal at best. But the Negro artist, in concentrating upon unrestrained variety and directness of three-dimensional effects, goes directly to the heart of his problem, and thus realizes the distinctive potentialities of sculpture."

Distortion and Stylization.—The third general quality of African sculpture comes as a corollary of the above. This is the obvious distortion of the human and animal figure and of nature patterns generally. This distortion, however, is what stands between the average person and an immediate appreciation of the qualities in African art which the experts rave over. Laymen continue to think, as was generally thought years ago, that these distortions are due to the crudity of the African's technique or his primitive child-like satisfaction with a caricature symbol. It is now realized that with the skill at his command, and obvious in other sides of his technique, the African artist could easily be realistically accurate in his art if he wished

101

to be. The distortion, then, has some other explanation. One critic (Graham) says: "African artists were never seduced by the desire to imitate or compete with nature, as they had, more than a thousand years before, travelled the long road from realism and exact representation to abstraction—a journey which we ourselves are only just ending. Steeped in their ancient tradition, the African sculptors produced works comparable, in their spiritual severity, to Gothic sculpture. Indeed a Gothic note will be felt in many of these exhibits." Another says: "One comes to regard the statue not as a distorted copy of natural forms, but as a purposeful creation of mass design, with free distortion of natural shapes into arbitrary, highly stylized forms expressing abstract design." Or finally, as James Sweeney Johnson puts it: "It is the vitality of the forms of Negro art that should speak to us, the simplification without impoverishment, the unerring emphasis on the essential, the consistent three-dimensional organization of structural planes in architectonic sequences, the uncompromising truth to material with a seemingly intuitive adaptation of it, and the tension achieved between the idea or emotion to be expressed through representation and the abstract principles of sculpture." In short, creation in Negro art is not imitation of nature, but free creative improvising on themes taken from nature and used to convey forcefully a selected mood or an intended idea. Primitive folk know nature too intimately and well to need to imitate it.

Regional Styles.—After this summary of the general characteristics of African Negro art, we need briefly to outline its principal regional styles. Students are only gradually approaching agreement on these matters, but all are agreed that "the finest work from a sculptural point of view may be considered as the product of the Negro proper" and that the geographical areas of this art are "precisely those areas most intensively covered by the African slave-trade, and thus, the home areas of the ancestors of the American and West Indian Negro populations." In general, this area is central Equatorial Africa and particularly the West African Ivory, Gold and Guinea Coasts. J. Sweeney Johnson says: "To describe roughly this area, a northern boundary might be drawn from the Atlantic Ocean on the west at the mouth of the Senegal, eastward through the upper bend of the Niger across to Lake Chad, southeast to the upper shores of Lake Victoria Nyanza and from there along the northern border of Tanganyika to the coast. The southern boundary may be said to follow that of the Belgian Congo province of Tanganyika westward, across southern Angola to the Atlantic."

The simplest way, especially since experts are not yet certain about their relative antiquity, and differ widely as to which they think artistically superior, is to follow the various art styles down the coast in seven main regional zones,—the art of the *Soudan,* of *Guinea,* of the *Ivory Coast,* of the *Gold Coast,* (which includes *Ashanti, Yoruban* and *Benin* art), of the *Cameroons, Gabon,* the *Congo* (French and Belgian), and of *Angola.* These in turn split up into tribal subdivisions, the more important of which will be mentioned in passing. Authoritative studies upon which certain statements are based will be cited in bracket mention.

The Soudan Art.—Much of the Soudanese art is of hybrid and mere craft character, with heavy Moslem influence. But certain regions, especially the Senoufo and Bambara tribes, show a singularly pure and seemingly ancient Negro sculptural art, mostly finely carved hardwood figurines or ancestor statuettes,

103

often in pairs (male and female), and elongated prong-horned dance-masks. Soudan art is one of the severest and most highly stylized of all the regional types, and is characterized by over-emphasized angularity, thin, sharp contours, elongated features, restrained straight-lined surface ornament, and an atmosphere of dignity, repose and even austerity. Its cultural emphasis is ancestor worship, phallic symbolism obviously associated with fertility rites, and animal totemism, the latter being particularly prominent in the dance mask motives. The Bambara Tribe, whom Kjersmeier thinks "the most artistic of all the African populations," have a most unique development of animal totem carvings; some used in the Koré, their great feast, every seventh year, of clan initiations, others, the famous antelope masks, used in the annual sowing and harvest festivals, where these elaborate crested male and female patterns of the antelope are the mounted head-dress for the celebrants who, in grass costumes, leap in the field grasses in rites symbolic of the earth's fertility. No modernistic art approaches these Bambara antelope crests in decorative use of severe curves. Some authorities (Frobenius) point out the analogies of Soudanese statuary art with archaic Greek sculpture; others (Apollinaire) suggest an Egyptian carry-over and survival: all agree that it is an art of great antiquity and powerful originality. Comparatively rare, its best pieces are in French collections, the Trocadero, and such private collections as Tzara, Fénéon, Chauvet and Guillaume, and in America, those of Frank Crowninshield and the Barnes Foundation.

The Guinea Art.—Uneven, but primitively strong in its best examples, the art typical of Guinea is almost the opposite of Soudanese art. It is rough surfaced, in irregular rhythms of tubular necks and extremities bulging suddenly out into bulbous curves of heads, breasts, hips and enlarged hands or feet, truly difficult for the novice to understand or appreciate. However, it is imporatnt in two respects; first as a rendition of strong primitive structural form, saying much in little, and conveying powerfully its desired emotional effects; then, as a sort of primitive anticipation of Cubism, its European analogue. Moreover, it is felt as an important element in the art of adjacent tribes, especially the Mendi and Temne of Sierra Leone and in much of the hinterland of Liberia. Sculptors prize it for its stark structuralism; ethnologists for its naive, almost simon-pure primitivism. Grotesque and generally to larger scale than most African sculpture, it is striking in its bold simplicity and crudity,—a crudity, however, associated with technical skill and unerring directness of attack. No art ever reduced art expression to barer or more basic essentials. The Fénéon, Chauvet, Tzara and Leonce Guerre collections have some of the fine examples of this still somewhat unfamiliar Guinea art.

The Ivory Coast Art.—Here we have one of the richest and most varied regions of native African art, so varied that the blanket term is almost a misnomer. Only one fact redeems it,—the striking refinement and sophistication commonly characteristic of nearly all its varieties. In fact, Ivory Coast art is oriental in its degree of technical and conceptual refinement. But it is no less African, for the double reason that the idioms of decoration are typically African, and that three of the five major types are found in a double strain, one heavily stylized, the other more naturalistic, indicating an obvious refinement of the same materials from a craft to a "fine art" level. The celebrated "Dán" masks are found in both styles; likewise the Baoule war and ceremonial drums; while

105

the Hein Collection has a number of beautiful oval wood plaques with low relief head decorations obviously copied from the Baoule ritual masks.

Michelet and Szecsi list five subdivisions of Ivory Coast art: Baoule, Dan, Guro, Senoufo and Ashanti, the latter two being mixed traditions, the one with Soudan, the other Dahomeyan style. The Dan style seems the oldest and severest, and is highly rated for its sculptural simplicity and power. Even the "terror masks," with metal inlay teeth and eyes, are artistically satisfactory over and above their apparent practical ceremonial function; while the more decorative Dan masks are among the most artistic of all African art types, and are prized treasures of the Barnes, Guillaume, Hein, and Ratton Collections. Baoule is essentially a style of exquisite decorative feeling and refinement, the product of generations of accumulative craftsmanship. However, the older Ivory Coast statuettes show basically the primitive Guinea Coast conception of form, refined and formalized by a more sensitive artistic group. Yet to a familiarized eye, Baoule could never be mistaken for anything else, with its decorative head crests, its characteristic tufted head dress, its linear hair ridges running in severe angularly contrasted patterns, its emphasized eyebrow arches, its use of tribal tattoo marks as raised ornamental design on face and body, and its subtle modelling and crisp curves. As with most styles, the severer and more sparing the modelling and the decorative ornament, the older and purer the specimen is likely to be. But after even centuries of such slow ripening, Ivory Coast art of comparatively recent times can hardly be classed as effete and decadent; and although shattered in the Europeanized zones, by the testimony of recent investigators like Dr. Hans Himmelheber and Professor Melville Herskovits, still flourishes in some degree of technical proficiency and purity of native idiom in parts of the West African hinterland. The refinement of this art was for a long time a puzzling inconsistency. Further investigation of native life and history, however, showed how old, sophisticated and elaborately conventional the life of the African West Coast tribes of the Ivory, Gold Coast and upper Nigerian regions really is. Their languages, rituals, social caste organization, folk-lore and elaborate tribal moral codes—all indicate seasoned traditions and an accumulative human experience of great antiquity. So, with a fuller notion of its cultural background, we see that the art fits it, and is not, as would at first seem, a miraculous exception. Though not yet fully established, it seems even likely that the artistic strain in the American Negro population is a vague echo and carry-over from the tropical homeland and its folk-ways.

Practically every new scientific notion of these cultures conforms to the art, many of which could have been discovered earlier, if the art had been seriously taken as clues. Benin art, for example, shows its patron class to have been proud, blood-thirsty, caste-loving, war-making, trophy-seeking, slaveholding, ancestor worshippers: Yoruban art reflects a more sensuous and superstitious culture, priest-ridden, ancestor-struck, but more inclined to nature-worship, serpent cults and totemism, loving gaudy polychrome objects rather than the austere bronzes of the Benin overlords. Similarly, the Ivory Coast art, with a multitude of small talismans, dancing accessories, personal ornaments, reflects a graceful, dance-loving and probably peacefully industrious set of folk, among whom the artisan, courtesan, dancer and voodoo man were as much at a social premium as the warrior king and his vassal knights or the priests and temple attendants were among their neighbors. Recent ethnology proves the Great Bend of the African continent to have such a rich variety and contrasts of culture, and the art of the region bristles with confirmations.

Gold Coast Art: Ifa and Benin.—Here, again, we have a cluster of art styles, yet undoubtedly organically related. As far as it has been pieced out, there is a definite genealogy;—first, ancient Ifa art, discovered by Frobenius, as the earliest basic form, then, its transfer by conquest to Benin and a long independent career as Benin art, meanwhile a side development with a different emphasis as modern Yoruban and Dahomey art, and a later collateral development of Benin art in the craft arts of the Ashanti or Gold Coast proper. Again, we have a highly sophisticated tradition, oddly enough more sophisticated and highly stylized in its earlier forms, and only unrestrained and sensuous in its late modern phases. Metal,—bronze or brass, is its predominant medium, and all the difficult processes from metal casting to metal engraving are at zenith development in this region. The same technical skill made large and small-scale ivory carving a matter of course, so that on the one hand, we have ten to eleven foot elephant tusks completely carved in low and high relief, incised filigree in block ivory, and on the other, miniature ivory and metal masks as delicate and difficult as any Chinese or Japanese carving affords. In short, technical virtuosity can be taken for granted in this region; leaving art style as the only test of the better and sounder art.

The famous Ifa heads, discovered by Frobenius, are in the Frankfort Museum, and the main repositories of the great classic Benin bronzes are, as we have already seen, the *British Museum* and the *Ethnographic Museum* of Berlin. America has a small but representative sample of this art in the *Museum of the*

108

University of Pennsylvania, and at the *Field Museum*, Chicago and the *Peabody Museum*, Harvard University. Two private collections, that of Louis Carré, recently exhibited in New York, and that of Corail-Stop, contain choice specimens of the rare classical Benin art. The Gold Coast art of other styles and periods, including the small-scale brass moulding and carvings of Dahomey—the best of which are the famous Ashanti gold-weights, are more available and give an ample idea of its general style,—naturalistic figures of human, animal, insect and plant forms, patterned over with delicate stippled surface design of dots or scrolls, perhaps an extension of the patterns of some of their favorite early subjects,—the crocodile, the leopard and the snake. Here again, ancestor worship and animal cults are by far the dominant motives, and yet in the latter periods of Gold Coast art realistic and even comic genre effects are found,—hunting, dancing, household and social activities scenes of great variety.

The Art of the Cameroons.—The Cameroons, next neighbors down the coast, furnish an art radically different, and more in accord with our earlier notions of the African spirit. Much of it is fiercely, almost savagely primitive, evoking terror and awe when effective and a sense of the grotesque when less impressive. Rich color decoration, and in the Bamum region, polychrome beads ingeniously sewn over stuffed and wooden figures in all-over casings, certainly give the idea of tropical flamboyancy. But the Cameroon art, in these phases very like Dahomean art of some periods, can at times have severe dignity and restraint as shown in more austere masks like those in the well-known Dutch collection of Von der Heydt or in the carved chieftain stools with caryatid heads that are more highly stylized than any other products of this

109

region. Bead and cowry shell costumes of this region are also unusually fine both in workmanship and color scheme and pattern design. So, if the Cameroon art does not stand out unusually, it is primarily because of the unusual virtuosity of primitive art with which it is bounded both on the north and the south.

The Congo Art: French and Belgian Congo.— Parts of the French Congo have an art with characteristics common to the prevailing art of the Belgian Congo; other parts are relatively unartistic. But a precious section of the French Congo,—Gabon, furnishes in the art of the Fang peoples,—the Pahouin, M'Pongwe and Ogoue, what most experts regard as the finest sculptural tradition in the whole range of primitive art. Nothing anywhere excels it in stylized simplicity and grace. The art of this region is a mystical art, with a baffling refinement and sophistication which will be beyond explanation until we know more about the religious thought in which it had its roots. More than the usual primitive ancestor worship, it had its source in a cult of the dead, as shown by the concave white moon-faced masks that are one of its distinctive phases. The same extreme simplifications are seen in the abstract brass and copper symbolic figures of the Ogoue district, which appear in male and female form but so conventionalized that except for nose and eyebrow lines, the original facial pattern is completely obliterated. In their wood statuettes, of fine surface finish, all head and body features are toned down to mere suggestions of contour masses, with long flowing curves that every commentator likens to elongated pears, for lack of any human art analogy. The Barnes, Guillaume, Ratton, Guerre and La Porte Collections have some magnificent Gabon statuary and masks.

The Belgian Congo.—Turning to the Belgian Congo, we have a more vigorous and varied art; again

110

richly subdivided, yet with marked common characters of design ornament and sculptural mannerisms. The one is a seemingly inexhaustible use of lozenge shape and criss-cross geometric line patterns common to all the Bushongo tribes, but with distinctive tribal variations; the other is the familiar squat-styled, foreshortened human figure, strong, sensuous but eloquent which characteristically marks Bakuba statuary. Bakuba statues and weaving are perhaps the climax of Congo artistry, although the Kasai, the Bassonge, Bashilele, Baluba, Bapende, Bena Lulua and Manyema tribes are all great sculptors and weavers. Pottery reaches its best development also in this region. The style runs from quite primitive, rough wood carvings in these idioms among the tribes adjacent to the Congo lakes to sophisticated and beautifully finished hardwood statuettes and ceremonial cups in the form of a hollow human head characteristic of the Bakuba, Baluba and Badjok. These cups for religious and blood brotherhood rites and the carved buffalo drinking-horns are gems of primitive art. Ceremonial masks of all types and materials are plentiful, carved chieftain's scepters, ceremonial chairs elaborately carved, portrait statues, ancestor fetiches, fertility fetiches, one-piece carved jewel boxes of exquisite design are only a few items of the range of Bushongo art, matched on the other hand by the skillful pile and raphia cloth weaving we have already mentioned and great smith-craft in decorative arms and weapons. The Belgian state *Museum of the Congo* at Tervueren, near Brussels, is the official temple of this art, but many other museums and collections have rare specimens. One of the best, the Blondiau Collection was purchased by Mrs. Edith Isaacs and exhibited in 1927 in New York as a *Theatre Arts Monthly* project, and in part purchased for the *Harlem Museum of African*

111

Art, now temporarily housed in the 135th St. Branch Public Library. The Ratton, Tzara, Carré, Barnes, Ward and Leipsig Collections have very fine specimens of Congo art.

Angola Art.—This province, under Portuguese control, could be passed over almost without mention,—for its average art yield is inferior and not too original, except for one startling province of strangely powerful art. Hardwood figurines of great distinction and power, ancestral images with conventionalized head cowls, come from this Vatchivoke district. They are among the finest and rarest of all the African art types. The rest of Angola art is an echo of the rather rude fertility and nail-studded witchcraft images of the Loanga and Congo lowland areas. It was on this level that the old notions of Africa and its art were formed; but today in the light of what the more representative art of Africa has revealed, we are forced to say with James Sweeney Johnson that: "We must agree with Frobenius who observed that the legend of the barbarous Negro current in Europe during the latter half of the Nineteenth Century is primarily the creation of European exploiters who needed some excuse for their depredations."

African Art and Modernism.—The common denominator between African art and modernist art is the cult of form for form's sake. That is to say form as a satisfaction in itself without reference to realistic representation or immediately intelligible symbolism. This is the same as to say that most primitive art and most modernist art are highly abstract or stylized. Of course the motives are different, but the results are startlingly the same. In primitive art, the motive is to express merely the essentials necessary to grasp the meaning and to speak with a direct naive simplicity. For modernist art the main motive has been to reach

112

this same goal by sophisticated means. But the contemporary artist cannot count on his audience grasping his symbolism, which is one way of saying that our artists are out of tune with their audience. In primitive tribes, the group is able to follow the artist for the double reason that they are able, like children, to reduce all their forms to their simplest components, and that they have closer contact with the mechanics of carving or decoration and therefore a feeling for the purely technical effects of these media,—in short they are themselves more artistic. They can understand symbols and appreciate technique intrinsically.

Cubism.—Cubism was the turning point in great modern art. As a style, it turned its back on realistic representation and the cult of color at one and the same time. It put in their place the cult of form and the search for simplification. Figures were to be reduced to their basic planes and lines, and a geometric, many-dimensional type of art was evolved experimentally. Perspective and realistic color were suddenly abandoned by Picasso and Braque beginning about 1907. Cubism proper was succeeded by Futurism,—an allied school in which movement or successive phases of objects were represented on the same canvas, and Vorticism was just another such technical and sophisticated breaking up of the units of sense experience. As yet, a great deal of this modernistic art is not appreciated by the majority of us western moderns. And yet Africans would prefer the type of art which is admired by our ultra-modern sophisticates to that which attracts the gaze and warms the heart of our "man in the street." The proof is clear if we put side by side some of the work of our representative but most misunderstood modernist artists with primitive African work. The difference could in many cases scarcely be recognized, so striking is the similarity.

113

However, for power of effect, directness, simplicity or economy of means, in many cases the award would have to go to the original genuine primitives, and some of the master artists of today are generous enough to admit this.

Sur-Realism.—A still more curious development in modern art took a step nearer toward the primitive. That step was this. It was an attempt to reduce to visible shape the forms of thought and feelings, or in more learned language to visualize the sub-conscious mind. This movement has been called Sur-Realism, and has been a strong movement sweeping from France to Germany to Russia to England to America in its strange influence. The primitive artist, without knowing anything about Freud and our modern theories of the sub-conscious gives concrete and symbolic form to his instinctive feelings. For example, in a mask designed to create terror, he would naively do what a nightmare or a hallucination would do,—that is, combine symbolically several elements associated in his experience with the mood of terror, no matter how incongruous that was from the point of view of conscious association. Taking as a base a human face in a mood of fear or attack, he would combine with it the ears and snout of a gorilla, the teeth of a crocodile and the mane of a lion. The composite would be the attempt to combine in one symbol a compounded impression of fear and terror. Intellectually, such an image would be ridiculous and incongruous. Emotionally, it would be effective and congruous. Although some primitive masks are stylistic combinations of symbols traditionally associated with the content of tribal rituals, many are the results of such naive emotional combination such as the Sur-Realists reconcoct out of the Freudian free association of their artistic imaginations. So the primitive and the sophisticate

114

meet on the level of the dream state and concur in each other's fantasies. One form or other of this type of modernist art has dominated European and American art expression between 1920 and 1935. It has been sustained by a fashionable vogue of primitivism and the now almost universal admiration for primitive and especially African art.

It is not to be assumed, however, that the appreciation for African art will fade out as the vogue of these modernist art schools changes. Of course the extreme appreciation of it which has characterized the last fifteen years must subside. But the fad for African art has permanently opened our eyes to its beauty, to its technical skill and to its historical significance in the evolution of our arts. Appreciation based on these three factors gives this art a permanent place in the history of art and in the scientific and technical appreciation of art. African art can count on this sustained interest and permanent significance even after the modernist vogue of abstract art and the contemporary cult of primitivism pass out in a new artistic style and philosophy, which they sooner or later must do.

Finally, if African art can be of such use and inspiration to modern artists of all nations and lands, it surely can and should be a matter of particular study, interest and inspiration to Negroes in general, and Negro artists in particular.

DISCUSSION QUESTIONS

In what sense is African art primitive? In what respects is a great deal of it "fine art?" Does African Negro art have its "classics" and classical periods? What is its estimated antiquity? How do experts regard its principles of form and design? Why has modernistic art revealed the true values of African art? What are its major forms? What are the main traditions or regions of African art? What ancient influences are suggested as possible sources of some African art styles? How is it related in form to Egyptian art? To Oriental art? What are the main characteristics of Soudan, Benin, Ivory Coast, Gold Coast, Yoruban, Dahomeyan, and Congo art? On what principles of aesthetics and art form are modern artists in agreement with the basic principles of African art? What museum collections and what private collections in Europe are great treasuries of Negro African art? What museums and private collections in America? What are the main differences between the native and the modernistic approach to art?

READING REFERENCES

Bean, E. M.: *A Dead People; A Living Art*—Amer. Magazine of Art —January, 1936.

Bell, Clive: *Negro Sculpture*—Arts and Decoration—August, 1920.

Carre, Louis: *The Royal Art of Benin*—Knoedler Gallery Catalogue— November, 1935.

Chauvet, Stephen: *Gold, Bronze & Ivories in Negro Art*—Cahiers D'Art No. 1, Paris—1930.

Cunard, Nancy: *Negro: An Anthology:* Wishart, London, 1934:— Section on Negro Art: *Negro Art* by Ladislaus Szecsi—pp. 679-681; *Bambara Sculpture* by Carl Kjersmeier—pp. 684-686; *Styles in the Statuary of the Belgian Congo*—Henri Lavachery—pp. 687-696; *Congo Sculpture*—Raymond Michelet—pp. 706-731.

Dunn, I.: *Principles of African Art*—School Arts—December, 1933.

Frobenius, Leo: *Kulturgeschichte Afrikas*—Phaidon Verlag, Zurich— 1933.

Graham, John: *Introduction to Jacques Seligmann Gallery Exhibit Catalogue*—January, 1936.

Guillaume, Paul and Thomas Munro: *Primitive Negro Sculpture*— Harcourt, Brace & Howe, N. Y.—1926.

Hardy, Georges: *L'Art Negré*—Henri Laurens, Paris—1927.

Herskovits, Melville & F. S.: *The Art of Dahomey*—American Magazine of Art—February and March, 1934.

Johnson, James Sweeney: *African Negro Art*—Museum of Modern Art, N. Y.—1935.

116

Locke, Alain: *A Note on African Art*—Opportunity Magazine—May, 1924; *A Collection of Congo Art*—The Arts—February, 1927; *African Art: Classic Style*—American Magazine of Art, May, 1935.

Maes, Joseph and H. Lavachery: *Negro Art at Paris Exposition*—Brussels—1930.

Opportunity Magazine: Special *Negro Art Number*—May, 1924.

von Luschan, Felix: *Antiquities of Benin*—London—1917.

von Sydow, Eckhardt: *Handbuch der Afrikanischen Plastik*—Berlin—1930.

X
THE FUTURE OF NEGRO ART

With such a distinctive past and such a promising present, what of the future of Negro art? Any future is a matter of time and patient waiting; the best prophecy can only approximate its realizations. However, we can note three trends that seem to point toward three desirable objectives. One is the encouraging growth of the Negro artist; another promises a vital promotion of Negro art; and a third indicates the development of the Negro theme and subject as a vital phase of the artistic expression of native American life. The net results of what we have already reviewed show that at least the Negro and his art are definitely upon the artistic map, and that the Negro subject is increasingly coming to the fore in the general art interest. Any review of today's art exhibitions, when compared with similar exhibitions of even five years ago, will unmistakably show this.

Someday, it is to be hoped, an exhibition of contemporary American art dealing with the Negro theme and subject will be assembled, irrespective of the racial affiliation of the artists. It is doubtful which trend a project of this sort would more clearly reveal: the increasing maturity of the Negro artist or the increased general interest in Negro subject matter in American art. It would really seem that fortunately the two advances have gone along together, with some evidence of having re-enforced each other.

A few years back, there were promising Negro artists, but little or no Negro art. Most Negro artists at that time regarded racialism in art as an unwarranted restriction. They either avoided racial

118

subjects or treated them in what have been aptly called "Nordic transcriptions." As a result, in contrast to the vital Negro self-expression in poetry, fiction, drama and music, there was nothing comparable in the field of the fine arts. While our poets, playwrights, writers and musicians were in the nourishing sunlight of a proud and positive race-consciousness, our artists were still for the most part in an eclipse of chilly doubt and disparagement.

Why was this? Mainly, I think, because social prejudice had seized on the stigma of color and racial feature, and the Negro artist became the oversensitive victim of this negative color-consciousness and its inhibitions. Sad as was the plight of Negro art in his hands, as long as the Negro artist was in this general frame of mind, his whole expression, even in non-racial subjects, was weak and to some extent apologetic in conception and spirit, because it was bound to be derivative, imitative and falsely sophisticated. But as the Negro subject has become more popular generally, a healthier atmosphere has been generated. Further, developments in Negro cultural life have led the Negro artist toward a very real and vital racialism. But such an adoption of the cause of Negro art does not, it must always be remembered, commit us to an artistic Ghetto or a restricted art province. It only signalizes a double emancipation from apologetic timidity and academic imitation. It binds the Negro artist only to express himself in originality and unhampered ·sincerity, and opens for him a relatively undeveloped field in which he has certain naturally intimate contacts and interests. Every successive step in the general popularity of the Negro theme brings the Negro and the white American artist closer together, therefore, in this common interest of the promotion of Negro art over the

119

common denominator of the development of native American art.

Holger Cahill, National Director of the Federal Art Project, in his sanely progressive introduction to *"New Horizons in American Life,"* signals out as distinctive in contemporary American art trends the "apparent trend toward social content in art" and hails the evidence of "a recovery of social context" as a symptom of American art's maturity and progress. "The organization of the project has proceeded on the principle," he says, "that it is not the solitary genius but a sound general movement which maintains art as a vital, functioning part of any cultural scheme." Any such program organically takes up the racial into the broader social context of an art aiming at a vital expression of contemporary social facts and values. That is why everything that Mr. Cahill advocates for a program of contemporary American art can be underscored for the advance program of contemporary Negro art. Both, as he says, need "a greater vigor, unity and clarity of statement, a search for an adequate symbolism in the expression of contemporary American experience, less dependence on the easily obvious in subject matter, and a definite relation to local and regional environments." This, that he so aptly calls "imaginative realism," might profitably be adopted as today's creed and gospel for the younger, progressive Negro artist.

But, however rightly and fully he may share in a program of public art support, temporary or permanent, a needed and logical step in the support of the Negro artist and the development of Negro art must come from an awakened interest of the Negro public in this matter. Negro churches, schools, organizations of all types should make Negro art vital and intimately effective in our group life by studying it,

120

circulating it and commissioning it. Only under such circumstances will it become truly representative. Only under such conditions can it work as the cultural leaven to support a general reawakening of the dormant art instincts which we may suppose still reside in the folk at large. Slight but encouraging beginnings have been made in this direction by such schools as Atlanta and Howard universities and Hampton Institute, by a few Negro churches and Y.M.C.A.'s and business concerns, even a few groups of private individuals organized for the express purpose of the promotion of Negro art. It is likely that the singular demonstration of the Federal Art Project will stimulate greatly this effort of private groups and private individuals to the eventual adequate support and encouragement of the younger Negro artists.

On the other hand, there are evidences of organization among the artists themselves; one of the most noteworthy being the founding of the Harlem Artists Guild. However, all but the youngest artists have been born to a transitional period and its inevitable confusions. Thus it is almost too much to expect, at present, that they should have any consistent platform or aesthetic, beyond being generally modernist in technical trends and tastes. They are children of the transition between "art for art's sake" and art as social interpretation and criticism. Later they will look keenly and powerfully at the scene of social and racial conflict and have something to say of social as well as artistic import. An occasional lynch-theme, or caricature of social protest and criticism, a sceptical study of a crowd-hypnotizing evangelist or a belligerent sketch of a Seventh Avenue soap-box orator show the beginnings of a period of socially interpretative art. Yet, for the moment, our artists, in spite of reformist and proletarian professions in some quarters, are only half-way down from their ivory towers to the street level of the masses and the contemporary social scene. Their main concern just now seems to be for spiritual freedom of expression, which but for the rather liberal P.W.A. program would simply mean under the present hard circumstances freedom to starve. The temporary present freedom and advance of the Negro artist, therefore, needs the creation of a wide base of popular support from the people themselves, which again depends on how rapidly and successfully the campaign for the popularization of good art can be carried forward.

Yet the trends everywhere are making for a more vital and popularly pivoted art. Primitive art traditions once thought dead are re-blossoming; even, as we have seen in West and Central Africa. A native Congo painter, Kalifala Sidibe, exhibiting in Paris and a West African woman painter, Suzanna Ogunjami, exhibiting in New York City are portents of great potential meaning. If the American Indian tribal arts can with little encouragement be revived and in a few year's time produce notable painters and art-craftsmen, the traditions of African native art are not necessarily lost either in Africa or among the American descendants. And more than this, the younger Negro artist is now nearly abreast of his generation in modernism of style and subject. From such vantage points Negro art and the Negro artist must go forward.

READING REFERENCES

Cahill, Holger: Introduction to *"New Horizons in American Art—* Museum of Modern Art Press, 1936.

Locke, Alain: *The Negro Takes His Place in American Art*—Harmon Catalogue, 1933, pp. 9-12.

"Schools and Universities Expand Art Courses," in Harmon Catalogue, 1935, p. 28pf.